The Academy Awards: A Pictorial History

The Academy Awards: A Pictorial History

by Paul Michael

THIRD REVISED EDITION

CROWN PUBLISHERS, INC. · New York

Library of Congress catalog card number: 68-9070

ISBN: 0-517-50118X
Designed by Judith Michael
Printed in the United States of America

Published simultaneously in Canada by
General Publishing Company Limited

acknowledgments

Grateful acknowledgment is made to the following for supplying photographs and invaluable assistance in the preparation of this volume: Mike Hutner, James Katz, United Artists Corp.; Florence Gilbert, Janus Films, Inc.; Al Adams, Donald Velde, Inc.; Frank Rodriguez, 20th Century-Fox Film Corp.; Harold Danziger, Columbia Pictures Corp.; Mary Pickford; John Sutherland, Warner Brothers; Olin Clark, Karla Davidson, Metro-Goldwyn-Mayer; David O. Selznick; Mike Berman, Paramount Pictures Corporation; William Klutz, Museum of Modern Art; Svensk Filmindustri; Samuel Goldwyn Productions; Michael Todd Corp.; Martin Schildkraut, Television Industries, Inc.; Lou Edelman, Embassy Pictures Corporation; Margaret Herrick, Academy of Motion Picture Arts and Sciences; Walt Disney; John G. Collins, Continental Distributing, Inc.; Buena Vista Distributing Co., Inc.; Canadian National Film Board; Paul Kamey, Universal Pictures Company, Inc.; Jerry Ludwig, The Mirisch Company, Inc.; Bryna Productions; Tom Brandon, Brandon Films; R. Pearson, Romulus Films Ltd.; John Groves, Central Office of Information; David Bloom, Hollywood Television Service (A Division of Republic Corp.); Mickie Meade, The Rank Organization, Ltd.; Barney Pitkin, Louis de Rochemont Associates, Inc.; The French Film Office; Fae R. Miske, Joseph Burstyn Company; Margot Forbes, Trans-Lux Distributing Corp.; Edward Harrison, Harrison Pictures Corporation; Barbara Jean Owens; Kathleen Padley; Roy Goin; Jean Andreola; Robert W. Taylor, National Broadcasting Company; John Strick, Laser Film Corporation; Penny Bergman, Stephen Bosustow Productions; Anne Marie Foran, Cinema 5 Ltd.; Ted Spiegel, Avco Embassy Pictures; Seymour Lesser; John Cocchi; James Robert Parish; Carol Schmidt, Cinerama Releasing Corporation; Mary Ann Forn, Walt Disney Productions; Bernard Kantor, Chairman, University of Southern California Cinema Department; Bernard Chevry, Midem; Pauline Klaw, Movie Star News, for her most generous help in supplying numerous stills from her vast collection.

A special word of thanks to James Robert Parish for his help in the revisions.

The idea for this book was conceived several years ago when I was part of the television audience of nearly 100,000,000 people watching the presentation of the annual Academy Awards. For me the most fascinating part of the program was the showing of some old photographs of early Oscar winners. I thought that there must be many people whose pleasant memories would be stirred by seeing pictures of Clark Gable and Claudette Colbert in "It Happened One Night"; Gary Cooper in "Sergeant York"; Vivien Leigh in "Gone With The Wind"; Mary Pickford in "Coquette"; Humphrey Bogart in "The African Queen"; Ingrid Bergman in "Anastasia"; or any of the other players and films honored since the inception of the Academy Awards.

I was surprised to learn that there was no book that brought together all the winners of the coveted Oscar, the most important and sought after of all film awards, given each year by The Academy of Motion Picture Arts and Sciences as the symbol of motion picture excellence.

Research for this book led to the discovery that the Oscar means different things to different people. To the public it is a badge of distinction. To the film maker it is the symbol of recognition by his toughest audience, his co-workers in the industry.

Physically the Academy's Oscar is not very imposing. He stands ten inches tall, weighs seven pounds, and is fashioned of gold plate over bronze. The cost of the statuette is approximately one hundred dollars. And yet it has been proven time and again that winning the Oscar is tremendously valuable. Take the case of "Lilies of the Field" starring Sidney Poitier. This film was expected to gross just over one million dollars, but it has almost tripled its profits since Poitier was named best actor of the year.

The Academy Awards: a Pictorial History is, as its name implies, a photographic survey of the Oscar winners. Therefore greater emphasis has been placed on actors, actresses, and films that have been honored than on producers, directors, writers, and technicians. This is not meant to minimize their Awards or achievements. It must be understood that any Award winning film is the result of the contributions and creative efforts of hundreds of dedicated people.

I would like to thank David O. Selznick who has contributed the foreword for this book. Mr. Selznick has received many Oscars for films such as "Gone With The Wind" and "Rebecca" among others. He is also the recipient of the Irving Thalberg Memorial Award for the "most consistent high quality of production."

In conclusion, I hope the readers of this book will enjoy reading and browsing through it as much as I have enjoyed writing it.

Paul Michael

foreword

The Academy of Motion Picture Arts and Sciences was the concept of the late Louis B. Mayer, who felt that such an organization would give status to the growing motion picture industry, the product of which had a far greater hold upon the public's affection than its respect. He secured the collaboration of other prominent figures in Hollywood, including Cecil B. DeMille, Douglas Fairbanks, Sr., Mary Pickford, and others whom I do not mention not because they contributed any less to the organization and early plans of the Academy, but because these initial meetings were informal and the respective contributions of the founders therefore are not a matter of record. A genuine "academy," devoted to technical research and an exchange of artistic and scientific views, was contemplated. But, as perhaps was inevitable in a group whose creative opportunities were then as now dependent upon public applause, the awards early became the prime function of the Academy; all too little is generally known of its substantial contributions to the inauguration and advancement of cinematic techniques. But since this volume is devoted solely to the "Oscars," the record of other activities of the Academy must be sought elsewhere by students of film and its uses.

All systems for selecting award recipients have their weaknesses, and those utilized to choose Oscar winners are not exceptions. Contributions of lasting significance to the advancement of motion pictures, as entertainment or as an art form, require the perspective of time for proper evaluation. It is undeniable that the Academy honored many films that it has already been proven were of only passing interest. Great films, and distinguished artists connected with them, were often bypassed, as we now know. To some extent these oversights were corrected many years later by special awards, as in the cases of D. W. Griffith, Mack Sennett, Ernst Lubitsch, Charles Chaplin, Buster Keaton, and Greta Garbo. The seeming slight to the work of some of these, and of others whose work was far in advance of their time, was not as insensitive or unknowing as might appear, for much of their work antedated the establishment of the annual Academy Awards; but it is no doubt true that in other cases there has been inadequately expressed appreciation by an electorate influenced unduly by transient tastes, by commercial success, by studio log-rolling, and by personal popularity in the community of Hollywood. This has been less true in recent years, because of the conscientious attempts of successive Boards of Governors of the Academy to eliminate voting pressures that grew with the increasing realization of the gigantic monetary value of the Awards. These corrections have to some extent made the selections at least more representative of the views of the people of the film world; and while the sincere attempts of the Academy executives to eliminate or at least reduce the sometimes shocking efforts to secure votes have unfortunately not been altogether successful, an objective evaluation, after the passing of years, would indicate that "the best" increasingly is to be found among the nominations, if not among the winners.

The members of each of the several branches of the Academy select, by secret vote, five nominees. Disregarding the factors mentioned above, it can therefore be assumed that the five winners of nominations in each branch are deemed by their colleagues to have done the "best" work in the industry within the Awards year. Again by secret vote, the entire Academy makes its selections of the winners from among the nominees in all divisions. Regrettably, those who are nominated, but do not win the final accolades, are too often regarded as "losers": it is the intention that each of the nominees is a "winner," having been one of the five "best" within his or her own craft. Thus, whatever may be said against the Awards and the systems utilized in their selection, they are unquestionably as close to being representative of the views of the Academy membership as ingenuity and sincere effort can make them.

As a senior producer of Hollywood, I take the liberty of intruding a tribute to that much-abused and sadly vanishing group—the creative producers, without whose imagination and talent, courage and resourcefulness, the work of many Academy Award winners would never have existed, or would have been presented to the public under far less advantageous circumstances. Space does not permit the listing of the many who contributed more than was always known even to many of those connected with the making of their films (because their ideas and directions were so often transmitted and executed through others). I therefore salute not only as individuals, but as outstanding examples of such craftsmen, J. Stuart Blackton and Thomas H. Ince; Irving G. Thalberg and Samuel Goldwyn; Sir Alexander Korda and Sir Michael Balcon.

The purpose and format of this book have no doubt been responsible for the emphasis upon "best pictures" and "best performances," with secondary attention to those major departments of film making, writing and direction. I therefore call the reader's attention to the complete listing of awards in each chapter. Also, I express respectful and limitless admiration for those others without whose devoted and often unsung efforts no motion picture could achieve distinction—for, to an extent far exceeding that of any other art form, cinema is a collaborative medium: the cameramen, the production and laboratory technicians, the musicians, the art directors, the costume designers, the wizards of "special effects" (these are, truly, the magicians of the movies), the film editors, the sound technicians, and all those others without whom producers and directors, writers and actors would of course be totally unable to function.

I am certain it was not the intention of Mr. Michael, in compiling this volume, to "second guess" the Academy electorate of the past. Rather it was presumably primarily to permit a nostalgic examination of film idols of yesteryear, and of at least some of those films that represent milestones in the development of motion pictures, especially in a more innocent era. I believe that the book should be of interest not only to the sadly diminishing but still large army of faithful film fans, but also to those who find pleasure in reminders of what sometimes appear to be the quaint tastes and preferences of even the recent past.

David O. Selznick

The Academy Awards: A Pictorial History

AWARDS

Production: "Wings," Paramount.

Actor: Emil Jannings in "The Way Of All Flesh," and "The Last Command," Paramount.

Actress: Janet Gaynor in "Seventh Heaven," "Street Angel," and "Sunrise," Fox.

Direction: Frank Borzage, "Seventh Heaven."

Direction (comedy): Lewis Milestone, "Two Arabian Knights," United Artists.

Writing (original story): Ben Hecht, "Underworld," Paramount.

Writing (adaptation): Benjamin Glazer, "Seventh Heaven."

Writing (title): Joseph Farnham, "Fair Co-Ed," "Laugh, Clown, Laugh," and "Telling The World," Metro-Goldwyn-Mayer.

Cinematography: Charles Rosher, Karl Struss, "Sunrise."

Art Direction: William Cameron Menzies, "The Dove," and "The Tempest," United Artists.

Engineering Effects: Roy Pomeroy, "Wings."

Artistic Quality of Production: "Sunrise."

SPECIAL AWARDS

Warner Brothers, for producing "The Jazz Singer," the pioneer talking picture, which has revolutionized the industry.

Charles Chaplin, for versatility and genius in writing, acting, directing and producing "The Circus."

2

1927 1928

first annual awards

"To Warner Brothers, for producing 'The Jazz Singer,' the pioneer talking picture, which has revolutionized the industry." These were the prophetic words that accompanied the presentation of a special Award of the then nameless statuette at the first Academy Awards banquet on May 16, 1929. They sounded the death knell of one Hollywood era and, at the same time, signalled a rebirth to even greater heights. Some of the people connected with the world of the silent screen would survive— but others, so many others, would fade into obscurity.

One man, who more than any other exemplified the magic of the silent silver screen, the peerless comedian Charlie Chaplin, was also honored with a special Award by the fledgling Academy for "his genius and versatility in writing, acting, directing, and producing 'The Circus'." This was the only Award that the great Chaplin ever won.

An epic film of war, romance, and daring in the air, "Wings," with Gary Cooper, Clara Bow, Charles "Buddy" Rogers, and Richard Arlen, was chosen best production. A further indication of the coming power of sound in the film industry was the fact that the biggest hit of the Awards banquet was a filmed dialogue between Douglas Fairbanks, President of the Academy, and Adolph Zukor, producer of "Wings." The short sound film had been produced in New York prior to the banquet.

"Wings" was not an easy victor in its category. There was stiff competition from a quartet of fine films: "Seventh Heaven," "The Way Of All Flesh," "The Racket," and "The Last Command."

Emil Jannings came to Hollywood from Germany, already acclaimed as one of the finest actors in the world on the strength of his admirable performances in "Variety," and "The Last Laugh." He walked away with the acting honors for his portrayal of an exiled Russian general in "The Last Command," and as an embittered family man in "The Way Of All Flesh." Two ranking Hollywood luminaries were also in contention: Richard Barthelmess for "The Noose" and "The Patent Leather Kid"; Charlie Chaplin for "The Circus"; but Jannings, at the peak of his acting abilities, was not to be denied.

Janet Gaynor received three of the five nominations for the best actress Award for her glowing performances in "Seventh Heaven," "Street Angel," and "Sunrise," and was chosen over such stalwarts as Gloria Swanson in her classic portrayal of "Sadie Thompson," and Louise Dresser in "A Ship Comes In."

Frank Borzage was named best director for "Seventh Heaven"; Ben Hecht, best original writer for "Underworld"; Benjamin Glazer, best adaptation for "Seventh Heaven"; Charles Rosher and Karl Struss honored for best cinematography for "Sunrise"; and William Cameron Menzies was cited for his art direction of "The Dove" and "The Tempest."

"Wings" (best production) with Charles "Buddy" Rogers and Clara Bow. Paramount

Janet Gaynor (best actress) and Charles Farrell in "Seventh Heaven." Fox

"Underworld" (best original story)
with Clive Brook. Paramount

"Sunrise" (best artistic quality of production)
with Janet Gaynor and George O'Brien. Fox

"Two Arabian Knights" (best comedy direction)
with Louis Wolheim and William Boyd. United Artists

"The Jazz Singer" (special award) with Richard Tucker,
Al Jolson, and May McAvoy. Warner Brothers

1928 1929

second annual awards

"Sound didn't do any more to the motion picture industry than turn it upside-down, shake the entire bag of tricks from its pocket, and advance Warner Brothers from last place (among the film companies) to first in the league." So said "Variety," with its tongue planted firmly in its cheek, just a little over a year after the explosive introduction of talking films. The bandwagon was rolling full steam ahead, and every studio was fighting for its share of the staggering box office receipts. They tried to outdo each other with such slogans as: "the first all-talking film," "the first 100% all-talking drama filmed outdoors," "the first all-Negro, all-talking film," "the first 100% talking, singing college picture," and so on. Even though certain motion picture executives felt that sound was just a passing fancy—it was a passing fancy that was bringing people into the theatres across the country in greater numbers than ever before.

In "Broadway Melody," voted best production of the year, Bessie Love, Anita Page, and Charles King cavorted in a tried and true story of two small-town girls lured to New York by the bright lights of Broadway — their ups, downs, and romantic tribulations. Although the film was not critically acclaimed, the box office returns were fabulous. Aside from the Academy Award, "Broadway Melody's" only claim to fame was the introduction of a song called "You Were Meant For Me."

Warner Baxter was one silent film idol who made a smooth transition from silent to talking pictures. His suave, darkly handsome features were matched by his fine voice, and for his portrayal of the dashing Cisco Kid in "In Old Arizona," he was named best actor. Also in contention were Paul Muni for "The Valiant," Chester Morris for "Alibi," Lewis Stone for "The Patriot," and George Bancroft for "Thunderbolt."

Another all-time silent screen favorite, Mary Pickford, came out of retirement to make "Coquette," and for her performance as a Southern belle, true to the man she loved, won best actress honors. Ruth Chatterton in "Madam X," Betty Compson in "The Barker," Jeanne Eagels in "The Letter," and Bessie Love in "Broadway Melody" were other nominees for best actress of the year.

Perhaps the finest film of the year, "The Bridge Of San Luis Rey," was not even nominated for best production — since it had committed the unforgivable sin of silence. The sensitive adaptation of the Thornton Wilder best-seller, had only the introduction and epilogue in sound. However, Cedric Gibbons won the first of his many Awards as best art director for this unforgettable film which starred Lili Damita, Ernest Torrence, and Duncan Renaldo.

Hans Kraly was cited for best writing achievement for "The Patriot," and Clyde De Vinna was named for his cinematography in "White Shadows In The South Seas."

AWARDS

Production: "Broadway Melody,"
  Metro-Goldwyn-Mayer.
Actor: Warner Baxter in "In Old Arizona," Fox.
Actress: Mary Pickford in "Coquette,"
  United Artists.
Direction: Frank Lloyd, "The Divine Lady,"
  First National.
Writing (achievement): Hans Kraly, "The Patriot,"
  Paramount.
Cinematography: Clyde De Vinna,
  "White Shadows In The South Seas,"
  Metro-Goldwyn-Mayer.
Art Direction: Cedric Gibbons,
  "The Bridge Of San Luis Rey,"
  Metro-Goldwyn-Mayer.

"The Bridge Of San Luis Rey" (best art direction)
with Raquel Torres and Emily Fitzroy. M-G-M

"The Patriot" (best writing achievement)
with Emil Jannings and Florence Vidor. Paramount

Mary Pickford
(best actress)
in "Coquette."
United Artists

"Broadway Melody"
(best production)
with Bessie Love and
Charles King. M-G-M

Warner Baxter (best actor)
and Lola Salvi (foreground)
in "In Old Arizona." Fox

AWARDS

Production: "All Quiet On The Western Front,"
Universal.

Actor: George Arliss in "Disraeli,"
Warner Brothers.

Actress: Norma Shearer in "The Divorcée,"
Metro-Goldwyn-Mayer.

Direction: Lewis Milestone,
"All Quiet On The Western Front."

Writing (achievement): Frances Marion,
"The Big House," Metro-Goldwyn-Mayer.

Cinematography: Willard Van Der Veer,
Joseph T. Rucker, "With Byrd At The
South Pole," Paramount.

Art Direction: Herman Rosse, "King Of Jazz,"
Universal.

Sound Recording: Douglas Shearer,
"The Big House."

1929
1930

The stark brutality and the utter senselessness of all war was brought home with sustained power and brilliant conviction in the most important anti-war, war film ever produced, "All Quiet On The Western Front," adapted from the Erich Remarque novel. Seen through the eyes of the little man—the line-soldiers, the men in the trenches—the war took on a new and much deeper meaning. It was no longer the grand struggle between great powers, but rather, a tough, grim battle between men — men who neither understood nor cared about the higher causes of war. The only thing they knew and understood were the bare facts that faced them: the glare of bursting shells above them, the hopeless desperation of staring into the no-man's-land in front of them. There was irony in the very title, for indeed, during the war, the news reports said "all quiet on the western front" when in reality, the war went on for these men, hour-by-hour, day-by-day. It was heartbreakingly certain that most would die. "All Quiet On The Western Front" was named best production.

Six actors of great stature were nominated for best acting laurels: Wallace Beery for "The Big House," Maurice Chevalier for "The Love Parade" and "The Big Pond," Lawrence Tibbett for "Rogue Song," George Arliss for "Disraeli" and "The Green Goddess," and Ronald Colman for "Bulldog Drummond" and "Condemned."

But it was veteran George Arliss' finely wrought portrait of England's Prime Minister, the witty, urbane, sophisticated, and sarcastic Benjamin Disraeli, that took the prize. Arliss had played the same role in a silent version of the film in 1921, but with the addition of sound, a new and brilliant dimension had been added that could not be overlooked by the Academy.

The biggest surprise of the Awards banquet was the fact that Greta Garbo did not win best actress honors for her grand performances in "Anna Christie" and "Romance." Rather, it was Norma Shearer in a rather nondescript film, "The Divorcée," who was acclaimed. She was ably abetted in this complicated and heavily plotted film by Chester Morris, Robert Montgomery, and Conrad Nagel.

But a change was taking place in the desires of the movie-going public. For the first time people were becoming interested in a purely American film phenomenon, the gangster-prison picture. With the production of "Little Caesar" early in 1930, a cycle of similar, hard-hitting, rough-and-tumble films were produced in rapid succession. "Variety" reported that there were more than fifty produced in a single year. One such film, "The Big House," starring Robert Montgomery, Chester Morris, and Wallace Beery was doubly honored by the Academy: Frances Marion for best writing achievement and Douglas Shearer for best sound recording.

Mention must be made of the Award-winning cinematography of Joseph T. Rucker and Willard Van Der Veer for the film "With Byrd At The South Pole"; a combination of actual footage of the expedition and new footage shot in the studio, telling the heroic story of man's fight against the elements.

"All Quiet On The Western Front" (best production) with Louis Wolheim, Slim Summerville, below; Lew Ayres and Raymond Griffith opposite. Universal

Norma Shearer (best actress) and Chester Morris in "The Divorcée." M-G-M

George Arliss (best actor)
in "Disraeli." Warner Brothers

"The Big House" (best writing achievement) with Chester Morris and Wallace Beery. M-G-M

1930
1931

This was definitely not the year for glamour at the Academy Awards presentations. No dashingly heroic, romantic leading man won acting honors; no ravishingly beautiful actress in luscious costumes garnered distaff laurels. Rather, it was the year of the character actor.

Lionel Barrymore, veteran of years on Broadway, the silent films, and now talking pictures was named best actor for his striking delineation of a free-drinking, free-thinking lawyer in "A Free Soul," a characterization of rare insight and intelligence. "A Free Soul" boasted an all-star supporting cast, including such luminaries as Norma Shearer, Clark Gable, Leslie Howard, and James Gleason. Also in contention for the top acting Award were Jackie Cooper, child actor and the youngest person ever nominated for a major Award, for "Skippy"; Richard Dix for "Cimarron"; Fredric March for "The Royal Family Of Broadway"; and suave Adolphe Menjou for "The Front Page."

Marie Dressler, a master of the shrug and the gesture, as well as an actress with a rare and unusual vocal quality, was singled out as best actress of the year for her deft and delightful performance in "Min And Bill," in which she starred opposite the irrepressible Wallace Beery. She had the power to elicit tears and laughs within moments of each other, and she used all these powers to their utmost in this film. Even such high-flying stars as Norma Shearer in "A Free Soul," Ann Harding in "Holiday," Irene Dunne in "Cimarron," and the ultra glamorous Marlene Dietrich in "Morocco" could not wrest the title from this honor graduate of the Mack Sennett Studio.

From Edna Ferber's thrilling novel of the men and women of the Old West and the land rush into Oklahoma, came "Cimarron," the film named best production. This epic film, covering forty years in the lives of the settlers, which starred Richard Dix, Irene Dunne, and Edna May Oliver, won two other Awards. Howard Estabrook was cited for best adaptation and Max Ree for best art direction.

Several other noteworthy films gained nominations: "East Lynne"; "Trader Horn"; the unforgettable story of the rough-and-tumble newspaper world, "The Front Page"; and "Skippy."

For his brilliant handling of the children, Jackie Cooper and Mitzi Green, in "Skippy," Norman Taurog was selected as best director of the year by the members of the Academy. John Monk Saunders won the Award for best original story for his "The Dawn Patrol," which starred Richard Barthelmess, Neil Hamilton and Douglas Fairbanks, Jr. as aviators.

When "Tabu" was first presented it was hailed as "one of the world's great art treasures." Here was a film of rare beauty and purity, shot on location in Tahiti — the combined directorial effort of Robert Flaherty and F. W. Murnau. Because "Tabu" was a silent film, with only a musical score as background, it could not possibly be in contention for best production honors, but Floyd Crosby was named for his cinematography. "Tabu" represented one beautiful, dying gasp of the silent film.

AWARDS

Production: "Cimarron," RKO Radio.

Actor: Lionel Barrymore in "A Free Soul,"
Metro-Goldwyn-Mayer.

Actress: Marie Dressler in "Min And Bill,"
Metro-Goldwyn-Mayer.

Direction: Norman Taurog, "Skippy," Paramount.

Writing (original story): John Monk Saunders,
"The Dawn Patrol," Warner Brothers.

Writing (adaptation): Howard Estabrook,
"Cimarron."

Cinematography: Floyd Crosby, "Tabu,"
Paramount.

Art Direction: Max Ree, "Cimarron."

Sound Recording: Paramount Studio Sound
Department.

SCIENTIFIC AND TECHNICAL AWARDS

Electrical Research Products, Inc.,
RCA-Photophone, Inc., and RKO Radio
Pictures, Inc., for noise reduction recording
equipment.

DuPont Film Manufacturing Corp. and
Eastman Kodak Co., for super-sensitive
panchromatic film.

Fox Film Corp., for effective use of
synchro-projection composite photography.

Electrical Research Products, Inc., for moving
coil microphone transmitters.

RKO Radio Pictures, Inc., for reflex type
microphone concentrators.

RCA-Photophone, Inc., for ribbon microphone
transmitters.

"Cimarron" (best production) with Estelle Taylor and Richard Dix. RKO Radio

Lionel Barrymore (best actor) and Norma Shearer in "A Free Soul." M-G-M

"The Dawn Patrol"
(best original story)
with Richard Barthelmess,
Clyde Cook,
Douglas Fairbanks, Jr.,
and Edmond Breon.
Warner Brothers

"Skippy"
(best direction)
with Jackie Cooper
and Mitzi Green.
Paramount

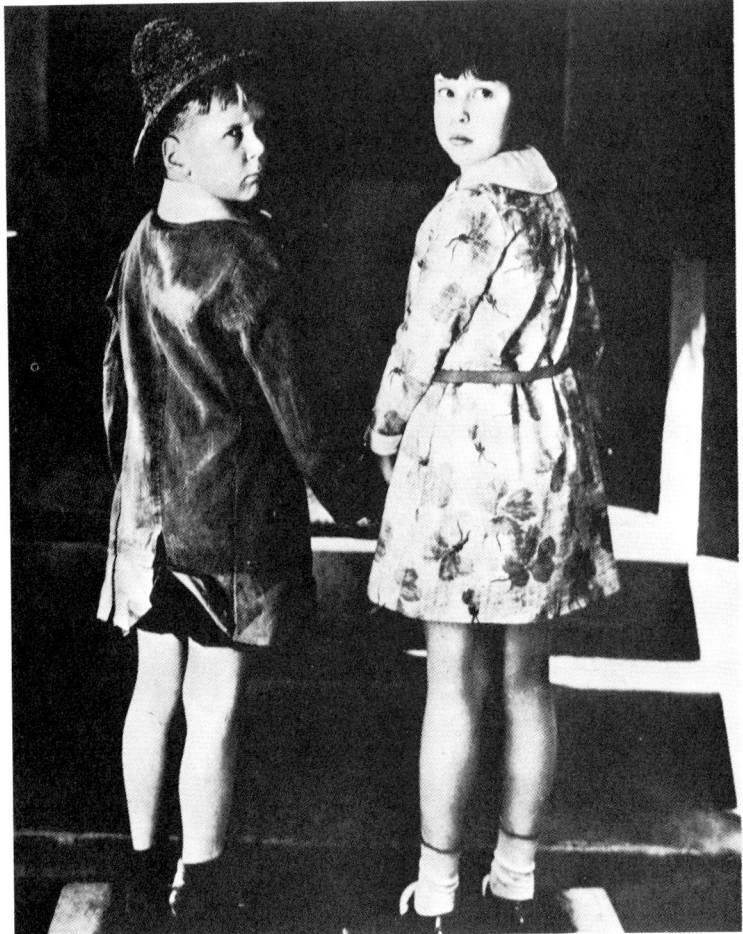

AWARDS

Production: "Grand Hotel," Metro-Goldwyn-Mayer.

Actor: Fredric March in "Dr. Jekyll And Mr. Hyde," Paramount. Wallace Beery in "The Champ," Metro-Goldwyn-Mayer.

Actress: Helen Hayes in "The Sin Of Madelon Claudet," Metro-Goldwyn-Mayer.

Direction: Frank Borzage, "Bad Girl," Fox.

Writing (original story): Frances Marion, "The Champ."

Writing (adaptation): Edwin Burke, "Bad Girl."

Cinematography: Lee Garmes, "Shanghai Express," Paramount.

Art Direction: Gordon Wiles, "Transatlantic," Fox.

Sound Recording: Paramount Studio Sound Department.

Short Subjects (cartoon): "Flowers And Trees," Disney, United Artists.

Short Subjects (comedy): "The Music Box," Roach, Metro-Goldwyn-Mayer.

Short Subjects (novelty): "Wrestling Swordfish," Sennett-Educational.

SPECIAL AWARD

Walt Disney, for the creation of Mickey Mouse.

SCIENTIFIC AND TECHNICAL AWARDS

Technicolor Motion Picture Corp., for their color cartoon process.

Eastman Kodak Co., for the Type II-B Sensitometer.

1931 1932

Take seven great stars: Lionel Barrymore, John Barrymore, Greta Garbo, Joan Crawford, Wallace Beery, Lewis Stone, and Jean Hersholt, each giving a glowing performance; take a scenario adapted from the popular Vicki Baum novel; stir them gently with the sure hand of director Edmund Goulding; add the spice of a torrid love scene between John and Greta; mix them together and you come up with the film cited as best production for the year, "Grand Hotel." Even today, more than thirty years after the official première of "Grand Hotel" on April 12, 1932, the film can still be viewed with pleasure.

For the first time in the history of the Awards the membership of the Academy was unable to decide which of two distinguished performances deserved the acting honors. The competition was so close that the Academy decided to give two Awards.

First, to Fredric March for his dual-role performance in "Dr. Jekyll And Mr. Hyde," the classic film of physical and psychological horror. Directed by Rouben Mamoulian, March's performance surpassed even the magnificent portrayal given by John Barrymore in an earlier silent version of the Robert Lewis Stevenson work.

But at the same time, Wallace Beery's sensitive and sympathetic characterization of a one-time heavyweight champion gone to ruin in "The Champ" could not be overlooked. The scenes between Beery and his son, ably played by young Jackie Cooper, are never to be forgotten.

As soon as the motion picture learned to talk, it became obvious that actors who could speak lines with authority in well-modulated tones would have to be recruited in a hurry. During the time it took for Hollywood personalities to frantically take vocal lessons, a group of Broadway players made the trek to Hollywood.

Of the three actresses nominated for top honors, two came from Broadway: Lynne Fontanne, nominated for "The Guardsman," and Helen Hayes, nominated for "The Sin Of Madelon Claudet." Only the irrepressible Marie Dressler, nominated for "Emma," was Hollywood trained. Helen Hayes was tapped for the Award.

Frank Borzage won the laurels as best director for the second time in the short history of the Academy for "Bad Girl," which was also honored for Edwin Burke's adaptation.

"Shanghai Express," under the direction of Josef von Sternberg, and starring Marlene Dietrich, Clive Brook, Anna May Wong, and Warner Oland, won the cinematography Award hands down. The camera work of Lee Garmes captured the feeling of revolutionary China—even though the entire film was shot in California.

This was the first year for short subjects Awards, and Walt Disney captured his first accolade by the Academy for his cartoon, "Flowers And Trees." Disney also won a special citation for the creation of Mickey Mouse. The best comedy short subject Award went to Laurel and Hardy's "The Music Box."

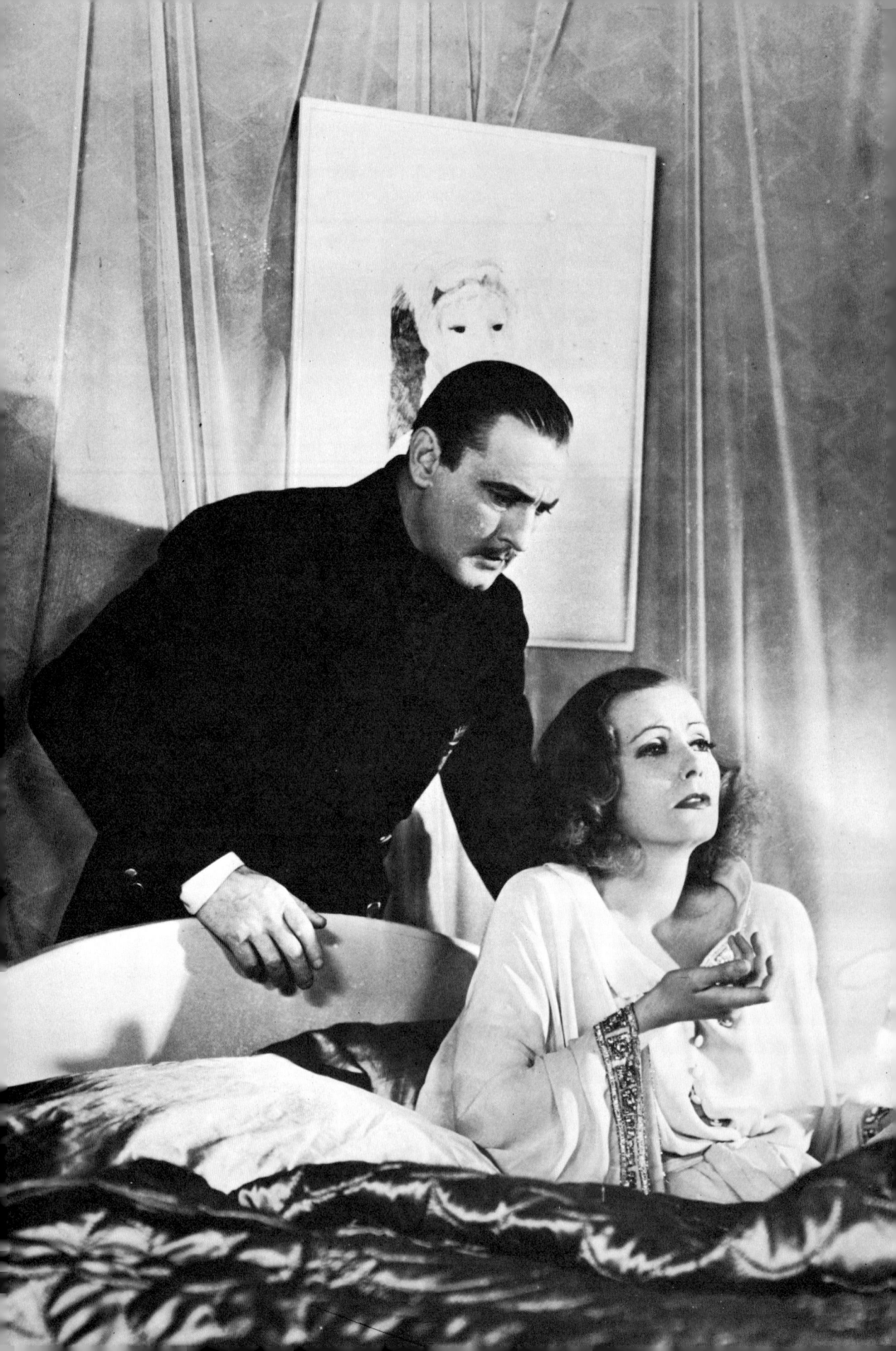

"Grand Hotel" (best production) with
John Barrymore, Greta Garbo, left;
Lionel and John Barrymore, above;
Wallace Beery, Joan Crawford, right. M-G-M

Wallace Beery (best actor) and Jackie Cooper in "The Champ." M-G-M

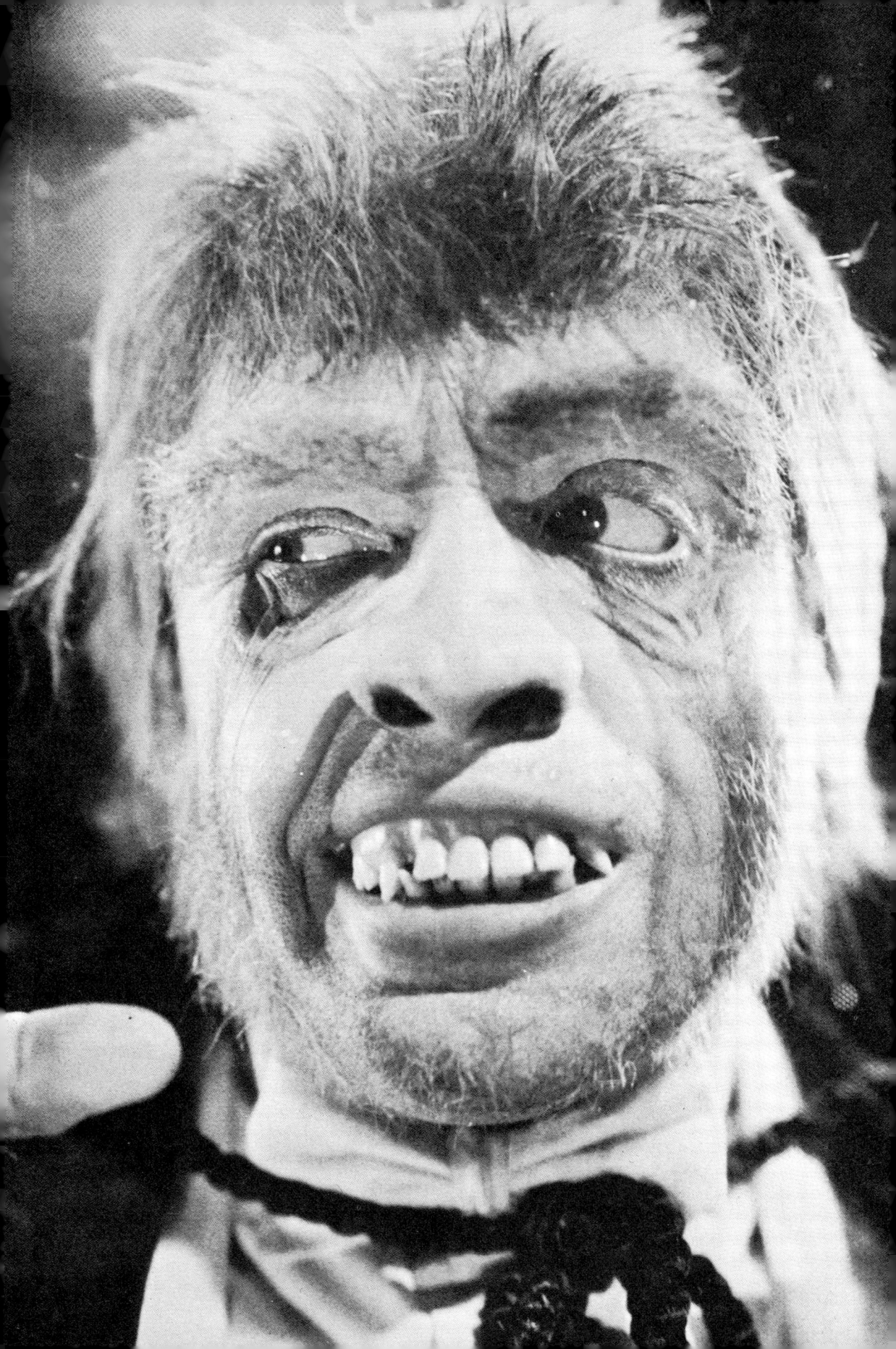

"Shanghai Express"
(best cinematography)
with Clive Brook
and Marlene Dietrich.
Paramount

Helen Hayes (best actress) and Lewis Stone in "The Sin Of Madelon Claudet." M-G-M

"Flowers And Trees" (best cartoon). Disney, United Artists

1932 1933

The spirit of the search for dignity, beauty, and peace, in a world which lacked the fundamental faith that these things were really possible, was the theme of Noel Coward's "Cavalcade," selected by the membership of the Academy as the best production of the year. Even though competing against such splendid films as Ernest Hemingway's "A Farewell To Arms," starring Gary Cooper and Helen Hayes; "The Private Life Of Henry VIII," England's contribution to costumed historical drama; and "I Am A Fugitive From A Chain Gang"—"Cavalcade" shone above all the rest by virtue, as one critic put it, "of its sheer luminosity, restraint in handling tragic detail, and its romantic adventurousness."

Seen through the eyes of a British family and their children, "Cavalcade" was a sensitive picture of a world in turmoil: more than thirty years sweeping before the cameras and across the screen; a relentless upheaval of the old order; the death and destruction of a way of life; the lulling, spurious peace; and, finally, the hope that things will be, must be, better in the future. This fine film won two other Oscars: Frank Lloyd was named best director, and William S. Darling, best art director.

The story of a stage-struck young girl who gives her "all" to her impresario, pounds the pavement in search of an acting job, finally gets the job as an understudy, and then, as if by magic, replaces the star on opening night, was the familiar and oft-told tale of "Morning Glory." And yet, Katharine Hepburn infused the film with such warmth and sincerity that it was a triumph. Whether drunkenly reciting the soliloquy from "Hamlet," or doing the balcony scene from "Romeo And Juliet," she glowed with an inner fire. She won the Oscar as best actress over Diana Wynyard in "Cavalcade," and May Robson in "Lady For A Day."

Still another virtuoso, Award-winning performance was given by Charles Laughton in "The Private Life Of Henry VIII," and for it he was named best actor. Directed by Alexander Korda, Laughton filled the screen with a portrayal that made the haughty, gluttonous king come to life. Winning the laurels for best actor was no mean accomplishment in a year that saw Paul Muni nominated for "I Am A Fugitive From A Chain Gang," and Leslie Howard nominated for "Berkeley Square."

"A Farewell To Arms," directed by two-time Award-winner Frank Borzage, was a film of rare tenderness, depth, and scope. It was doubly honored: both for its cinematography by Charles Bryant Lang, Jr., and for its sound recording by Harold Lewis.

The trophy for best adaptation went to Victor Heerman and Sarah Y. Mason for their "Little Women," with an all-star cast including Katharine Hepburn, Joan Bennett, Paul Lukas, and Spring Byington.

Once again, Walt Disney was tapped for the cartoon honors for his delightful "The Three Little Pigs," while the other two short subject Awards went to "So This Is Harris," and "Krakatoa."

AWARDS

Production: "Cavalcade," Fox.

Actor: Charles Laughton in "The Private Life Of Henry VIII," London Films, United Artists.

Actress: Katharine Hepburn in "Morning Glory," RKO Radio.

Direction: Frank Lloyd, "Cavalcade."

Writing (original story): Robert Lord, "One Way Passage," Warner Brothers.

Writing (adaptation): Sarah Y. Mason, Victor Heerman, "Little Women," RKO Radio.

Cinematography: Charles Bryant Lang, Jr., "A Farewell To Arms," Paramount.

Art Direction: William S. Darling, "Cavalcade."

Sound Recording: Harold C. Lewis, "A Farewell To Arms."

Assistant Director: Charles Dorian, Metro-Goldwyn-Mayer; Gordon Hollingshead, Warner Brothers; Dewey Starkey, RKO Radio; Charles Barton, Paramount; Scott Beal, Universal; Fred Fox, United Artists; William Tummel, Fox.

Short Subjects (cartoon): "The Three Little Pigs," Disney, United Artists.

Short Subjects (comedy): "So This Is Harris," RKO Radio.

Short Subjects (novelty): "Krakatoa," Educational.

SCIENTIFIC AND TECHNICAL AWARDS

Electrical Research Products, Inc., for their wide range recording and reproducing system.

RCA-Victor Co., Inc., for their high-fidelity recording and reproducing system.

Fox Film Corp., Fred Jackman and Warner Bros. Pictures, Inc., and Sidney Sanders of RKO Studios, Inc., for their development and effective use of the translucent cellulose screen in composite photography.

"Cavalcade" (best production) with Herbert Mundin,
Diana Wynyard, Clive Brook, and Una O'Connor. Fox

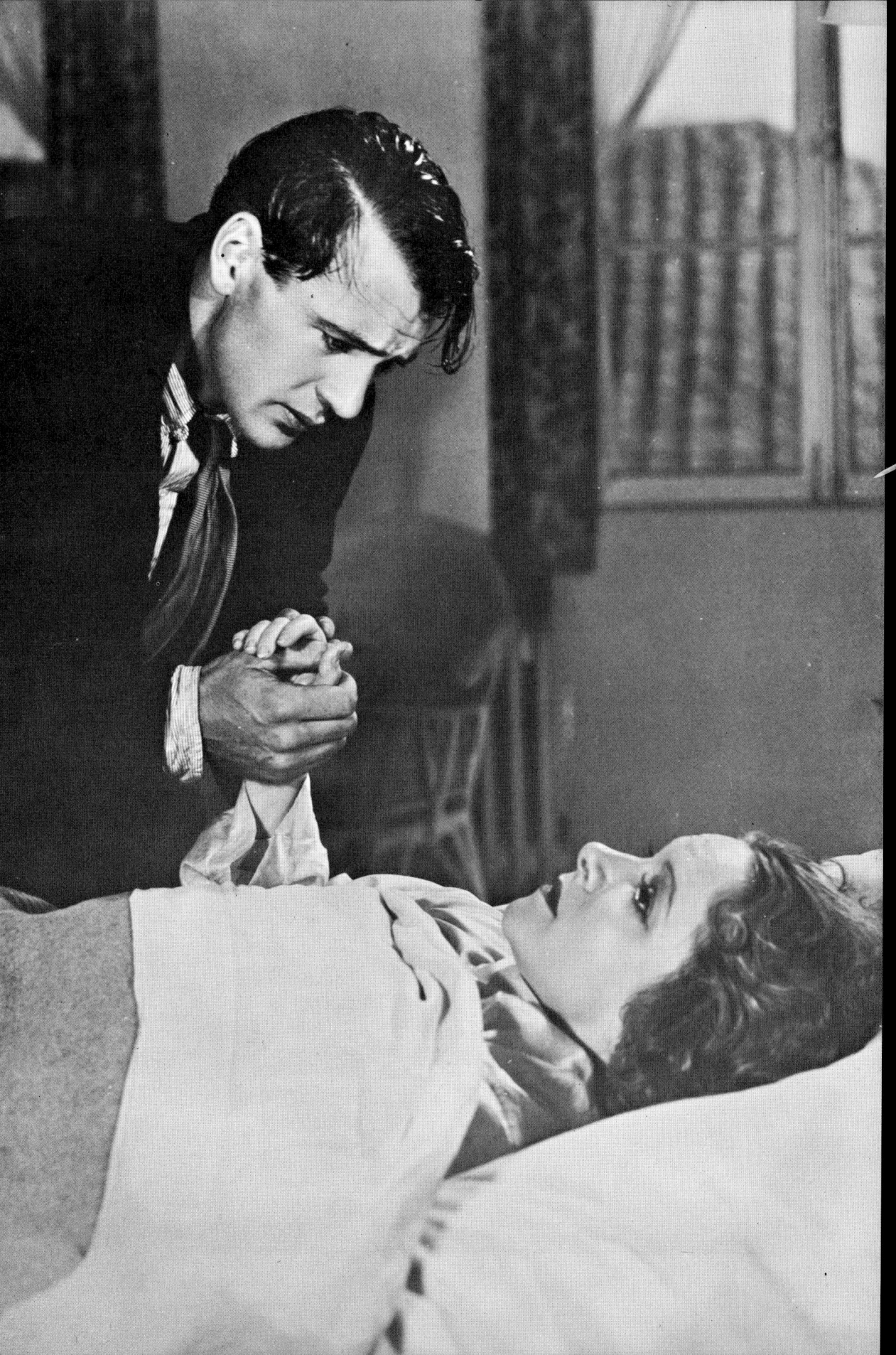

Katharine Hepburn (best actress) and Douglas Fairbanks, Jr.
in "Morning Glory." RKO Radio

"One Way Passage" (best original story) with Warren Hymer, William Powell, and Kay Francis. Warner Brothers

"One Way Passage" (best original story) with Warren Hymer, William Powell, and Kay Francis. Warner Brothers

"The Three Little Pigs" (best cartoon). Disney, RKO Radio

AWARDS

Production: "It Happened One Night," Columbia.

Actor: Clark Gable in "It Happened One Night."

Actress: Claudette Colbert in "It Happened One Night."

Direction: Frank Capra, "It Happened One Night."

Writing (original story): Arthur Caesar, "Manhattan Melodrama," Metro-Goldwyn-Mayer.

Writing (adaptation): Robert Riskin, "It Happened One Night."

Cinematography: Victor Milner, "Cleopatra," Paramount.

Art Direction: Cedric Gibbons, Frederic Hope, "The Merry Widow," Metro-Goldwyn-Mayer.

Sound Recording: Paul Neal, "One Night Of Love," Columbia.

Film Editing: Conrad Nervig, "Eskimo," Metro-Goldwyn-Mayer.

Assistant Director: John Waters, "Viva Villa," Metro-Goldwyn-Mayer.

Music (score): Louis Silvers, "One Night Of Love."

Music (song): Herb Magidson (lyrics), Con Conrad (music), "The Continental" from "The Gay Divorcee," RKO Radio.

Short Subjects (cartoon): "The Tortoise And The Hare," Disney.

Short Subjects (comedy): "La Cucaracha," RKO Radio.

Short Subjects (novelty): "City Of Wax," Educational.

SPECIAL AWARD

Shirley Temple, presented in grateful recognition of her outstanding contribution to screen entertainment during the year 1934.

SCIENTIFIC AND TECHNICAL AWARDS

Electrical Research Products, Inc., for their development of the vertical cut disc method of recording sound for motion pictures (hill and dale recording).

Columbia Pictures Corp., for their application of the vertical cut disc method (hill and dale recording) to actual studio production, with their recording of the sound on the picture, "One Night Of Love."

Bell and Howell Co., for their development of the Bell and Howell fully automatic sound and picture printer.

1934

A classic of American film-making was born when "It Happened One Night" opened, almost unheralded in Hollywood. There was no indication that this comedy about the adventures of a newspaperman and an heiress would take its place among the masterpieces of cinema art. Claudette Colbert and Clark Gable had never demonstrated any particular comic talents. Neither was the reigning favorite among the millions of film fans. Frank Capra was considered only one of several better-than-average directors. Even Robert Riskin's screenplay—the story of two people from different worlds meeting on a night-bus, and their merry madcap adventures—was not particularly unique.

The night that the Awards were presented there were two favorites: William Powell and Myrna Loy's mystery-comedy, "The Thin Man," and "The Gay Divorcee," starring Ginger Rogers and Fred Astaire. "One Night Of Love," with Grace Moore, and "Flirtation Walk," starring Dick Powell, were given an outside chance.

And yet, "It Happened One Night" walked off with every major Award. Clark Gable and Claudette Colbert won Oscars for their acting; Frank Capra for his direction; Robert Riskin for his screenplay; and the film, named best production of the year.

What was it about "It Happened One Night" that made it a masterpiece, an Award-winner? The answer is not simple. Part of the answer could be found in the emergence of the writer-director team as a force in the medium. Together, Capra and Riskin built scenes that were unforgettable, where the use of the camera heightened the effectiveness of the dialogue. Two scenes particularly, the hitch-hiking scene and the Walls of Jericho scene, served as models for film comedy through the years. In all, "It Happened One Night" was the perfect blending of all aspects of film making.

The cinematography Award went to Victor Milner for "Cleopatra," which was an all-star production from top to bottom, under the sure directorial hand of C. B. De Mille, with Claudette Colbert as Cleo, Warren William as Caesar, and matinee-idol Henry Wilcoxon as Antony.

The number of Awards was beginning to grow, and for the first time, the important role of music in motion pictures was recognized by the Academy. "One Night Of Love" was honored for its musical score, and "The Continental" from "The Gay Divorcee" was named best song.

Walt Disney, for the third straight year, took the cartoon award with "The Tortoise And The Hare"; and Shirley Temple, the darling of millions, won a special Award for her winning performances in "Little Miss Marker" with Adolphe Menjou, "Now And Forever" with Gary Cooper and Carole Lombard, and "Stand Up And Cheer" with James Dunn.

"It Happened One Night" (best production) with Claudette Colbert
(best actress) and Clark Gable (best actor). Columbia

"Cleopatra" (best cinematography) with Henry Wilcoxon, Claudette Colbert, and a cast of thousands. Paramount

"The Tortoise And The Hare" (best cartoon). Disney

1935

If, during the course of any year, one really great film is produced, it is fortunate. During this year, however, there were two truly magnificent films made; two films which were much more than mere entertainment; two films which achieved the stature of art; they, in fact, transcended film toward art.

First, "Mutiny On The Bounty," a rugged, sometimes brutal and disquieting film. Here was a film true to its source, the Nordhoff-Hall novel, and thus, true to itself. It was an uncompromising film directed by Frank Lloyd, and it did not hesitate to show, in graphic detail, the harshness and tyranny of the sea and the men who dedicated themselves to it.

It was produced on the grand scale, and, aided by the brilliant performances of Charles Laughton as Captain Bligh and Clark Gable as Mr. Christian, "Mutiny On The Bounty" was named best production of the year.

The second great film of the year was "The Informer," and although it did not take the top honor, it has remained a classic of film making, even more highly regarded than "Mutiny On The Bounty," in retrospect.

"The Informer" is the story of man's temptation, transgression, fear, remorse, retribution, forgiveness, and death—and all of this in a single dreary night in Dublin. As Gypo Nolan, Victor McLaglen created one of the most unforgettable characters ever presented on film, and for it he was rewarded with the accolade for best actor. John Ford directed this symbolic drama and was named best director. Ford said, when interviewed, that "The Informer" was "the easiest film" he ever directed. "No wonder," said Ford. "I had been dreaming of it for five years." "The Informer" was also named for two other awards: for musical score by Max Steiner, and for screen adaptation by Dudley Nichols.

The selection of the year's best actress was most difficult. Elisabeth Bergner was nominated for "Escape Me Never," Claudette Colbert for "Private Worlds," Bette Davis for "Dangerous," Katharine Hepburn for "Alice Adams," Miriam Hopkins for "Becky Sharp," and Merle Oberon for "The Dark Angel."

Bette Davis, portraying an actress whose talents are diminished by her love of hard liquor, lechery, and off-stage exhibitionism, won the Award as best actress. Once again she proved that she was Hollywood's No. 1 femme fatale, as she had already shown in "Of Human Bondage." It was a rare performance which lifted an otherwise ordinary film into a higher bracket.

Once again Walt Disney was named as cartoon-master, with his fourth consecutive Award in the category; this time for "Three Orphan Kittens."

Hal Mohr was honored for his cinematography in "A Midsummer Night's Dream."

David Wark Griffith, perhaps the greatest director and innovator ever produced in Hollywood, the director responsible for such classic films as "The Birth Of A Nation," "Intolerance," "Way Down East," and "Orphans Of The Storm," was honored by a special Award from the Academy.

AWARDS

Production: "Mutiny On The Bounty,"
Metro-Goldwyn-Mayer.

Actor: Victor McLaglen in "The Informer,"
RKO Radio.

Actress: Bette Davis in "Dangerous,"
Warner Brothers.

Direction: John Ford, "The Informer."

Writing (original story): Ben Hecht, Charles
MacArthur, "The Scoundrel," Paramount.

Writing (best written screenplay): Dudley Nichols,
"The Informer."

Cinematography: Hal Mohr, "A Midsummer Night's
Dream," Warner Brothers.

Art Direction: Richard Day, "The Dark Angel,"
Goldwyn, United Artists.

Sound Recording: William Steinkampf, "Naughty
Marietta," Metro-Goldwyn-Mayer.

Film Editing: Ralph Dawson, "A Midsummer
Night's Dream."

Assistant Director: Clem Beauchamp, Paul Wing,
"Lives Of A Bengal Lancer," Paramount.

Music (score): Max Steiner, "The Informer."

Music (song): Al Dubin (lyrics), Harry Warren
(music), "Lullaby Of Broadway" from
"Golddiggers Of 1935," Warner Brothers.

Dance Direction: Dave Gould, "I've Got A Feeling
You're Fooling" number from "Broadway Melody
Of 1936," Metro-Goldwyn-Mayer. "Straw Hat"
number from "Folies Bergere," 20th Century,
United Artists.

Short Subjects (cartoon): "Three Orphan Kittens,"
Disney, United Artists.

Short Subjects (comedy): "How To Sleep,"
Metro-Goldwyn-Mayer.

Short Subjects (novelty): "Wings Over Mt.
Everest," Gaumont British, Educational.

SPECIAL AWARD

David Wark Griffith, for his distinguished creative
achievements as director and producer and his
invaluable initiative and lasting contributions
to the progress of the motion picture arts.

SCIENTIFIC AND TECHNICAL AWARDS

Agfa Ansco Corp., for their development of the
Agfa infra-red film.

Eastman Kodak Co., for their development of the
Eastman Pola-Screen.

Metro-Goldwyn-Mayer Studio, for the development
of anti-directional negative and positive
development by means of jet turbulation, and
the application of the method to all negative
and print processing of the entire product of a
major producing company.

William A. Mueller of Warner Bros.-First National
Studio Sound Department, for his method of
dubbing, in which the level of the dialogue
automatically controls the level of the
accompanying music and sound effects.

Mole-Richardson Co., for their development of the
"Solar-spot" spot lamps.

Douglas Shearer and Metro-Goldwyn-Mayer Studio
Sound Department, for their automatic control
system for cameras and sound recording
machines and auxiliary stage equipment.

Electrical Research Products, Inc., for their study
and development of equipment to analyze and
measure flutter resulting from the travel of the
film through the mechanisms used in the
recording and reproduction of sound.

Paramount Productions, Inc., for the design and
construction of the Paramount transparency air
turbine developing machine.

Nathan Levinson, Director of Sound Recording for
Warner Bros.-First National Studio, for the
method of intercutting variable density and
variable area sound tracks to secure an increase
in the effective volume range of sound recorded
for motion pictures.

Victor McLaglen (best actor) and Margot Grahame
in "The Informer" (best direction). RKO Radio

"Mutiny On The Bounty" (best production) with Franchot Tone, below;
Charles Laughton and Clark Gable, opposite. M-G-M

Bette Davis (best actress)
in "Dangerous." Warner Brothers

"A Midsummer Night's Dream" (best cinematography)
with Hugh Herbert, Frank McHugh, Arthur Treacher, Otis Harlan,
Dewey Robinson, James Cagney, and Joe E. Brown. Warner Brothers

AWARDS

Production: "The Great Ziegfeld,"
Metro-Goldwyn-Mayer.

Actor: Paul Muni in "The Story Of Louis Pasteur,"
Warner Brothers.

Actress: Luise Rainer in "The Great Ziegfeld."

Supporting Actor: Walter Brennan in "Come And
Get It," Goldwyn, United Artists.

Supporting Actress: Gale Sondergaard in
"Anthony Adverse," Warner Brothers.

Direction: Frank Capra, "Mr. Deeds Goes To Town,"
Columbia.

Writing (original story): Pierre Collings, Sheridan
Gibney, "The Story Of Louis Pasteur."

Writing (best written screenplay): Pierre Collings,
Sheridan Gibney, "The Story Of Louis Pasteur."

Cinematography: Tony Gaudio, "Anthony Adverse."

Art Direction: Richard Day, "Dodsworth," Goldwyn,
United Artists.

Sound Recording: Douglas Shearer,
"San Francisco," Metro-Goldwyn-Mayer.

Film Editing: Ralph Dawson, "Anthony Adverse."

Assistant Director: Jack Sullivan, "The Charge Of
The Light Brigade," Warner Brothers.

Music (score): Leo Forbstein, "Anthony Adverse."

Music (song): Dorothy Fields (lyrics), Jerome Kern
(music), "The Way You Look Tonight" from
"Swing Time," RKO Radio.

Dance Direction: Seymour Felix, "A Pretty Girl Is
Like A Melody" number from "The Great
Ziegfeld."

Short Subjects (cartoon): "Country Cousin,"
Disney, United Artists.

Short Subjects (color): "Give Me Liberty,"
Warner Brothers.

Short Subjects (1-reel): "Bored Of Education,"
Roach, Metro-Goldwyn-Mayer.

Short Subjects (2-reel): "The Public Pays,"
Metro-Goldwyn-Mayer.

SPECIAL AWARDS

The March Of Time, for its significance to motion
pictures and for having revolutionized one of
the most important branches of the industry—
the newsreel.

W. Howard Greene and Harold Rosson, for the
color cinematography of the Selznick
International production, "The Garden Of Allah."

SCIENTIFIC AND TECHNICAL AWARDS

Douglas Shearer and the Metro-Goldwyn-Mayer
Studio Sound Department, for the development
of a practical two-way horn system, and a biased
Class A push-pull recording system.

E. C. Wente and the Bell Telephone Laboratories,
for their multi-cellular high-frequency horn
and receiver.

RCA Manufacturing Co., Inc., for their rotary
stabilizer sound head.

RCA Manufacturing Co., Inc., for their
development of a method of recording and
printing sound records utilizing a restricted
spectrum (known as ultra-violet light recording).

Electrical Research Products, Inc., for the ERPI
"Type Q" portable recording channel.

RCA Manufacturing Co., Inc., for furnishing a
practical design and specifications for a
non-slip printer.

United Artists Studio Corp., for the development
of a practical, efficient and quiet wind machine.

1936

The race for acting honors in the Academy sweepstakes was a wide open affair with Gary Cooper nominated for "Mr. Deeds Goes To Town," Walter Huston for "Dodsworth," Paul Muni for "The Story Of Louis Pasteur," William Powell for "My Man Godfrey," and Spencer Tracy for "San Francisco."

But it was Paul Muni, a graduate of the Yiddish Art Theatre and Broadway, nominated in 1933 for his stirring performance in "I Was A Fugitive From A Chain Gang," who garnered the Oscar for his portrayal of Louis Pasteur. Muni filled the screen with a portrait of lasting and sensitive understanding of the country chemist who plodded and prayed, and who defied the scoffing doctors and academicians of all Europe to give the world lifesaving vaccines and serums.

It was the year of film biographies in the motion picture industry. As best production, the Academy members chose "The Great Ziegfeld," a film that was very nearly not made.

Almost as soon as Flo Ziegfeld died in 1932, every studio wanted to film his glamorous life. Here was a man who had become a legend in his own time, one of the most colorful and astute showmen the theatre ever knew. His "Follies" were the toast of New York and the talk of the world. But, somehow an acceptable screenplay could not be found until William Anthony McGuire, a playwright and friend of Ziegfeld's, hit the jackpot.

Here was all the excitement of the great Ziegfeld (played by William Powell), and the famous people who surrounded him: Billie Burke (played by Myrna Loy), Fannie Brice, Eddie Cantor, and Will Rogers. For her portrayal of Anna Held, Luise Rainer, recently brought to Hollywood from Austria, was named best actress. Here was a perfect blending of drama and music, human interest and spectacle.

Frank Capra who had already won one Academy citation for "It Happened One Night," was named best director for "Mr. Deeds Goes To Town."

Another film that must be mentioned is "Anthony Adverse," a giant production made from Hervey Allen's mammoth novel. In all, over 700,000 feet of film passed through the cameras; there were over ninety-eight speaking parts; over 130 different sets. Directed by Mervyn LeRoy, "Anthony Adverse" had a cast led by Fredric March, Olivia de Havilland, Anita Louise, Donald Woods, Edmund Gwenn, Claude Rains, Louis Hayward, and Gale Sondergaard.

For her performance in this epic film, Gale Sondergaard won a new Oscar offered by the Academy, best supporting actress. "Anthony Adverse" was also cited for its cinematography by Tony Gaudio; its film editing by Ralph Dawson; and its musical score by Leo Forbstein.

Veteran character actor Walter Brennan was named best supporting actor for his performance in "Come And Get It," which had been adapted from an Edna Ferber novel. Walt Disney, who had the Award habit, was again named for the best cartoon, this time for "Country Cousin."

"The Great Ziegfeld" (best production) with Frank Morgan, William Powell and Jean Chatburn. M-G-M

Luise Rainer
(best actress),
William Powell and Robert Grieg
in "The Great Ziegfeld."
M-G-M

Paul Muni (best actor) in
"The Story Of Louis Pasteur."
Warner Brothers

Gale Sondergaard (best supporting actress) with Claude Rains and Fredric March
in "Anthony Adverse" (best cinematography). Warner Brothers

Walter Brennan (best supporting actor)
and Frances Farmer in "Come And Get It."
Goldwyn, United Artists

"Mr. Deeds
Goes To Town"
(best direction)
with Gary Cooper.
Columbia

1937

"The Life Of Emile Zola" caught the spirit of the crusading French novelist for posterity on film. Paul Muni, as Zola, dominated the production, with his unbelievable ability to get under the skin of a character and make it his own. It traced Zola's life from his youth, when as a friend of impressionist painter, Cezanne, he starved in an attic in Paris, to the peak of his career when he was on the threshold of membership in the French Academy, only to face almost certain defamation by joining the defense of controversial Captain Alfred Dreyfus. This brilliant biography was named best production, Norman Reilly Raine, Heinz Herald and Geza Herczeg were honored for their screenplay, and Joseph Schildkraut was cited as best supporting actor for his performance as Dreyfus, the army officer falsely accused of treason and sent to Devil's Island.

Once again Luise Rainer was named best actress, this time for her triumphant portrayal of O-lan, a mute and humble Chinese bride. She conveyed all the suffering, courage, pain, and transient moments of joy in the life of China's women, almost completely without the help of words. Paul Muni was once again marvelous as Wang, her husband.

"The Good Earth," the poignant dramatization of Pearl S. Buck's mighty novel of China, showed in telling words and pictures the struggle of man pitted against Nature. The swarming locust, the wind, rain, and hail storms rushing down on the plains, the stampede of people driven to desperation by raw hunger, and vivid and compelling pictures of revolution, were startling and penetrating. It was filmed partially on location in China, and Karl Freund was honored for his splendid cinematography.

Although there could be no doubt that Paul Muni was in top form in both "The Life Of Emile Zola" and "The Good Earth," he, along with such other nominees for acting laurels as Charles Boyer for "Conquest," Fredric March for "A Star Is Born," and Robert Montgomery for "Night Must Fall," went down to defeat at the hands of Spencer Tracy.

Tracy's performance in "Captains Courageous" was nothing short of superb, and for it he was awarded the Oscar as best actor by the Academy membership.

Alice Brady was named best supporting actress for her performance with Tyrone Power in "In Old Chicago"; Leo McCarey was cited as best director for "The Awful Truth"; and Robert Carson and William A. Wellman were named for best original writing in "A Star Is Born."

The name of Mack Sennett and the world of filmed comedy are so closely intertwined that it is impossible to separate them. The custard pie and the harrowing chases of the Keystone Kops were his trademark, but he was much more than that, he was a consummate artist, adept at every phase of filmmaking. The Academy gave him a special Award for his contributions to the art of motion pictures.

AWARDS

Production: "The Life Of Emile Zola,"
Warner Brothers.

Actor: Spencer Tracy in "Captains Courageous,"
Metro-Goldwyn-Mayer.

Actress: Luise Rainer in "The Good Earth,"
Metro-Goldwyn-Mayer.

Supporting Actor: Joseph Schildkraut in "The Life
Of Emile Zola."

Supporting Actress: Alice Brady in "In Old
Chicago," 20th Century-Fox.

Direction: Leo McCarey, "The Awful Truth,"
Columbia.

Writing (original story): Robert Carson, William A.
Wellman, "A Star Is Born," Selznick, United
Artists.

Writing (best written screenplay): Norman Reilly
Raine, Heinz Herald, Geza Herczeg, "The Life
Of Emile Zola."

Cinematography: Karl Freund, "The Good Earth."

Art Direction: Stephen Goosson, "Lost Horizon,"
Columbia.

Sound Recording: Thomas T. Moulton,
"Hurricane," Goldwyn, United Artists.

Film Editing: Gene Milford, Gene Havlick,
"Lost Horizon."

Assistant Director: Robert Webb, "In Old Chicago."

Music (score): Charles Previn, "One Hundred
Men And A Girl," Universal.

Music (song): Harry Owens (lyrics and music),
"Sweet Leilani" from "Waikiki Wedding,"
Paramount.

Dance Direction: Hermes Pan, "Fun House"
number from "A Damsel In Distress,"
RKO Radio.

Short Subjects (cartoon): "The Old Mill," Disney,
RKO Radio.

Short Subjects (color): "Penny Wisdom,"
Metro-Goldwyn-Mayer.

Short Subjects (1-reel): "Private Life Of The
Gannets," Educational.

Short Subjects (2-reel): "Torture Money,"
Metro-Goldwyn-Mayer.

Irving G. Thalberg Memorial Award: Darryl F.
Zanuck.

SPECIAL AWARDS

The Museum of Modern Art Film Library, for
making available to the public the means of
studying the development of the motion picture
as one of the major arts.

Mack Sennett, for his lasting contribution to the
comedy technique of the screen.

Edgar Bergen, for his outstanding comedy
creation, Charlie McCarthy.

W. Howard Greene, for the color cinematography
of "A Star Is Born."

SCIENTIFIC AND TECHNICAL AWARDS

Agfa Ansco Corp., for Agfa Supreme and Agfa
Ultra Speed pan motion picture negatives.

Walt Disney Prods., Ltd., for the Multi-Plane
Camera.

Eastman Kodak Co., for two fine-grain duplicating
film stocks.

Farciot Edouart and Paramount Pictures, Inc., for
the development of the Paramount dual screen
transparency camera setup.

Douglas Shearer and the Metro-Goldwyn-Mayer
Studio Sound Department, for a method of
varying the scanning width of variable density
sound tracks (squeeze tracks) for obtaining an
increased amount of noise reduction.

John Arnold and Metro-Goldwyn-Mayer Studio
Camera Department, for their improvement of
the semi-automatic follow focus device and its
application to all of the cameras used by M-G-M.

John Livadary, Director of Sound Recording for
Columbia Pictures Corp., for the application of
the bi-planar light valve to motion picture
sound recording.

Thomas T. Moulton and the United Artists Studio
Sound Department, for the application to motion
picture sound recording of volume indicators
which have peak reading response and linear
decibel scales.

RCA Manufacturing Co., Inc., for the introduction
of the modulated high-frequency method of
determining optimum photographic processing
conditions for variable width sound tracks.

Joseph E. Robbins and Paramount Pictures, Inc.,
for an exceptional application of acoustic
principles to the soundproofing of gasoline
generators and water pumps.

Douglas Shearer and the Metro-Goldwyn-Mayer
Studio Sound Department, for the design of the
film drive mechanism as incorporated in the
ERPI 1010 reproducer.

Alice Brady (best supporting actress) and Tyrone Power in "In Old Chicago." 20th Century-Fox

"The Life Of Emile Zola" (best production) with Paul Muni, Henry O'Neill, below;
Joseph Schildkraut (best supporting actor), right. Warner Brothers

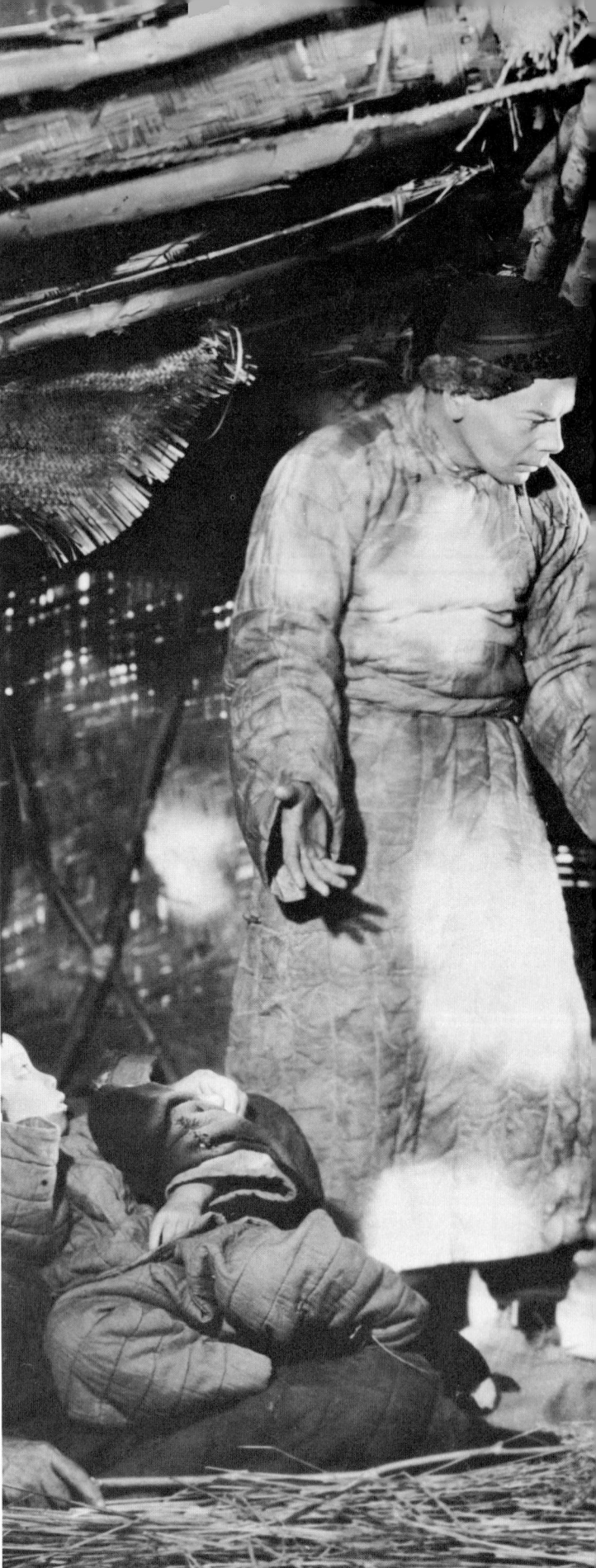

Luise Rainer (best actress)
and Paul Muni in "The Good Earth"
(best cinematography). M-G-M

Spencer Tracy (best actor) and Freddie Bartholomew in "Captains Courageous." M-G-M

AWARDS

Production: "You Can't Take It With You," Columbia.

Actor: Spencer Tracy in "Boys' Town," Metro-Goldwyn-Mayer.

Actress: Bette Davis in "Jezebel," Warner Brothers.

Supporting Actor: Walter Brennan in "Kentucky," 20th Century-Fox.

Supporting Actress: Fay Bainter in "Jezebel."

Direction: Frank Capra, "You Can't Take It With You."

Writing (original story): Dore Schary, Eleanore Griffin, "Boys' Town."

Writing (adaptation): W. P. Lipscomb, Cecil Lewis, Ian Dalrymple, "Pygmalion," Metro-Goldwyn-Mayer.

Writing (best written screenplay): George Bernard Shaw, "Pygmalion."

Cinematography: Joseph Ruttenberg, "The Great Waltz," Metro-Goldwyn-Mayer.

Art Direction: Carl Weyl, "The Adventures Of Robin Hood," Warner Brothers.

Sound Recording: Thomas T. Moulton, "The Cowboy And The Lady," Goldwyn, United Artists.

Film Editing: Ralph Dawson, "The Adventures Of Robin Hood."

Music (best score): Alfred Newman, "Alexander's Ragtime Band," 20th Century-Fox.

Music (original score): Erich Wolfgang Korngold, "The Adventures Of Robin Hood."

Music (song): Leo Robin (lyrics), Ralph Rainger (music), "Thanks For The Memory" from "Big Broadcast Of 1938," Paramount.

Short Subjects (cartoon): "Ferdinand The Bull," Disney, RKO Radio.

Short Subjects (1-reel): "That Mothers Might Live," Metro-Goldwyn-Mayer.

Short Subjects (2-reel): "Declaration Of Independence," Warner Brothers.

Irving G. Thalberg Memorial Award: Hal B. Wallis.

SPECIAL AWARDS

Deanna Durbin and Mickey Rooney, for their significant contribution in bringing to the screen the spirit and personification of youth, and as juvenile players setting a high standard of ability and achievement.

Harry M. Warner, in recognition of patriotic service in the production of historical short subjects presenting significant episodes in the early struggle of the American people for liberty.

Walt Disney, for "Snow White And The Seven Dwarfs," recognized as a significant screen innovation which has charmed millions and pioneered a great new entertainment field for the motion picture cartoon.

SCIENTIFIC AND TECHNICAL AWARDS

John Aalberg and the RKO Radio Studio Sound Department, for the application of compression to variable area recording in motion picture production.

Byron Haskin and the Special Effects Department of Warner Bros. Studio, for pioneering the development, and for the first practical application to motion picture production of the triple head background projector.

1938

The fulfillment of the dream of the man who said "... there is no such thing as a bad boy" was the subject matter of one of the finest films of the year, "Boys' Town," a film which gave Spencer Tracy the opportunity to win his second Oscar in a row as best actor. As Father Flanagan, the good priest who took wayward and delinquent boys from the overcrowded cities, educated them, and then sent them out into the world again, better people for their experience, Spencer Tracy was magnificent. Whether desperately trying to raise money for his Boys' Town project, or working closely with the delinquent children, Tracy's performance was skillful and radiant. He "was" Father Flanagan.

And, it might be added that Tracy was honored over some top stars giving excellent performances from both Hollywood and England: Leslie Howard in "Pygmalion," Robert Donat in "The Citadel," James Cagney in "Angels With Dirty Faces," and Charles Boyer in "Algiers."

"Boys' Town" was also honored for its original story by Dore Schary and Eleanore Griffin.

For the first time since 1934, a full-fledged comedy was named best production. "You Can't Take It With You," starring screen favorites Jean Arthur, Jimmy Stewart, and Lionel Barrymore, carried away the Oscar. It was a comedy with a difference, and the difference was Frank Capra, honored as best director for the third time in five years. Capra was a master of the comedy film as he had proven before with "It Happened One Night" and "Mr. Deeds Goes To Town." Capra had the uncanny ability to whip dialogue and picture into a frothy delight. He was not afraid of words, and never buried them under fancy camera angles. Capra also had the knack of getting the best possible performance out of each actor.

Margaret Sullavan in "Three Comrades," Norma Shearer in "Marie Antoinette," Wendy Hiller in "Pygmalion," Bette Davis in "Jezebel," and Fay Bainter in "White Banners," were all nominated for best actress, but it was Miss Davis, essaying one of the most difficult roles of her career—the head-strong, self-centered, and spiteful Southern belle in "Jezebel"—who was chosen by the Academy membership. The film, set in the Deep South in pre-Civil War days, was a diffuse film to say the least, a series of incidents sewn together on the fine, silken thread of Bette Davis' brilliant characterization.

Supporting Oscars went to Fay Bainter for her performance in "Jezebel," and Walter Brennan for "Kentucky."

Two special Awards of the Academy were particularly important. First, Walt Disney, who also took the regular cartoon Award for the classic "Ferdinand The Bull," was awarded one regular Oscar and seven miniature Oscars for his charming "Snow White And The Seven Dwarfs," which still delights millions of youngsters every year.

Mickey Rooney and Deanna Durbin were also the recipients of special Awards for their performances over the years, which had brought great joy to millions of movie-goers across the nation.

"You Can't Take It With You" (best production)
with Edward Arnold, James Stewart, and Lionel Barrymore. Columbia

Spencer Tracy (best actor)
and Mickey Rooney
in "Boys' Town." M-G-M

Walter Brennan
(best supporting actor)
and Loretta Young
in "Kentucky."
20th Century-Fox

Bette Davis (best actress)
left, and Fay Bainter
(best supporting actress)
in "Jezebel." Warner Brothers

"The Adventures Of Robin Hood" (best art direction)
with Basil Rathbone and Errol Flynn. Warner Brothers

"Ferdinand The Bull" (best cartoon). Disney, RKO Radio

1939

From the turbulent pages of Margaret Mitchell's best-selling Civil War novel, came the outstanding film of the decade, David O. Selznick's "Gone With The Wind." All America waited anxiously for the world première, and at the opening in New York it took a force of over 300 policemen to control the crowds that wanted to get a glimpse of the celebrities attending. Appetites had been whetted by a world-wide search for the right girl to play Scarlett O'Hara, and Clark Gable was everyone's choice to play Rhett Butler. No motion picture had ever garnered as much advance publicity or lived up to expectations so well.

In every respect "Gone With The Wind" was a superlative motion picture: magnificent performances from each member of the huge cast, stunning Technicolor cinematography and art direction, a highly literate screenplay that captured the story of the South in the fateful decade of secession, war, and reconstruction in terms of the people involved, all blended with artistry by David O. Selznick and director Victor Fleming.

"Gone With The Wind" was hailed by the public and the critics alike, and the members of the Academy voted it the Award as the best production of the year along with eight other regular Oscars and two special citations.

Vivien Leigh as the self-centered, unconquerable Scarlett O'Hara, the representative of a dying aristocratic society, was named best actress. Even though she was a relative newcomer to American audiences before her imperious portrayal of Scarlett, she was honored over such favorites as Irene Dunne in "Love Affair," Greer Garson in "Goodbye, Mr. Chips," Bette Davis in "Dark Victory," and Greta Garbo in "Ninotchka."

Clark Gable as Rhett, Leslie Howard as Ashley, and Olivia de Havilland as Melanie were so true to the novel that it gave audiences the feeling that Margaret Mitchell had written the novel with them in mind. This was also the case with Hattie McDaniel's unforgettable performance as Mammy for which she was honored as best supporting actress.

In all, "Gone With The Wind" left a lasting mark of excellence that Hollywood could point to with pride.

Although it seemed that way, "Gone With The Wind" did not win all the Awards. Clark Gable had been nominated for acting honors but he, along with James Stewart in "Mr. Smith Goes To Washington," Mickey Rooney in "Babes In Arms," and Laurence Olivier in "Wuthering Heights," could not take the honors from Robert Donat's performance as the shy, revered English schoolteacher in "Goodbye, Mr. Chips."

Thomas Mitchell was cited as best supporting actor for his work in John Ford's style-setting Western, "Stagecoach."

For the eighth consecutive year, Walt Disney won the Oscar for the best cartoon short subject, this time for "The Ugly Duckling."

AWARDS

Production: "Gone With The Wind," Selznick.

Actor: Robert Donat in "Goodbye, Mr. Chips," Metro-Goldwyn-Mayer.

Actress: Vivien Leigh in "Gone With The Wind."

Supporting Actor: Thomas Mitchell in "Stagecoach," Wanger, United Artists.

Supporting Actress: Hattie McDaniel in "Gone With The Wind."

Direction: Victor Fleming, "Gone With The Wind."

Writing (original story): Lewis R. Foster, "Mr. Smith Goes To Washington," Columbia.

Writing (best written screenplay): Sidney Howard, "Gone With The Wind."

Cinematography (black-and-white): Gregg Toland, "Wuthering Heights," Goldwyn, United Artists.

Cinematography (color): Ernest Haller, Ray Rennahan, "Gone With The Wind."

Art Direction: Lyle Wheeler, "Gone With The Wind."

Sound Recording: Bernard B. Brown, "When Tomorrow Comes," Universal.

Film Editing: Hal C. Kern, James E. Newcom, "Gone With The Wind."

Music (best score): Richard Hageman, Franke Harling, John Leipold, Leo Shuken, "Stagecoach."

Music (original score): Herbert Stothart, "The Wizard Of Oz," Metro-Goldwyn-Mayer.

Music (song): E. Y. Harburg (lyrics), Harold Arlen (music), "Over The Rainbow" from "The Wizard Of Oz."

Short Subjects (cartoon): "The Ugly Duckling," Disney, RKO Radio.

Short Subjects (1-reel): "Busy Little Bears," Paramount.

Short Subjects (2-reel): "Sons Of Liberty," Warner Brothers.

Irving G. Thalberg Memorial Award: David O. Selznick.

SPECIAL AWARDS

Douglas Fairbanks (Commemorative Award), recognizing the unique and outstanding contribution of Douglas Fairbanks, first President of the Academy, to the international development of the motion picture.

The Technicolor Company, for its contributions in successfully bringing three-color feature production to the screen.

Motion Picture Relief Fund, acknowledging the outstanding services to the industry during the past year of the Motion Picture Relief Fund and its progressive leadership.

Judy Garland, for her outstanding performance as a screen juvenile during the past year.

William Cameron Menzies, for outstanding achievement in the use of color for the enhancement of dramatic mood in the production of "Gone With The Wind."

SCIENTIFIC AND TECHNICAL AWARDS

George Anderson of Warner Bros. Studio, for an improved positive head for sun arcs.

John Arnold of Metro-Goldwyn-Mayer Studio, for the M-G-M mobile camera crane.

Thomas T. Moulton, Fred Albin and the Sound Department of the Samuel Goldwyn Studio, for the origination and application of the Delta db test to sound recording in motion pictures.

Farciot Edouart, Joseph E. Robbins, William Rudolph and Paramount Pictures, Inc., for the design and construction of a quiet portable treadmill.

Emery Huse and Ralph B. Atkinson of Eastman Kodak Co., for their specifications for chemical analysis of photographic developers and fixing baths.

Harold Nye of Warner Bros. Studio, for a miniature incandescent spot lamp.

A. J. Tondreau of Warner Bros. Studio, for the design and manufacture of an improved sound track printer.

Multiple Award for important contributions in cooperative development of new improved process Projection Equipment:

F. R. Abbott, Haller Belt, Alan Cook and Bausch & Lomb Optical Co., for faster projection lenses.

Mitchell Camera Co., for a new type process projection head.

Mole-Richardson Co., for a new type automatically controlled projection arc lamp.

Charles Handley, David Joy and National Carbon Co., for improved and more stable high-intensity carbons.

Winton Hoch and Technicolor Motion Picture Corp., for an auxiliary optical system.

Don Musgrave and Selznick International Pictures, Inc., for pioneering in the use of coordinated equipment in the production, "Gone With The Wind."

"Wuthering Heights"
(best cinematography,
black and white)
with Laurence Olivier
and Merle Oberon.
Goldwyn, United Artists

"Mr. Smith Goes To Washington"
(best original story)
with James Stewart
and Jean Arthur. Columbia

"Sons Of Liberty"
(best short subject, 2-reel)
with Gale Sondergaard
and Claude Rains.
Warner Brothers

Vivien Leigh (best actress)
with Clark Gable, left,
and with Leslie Howard, below,
in "Gone With The Wind"
(best production). Selznick

Hattie McDaniel
(best supporting actress)
and Clark Gable in
"Gone With The Wind."
Selznick

Thomas Mitchell
(best supporting
actor), center, with
George Bancroft,
and John Wayne
in "Stagecoach."
Wanger, United Artists

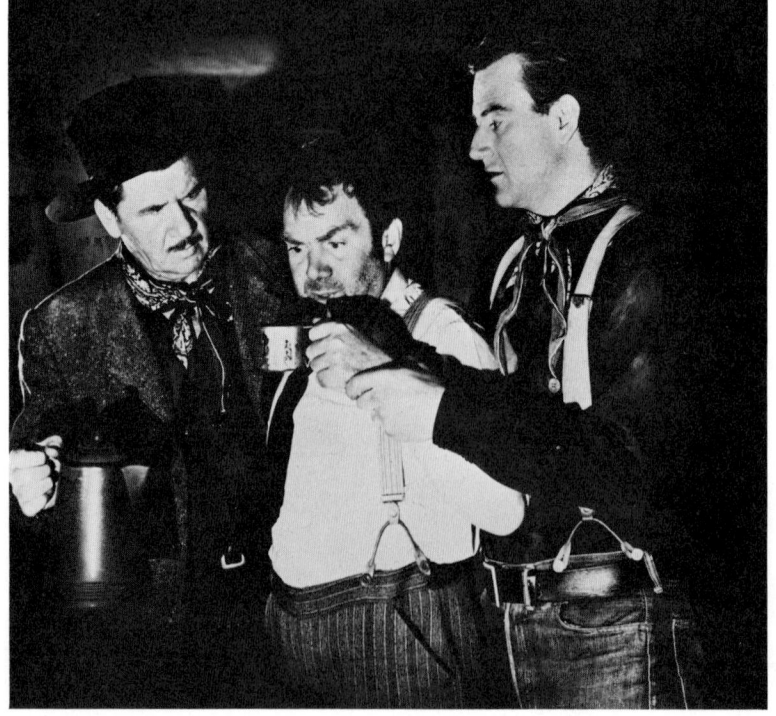

AWARDS

Production: "Rebecca," Selznick, United Artists.

Actor: James Stewart in "The Philadelphia Story," Metro-Goldwyn-Mayer.

Actress: Ginger Rogers in "Kitty Foyle," RKO Radio.

Supporting Actor: Walter Brennan in "The Westerner," Goldwyn, United Artists.

Supporting Actress: Jane Darwell in "The Grapes Of Wrath," 20th Century-Fox.

Direction: John Ford, "The Grapes Of Wrath."

Writing (original story): Benjamin Glazer, John S. Toldy, "Arise, My Love," Paramount.

Writing (original screenplay): Preston Sturges, "The Great McGinty," Paramount.

Writing (best written screenplay): Donald Ogden Stewart, "The Philadelphia Story."

Cinematography (black-and-white): George Barnes, "Rebecca."

Cinematography (color): George Perrinal, "The Thief Of Bagdad," Korda, United Artists.

Art Direction (black-and-white): Cedric Gibbons, Paul Groesse, "Pride And Prejudice," Metro-Goldwyn-Mayer.

Art Direction (color): Vincent Korda, "The Thief Of Bagdad."

Sound Recording: Douglas Shearer, "Strike Up The Band," Metro-Goldwyn-Mayer.

Film Editing: Anne Bauchens, "North West Mounted Police," Paramount.

Special Effects: Lawrence Butler (photographic), Jack Whitney (sound), "The Thief Of Bagdad."

Music (best score): Alfred Newman, "Tin Pan Alley," 20th Century-Fox.

Music (original score): Leigh Harline, Paul J. Smith, Ned Washington, "Pinocchio," Disney, RKO Radio.

Music (song): Ned Washington (lyrics), Leigh Harline (music), "When You Wish Upon A Star," from "Pinocchio."

Short Subjects (cartoon): "The Milky Way," Metro-Goldwyn-Mayer.

Short Subjects (1-reel): "Quicker 'N A Wink," Metro-Goldwyn-Mayer.

Short Subjects (2-reel): "Teddy, The Rough Rider," Warner Brothers.

SPECIAL AWARDS

Bob Hope, in recognition of his unselfish services to the Motion Picture Industry.

Colonel Nathan Levinson, for his outstanding services to the industry and the Army which made possible the present efficient mobilization of the Motion Picture Industry facilities for the production of Army training films.

SCIENTIFIC AND TECHNICAL AWARDS

20th Century-Fox Film Corp., for the design and construction of the 20th Century Silenced Camera, developed by Daniel Clark, Grover Laube, Charles Miller and Robert W. Stevens.

Warner Bros. Studio Art Department and Anton Grot, for the design and perfection of the water ripple and wave illusion machine.

1940

For the second consecutive year, David O. Selznick brought an adaptation of a best-selling novel to the screen with precisely the same results. "Rebecca," an intensely interesting and dramatic psychological drama won the Oscar as best production. Writers Robert E. Sherwood and Joan Harrison were almost completely faithful in their transfer of the Daphne du Maurier book to the screen, and "Rebecca" had the distinction of serving as Alfred Hitchcock's directorial debut in American films.

Rebecca, the first wife of Maxim de Winter, was already dead at the opening, but her spirit hovered everywhere; in every room of de Winter's castle-like house, Manderley; coming at every turn between de Winter, expertly played by a brooding Laurence Olivier, and his young, impressionable new wife. Joan Fontaine moved close to stardom with her finely drawn portrait of the fragile, embarrassed bride.

The overall somber effect of the film was heightened by George Barnes' cinematography, which was named best in the category, but it was the masterly direction of Hitchcock that made "Rebecca" a prize-winner.

Laurence Olivier was nominated for top acting honors for his performance in "Rebecca," along with Charles Chaplin for "The Great Dictator," James Stewart for "The Philadelphia Story," Henry Fonda for "The Grapes Of Wrath," and Raymond Massey for his unforgettable characterization of Lincoln in "Abe Lincoln in Illinois."

It was Stewart, however, who captured the gold statuette, playing opposite Katharine Hepburn in "The Philadelphia Story."

The race for best actress was a free-for-all among Bette Davis, nominated for "The Letter," Joan Fontaine for "Rebecca," Martha Scott for "Our Town," Ginger Rogers for "Kitty Foyle," and Katharine Hepburn for "The Philadelphia Story."

Ginger Rogers, an actress better known for her charming performances in a series of song and dance features, was honored by the Academy membership. Miss Rogers breathed life into the rather tepid story of Kitty, a poor Irish working girl who suffered numerous romantic trials and tribulations.

"The Grapes Of Wrath," adapted from John Steinbeck's powerful novel, came to the screen with shattering realism; a semi-documentary bursting with truth. Under the lean, hard, and stark direction of John Ford, the saga of the migratory worker in California was so compellingly told, that the unbelievable hardships of the nomadic, hopeless men and women were indelibly etched on the minds and hearts of every viewer. Ford was named best director, and Jane Darwell best supporting actress for her performance as the mother of the wandering Joad family.

Walter Brennan was once again honored as the best supporting actor in William Wyler's "The Westerner."

"The Milky Way," an M-G-M cartoon, finally broke Walt Disney's winning streak after eight straight years, when it was named best cartoon; and "Teddy, The Rough Rider," was cited as the best 2-reel short subject.

"Rebecca" (best production)
with Laurence Olivier, Joan Fontaine, and Judith Anderson, below;
Olivier and Fontaine, opposite. Selznick, United Artists

James Stewart (best actor), Katharine Hepburn, and Ruth Hussey
in "The Philadelphia Story." M-G-M

Walter Brennan (best supporting actor)
in "The Westerner." Goldwyn, United Artists

Jane Darwell (best supporting actress) and Henry Fonda
in "The Grapes Of Wrath" (best direction). 20th Century-Fox

1941

"How Green Was My Valley" sprang to life from the pages of Richard Llewellyn's novel full-blown, and brought to the screen a film of unsurpassed beauty, sensitivity, and intelligence. Here was a story of joy and sorrow, of life and death, seen in a microcosm of a Welsh mining village. A brilliant cast headed by young Roddy McDowall; Donald Crisp as the father, the "head" of the Morgan family; Sara Allgood as the mother, the strong "heart" of the family; Walter Pidgeon as the sincere, straightforward minister; Maureen O'Hara as the lovely sister; and Anna Lee as the pretty wife; all under the subtle direction of John Ford, made "How Green Was My Valley" one of the finest films of all time.

"How Green Was My Valley" was honored with seven Oscars, including the top Award as best production and the supporting actor Oscar for Donald Crisp.

Sergeant Alvin York, one of America's great heroes in World War I, a modest, good-natured man from the mountain country of Tennessee, had, for years, refused to allow film makers to bring his life story to the screen. Finally, under the pressure that the film was his patriotic duty, he capitulated, but with certain conditions: first, that Gary Cooper portray him; second, that no oomphy (or any other kind of grunt) girl portray his wife; and last, that the film be accurate.

The resulting film, "Sergeant York," was everything that York could have wanted. Gary Cooper, with consummate skill, charm, and good nature, played York to perfection; and for this performance he was named best actor, over such favorites as Cary Grant in "Penny Serenade," Walter Huston in "All That Money Can Buy," Robert Montgomery in "Here Comes Mr. Jordan," and Orson Welles in "Citizen Kane."

This last performance and film deserves special mention even though "Citizen Kane" won only one Award: best original screenplay by Herman J. Mankiewicz and Orson Welles.

"Citizen Kane" was one of the most remarkable films ever made, a rare combination of originality, excitement, and entertainment; the personal film statement of its producer, director, star, and co-author, Orson Welles. This was Welles' first film, and yet, on a small budget, he made a masterpiece of cinematic art. The critics said that he had broken all the Hollywood rules — only a few close-ups, playing whole scenes with the actors' faces in shadow, using lighting to create dramatic values instead of actors, using flash-backs throughout — but nevertheless, "Citizen Kane" was and is a great film.

Joan Fontaine was named best actress for her portrayal of a rather peculiar, ripe-for-love spinster, who, after a most unusual courtship, married and continued to love a strange half man, half child, in "Suspicion."

Mary Astor as a sharp-tongued, stylish pianist, was cited as best supporting actress for "The Great Lie."

Walt Disney was back on the track again with a victory in the cartoon category with his "Lend A Paw," and a special Oscar for "Fantasia"; while "Churchill's Island" and "Target For Tonight" were named for special documentary Awards.

AWARDS

Production: "How Green Was My Valley,"
20th Century-Fox.

Actor: Gary Cooper in "Sergeant York,"
Warner Brothers.

Actress: Joan Fontaine in "Suspicion," RKO Radio.

Supporting Actor: Donald Crisp in "How Green
Was My Valley."

Supporting Actress: Mary Astor in "The Great Lie,"
Warner Brothers.

Direction: John Ford, "How Green Was My Valley."

Writing (original story): Harry Segall, "Here Comes
Mr. Jordan," Columbia.

Writing (original screenplay): Herman J.
Mankiewicz, Orson Welles, "Citizen Kane,"
Mercury, RKO Radio.

Writing (best written screenplay): Sidney
Buchman, Seton I. Miller, "Here Comes Mr.
Jordan."

Cinematography (black-and-white): Arthur Miller,
"How Green Was My Valley."

Cinematography (color): Ernest Palmer, Ray
Rennahan, "Blood And Sand," 20th Century-Fox.

Art Direction (black-and-white): Richard Day,
Nathan Juran, "How Green Was My Valley."

Art Direction (color): Cedric Gibbons, Urie
McCleary, "Blossoms In The Dust,"
Metro-Goldwyn-Mayer.

Interior Decoration (black-and-white): Thomas
Little, "How Green Was My Valley."

Interior Decoration (color): Edwin B. Willis,
"Blossoms In The Dust."

Sound Recording: Jack Whitney (general service),
"That Hamilton Woman," Korda, United Artists.

Film Editing: William Holmes, "Sergeant York."

Special Effects: Farciot Edouart, Gordon Jennings
(photographic), Louis Mesenkop (sound),
"I Wanted Wings," Paramount.

Music (scoring dramatic picture): Bernard
Herrmann, "All That Money Can Buy,"
RKO Radio.

Music (scoring musical picture): Frank Churchill,
Oliver Wallace, "Dumbo," Disney, RKO Radio.

Music (song): Oscar Hammerstein II (lyrics),
Jerome Kern (music), "The Last Time I Saw
Paris" from "Lady Be Good,"
Metro-Goldwyn-Mayer.

Short Subjects (cartoon): "Lend A Paw," Disney,
RKO Radio.

Short Subjects (1-reel): "Of Pups And Puzzles,"
Metro-Goldwyn-Mayer.

Short Subjects (2-reel): "Main Street On The
March," Metro-Goldwyn-Mayer.

Irving G. Thalberg Memorial Award:
Walt Disney.

SPECIAL AWARDS

"Churchill's Island," Canadian National Film
Board, citation for distinctive achievement.

Rey Scott, for his extraordinary achievement
in producing "Kukan."

The British Ministry of Information, for
"Target For Tonight."

Leopold Stokowski and his associates, for their
unique achievement in the creation of a
new form of visualized music in "Fantasia."

Walt Disney, William Garity, John N. A. Hawkins
and the RCA Manufacturing Company, for their
outstanding contribution to the advancement
of the use of sound in motion pictures
through the production of "Fantasia."

SCIENTIFIC AND TECHNICAL AWARDS

Electrical Research Products Division of
Western Electric Co., Inc., for the development
of the precision integrating sphere
densitometer.

RCA Manufacturing Co., for the design and
development of the MI-3043 Uni-directional
microphone.

Ray Wilkinson and the Paramount Studio
Laboratory, for pioneering in the use of and
for the first practical application to release
printing of fine grain positive stock.

Charles Lootens and the Republic Studio Sound
Department, for pioneering Class B push-pull
variable area recording.

Wilbur Silvertooth and the Paramount Studio
Engineering Department, for the design and
computation of a relay condenser system
applicable to transparency process projection,
delivering considerably more usable light.

Paramount Pictures, Inc., and 20th Century-Fox
Film Corp., for the development and first
practical application to motion picture
production of an automatic scene slating device.

Douglas Shearer and the Metro-Goldwyn-Mayer
Studio Sound Department, and to Loren Ryder
and the Paramount Studio Sound Department,
for pioneering the development of fine grain
emulsions for variable density original sound
recording in studio production.

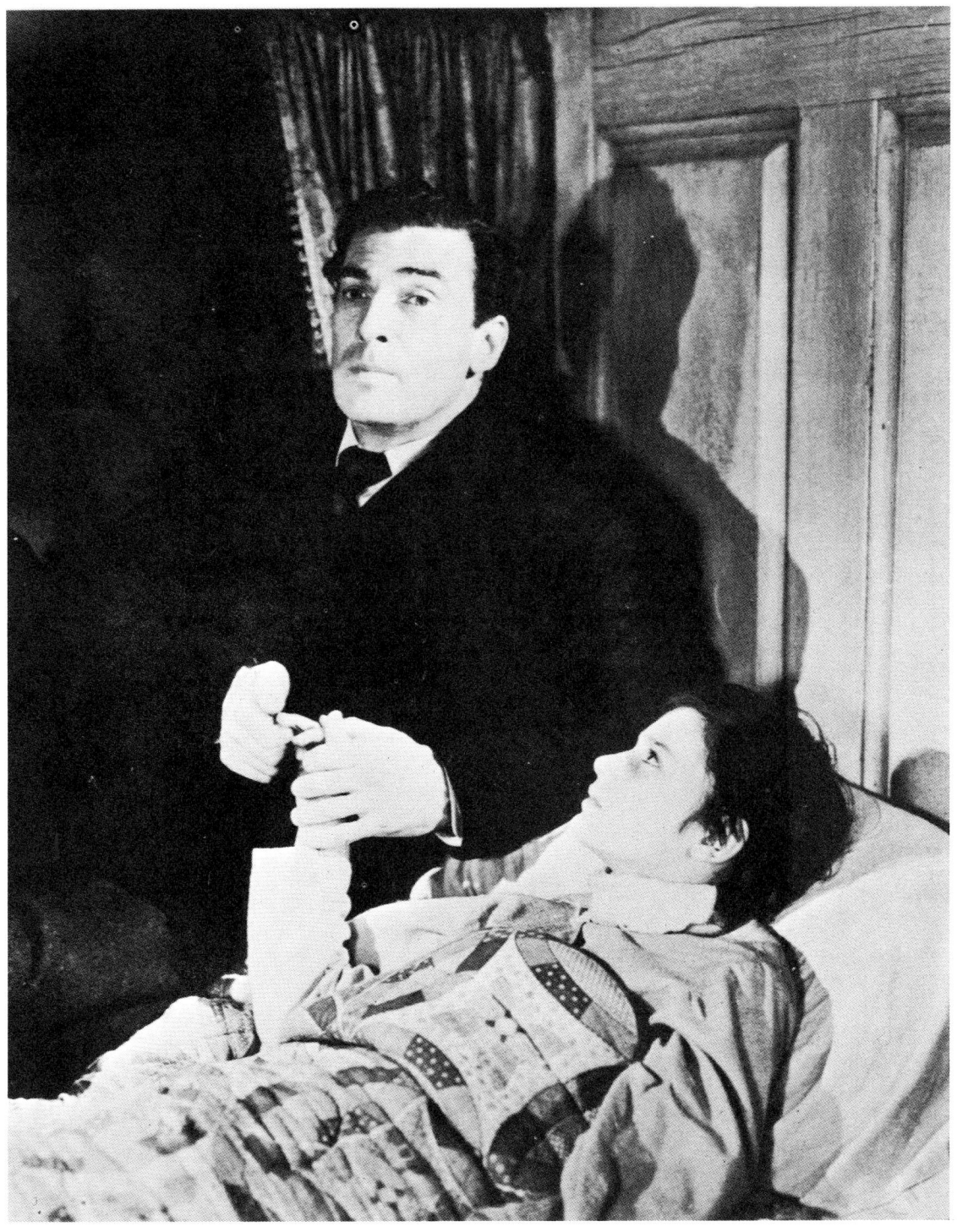

"How Green Was My Valley" (best production) with Walter Pidgeon
Donald Crisp (best supporting actor), and Roddy McDowall. 20th Century-Fox

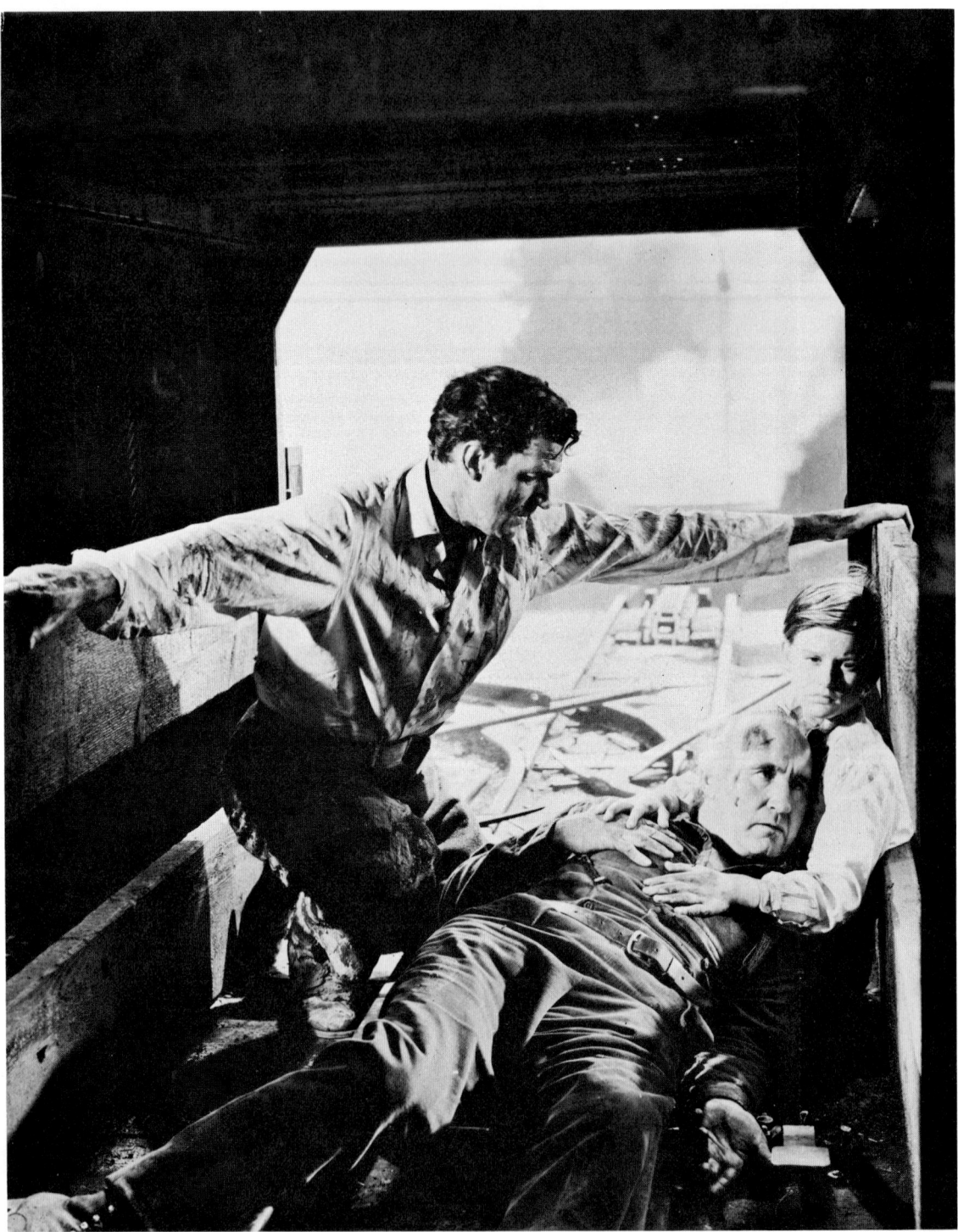

"Citizen Kane" (best original screenplay) with Orson Welles. Mercury, RKO Radio

Gary Cooper (best actor) and Joan Leslie in "Sergeant York." Warner Brothers

"Blood And Sand"
(best cinematography, color)
with Tyrone Power,
J. Carrol Naish,
and John Carradine.
20th Century-Fox

"Churchill's Island"
(special award)
with Max Schmeling
and Nazi paratroopers.
Canadian National Film Board

Mary Astor
(best supporting actress)
and Bette Davis
in "The Great Lie."
Warner Brothers

"Here Comes Mr. Jordan"
(best written screenplay)
with Edward Everett Horton,
Robert Montgomery,
and Claude Rains. Columbia

AWARDS

Production: "Mrs. Miniver," Metro-Goldwyn-Mayer.

Actor: James Cagney in "Yankee Doodle Dandy," Warner Brothers.

Actress: Greer Garson in "Mrs. Miniver."

Supporting Actor: Van Heflin in "Johnny Eager," Metro-Goldwyn-Mayer.

Supporting Actress: Teresa Wright in "Mrs. Miniver."

Direction: William Wyler, "Mrs. Miniver."

Writing (original story): Emeric Pressburger, "The Invaders," Ortus, Columbia.

Writing (original screenplay): Ring Lardner, Jr., Michael Kanin, "Woman Of The Year," Metro-Goldwyn-Mayer.

Writing (best written screenplay): Arthur Wimperis, George Froeschel, James Hilton, Claudine West, "Mrs. Miniver."

Cinematography (black-and-white): Joseph Ruttenberg, "Mrs. Miniver."

Cinematography (color): Leon Shamroy, "The Black Swan," 20th Century-Fox.

Art Direction (black-and-white): Richard Day, Joseph Wright, "This Above All," 20th Century-Fox.

Art Direction (color): Richard Day, Joseph Wright, "My Gal Sal," 20th Century-Fox.

Interior Decoration (black-and-white): Thomas Little, "This Above All."

Interior Decoration (color): Thomas Little, "My Gal Sal."

Sound Recording: Nathan Levinson, "Yankee Doodle Dandy."

Film Editing: Daniel Mandell, "The Pride Of The Yankees," Goldwyn, RKO Radio.

Special Effects: Gordon Jennings, Farciot Edouart, William L. Pereira (photographic), Louis Mesenkop (sound), "Reap The Wild Wind," Paramount.

Music (scoring dramatic or comedy picture): Max Steiner, "Now Voyager," Warner Brothers.

Music (scoring musical picture): Ray Heindorf, Heinz Roemheld, "Yankee Doodle Dandy."

Music (song): Irving Berlin (lyrics and music), "White Christmas" from "Holiday Inn," Paramount.

Short Subjects (cartoon): "Der Fuehrer's Face," Disney, RKO Radio.

Short Subjects (1-reel): "Speaking Of Animals And Their Families," Paramount.

Short Subjects (2-reel): "Beyond The Line Of Duty," Warner Brothers.

Documentary (short subject): "Kokoda Front Line," Australian News Information Bureau.
"Battle of Midway," U.S. Navy, 20th Century-Fox.
"Moscow Strikes Back," Artkino.

Documentary (feature length): "Prelude To War," U.S. Army Special Services.

Irving G. Thalberg Memorial Award: Sidney Franklin.

SPECIAL AWARDS

Charles Boyer for his progressive cultural achievement in establishing the French Research Foundation in Los Angeles.

Noel Coward for his outstanding production achievement in "In Which We Serve."

Metro-Goldwyn-Mayer Studio, for its achievement in representing the American Way of Life in the production of the "Andy Hardy" series of films.

SCIENTIFIC AND TECHNICAL AWARDS

Carroll Clark, F. Thomas Thompson and the RKO Radio Studio Art and Miniature Departments, for the design and construction of a moving cloud and horizon machine.

Daniel B. Clark and the 20th Century-Fox Film Corp., for the development of a lens calibration system and the application of this system to exposure control in cinematography.

Robert Henderson and the Paramount Studio Engineering and Transparency Departments, for the design and construction of adjustable light bridges and screen frames for transparency process photography.

Daniel J. Bloomberg and the Republic Studio Sound Department, for the design and application to motion picture production of a device for making action negative for pre-selection purposes.

1942

"Mrs. Miniver" was a film about war—not the story of the men in the trenches with bullets flying over their heads, but the story of war as it affected the daily lives of an upper-middle class English family, the Miniver family. At a time when the American people were just beginning to learn what war was all about, and what it meant to the individual, what better example could they have than the British people?

"Mrs. Miniver" told the story of the British people fighting for their lives and their way of life in personal terms. The cast, guided superbly by director William Wyler, rose to great heights. Greer Garson played Mrs. Miniver; Walter Pidgeon, her husband; and Teresa Wright and Richard Ney, young lovers.

Greer Garson brought off the transition in Mrs. Miniver's character with grace, charm, and convincing reality; from the pre-war representative of her caste, concerned with inconsequential matters, to a woman who aids in the rescue work at Dunkirk, captures a German, and calmly reads stories to the children as the blitz continues.

In all, "Mrs. Miniver" garnered six Oscars: best production; Greer Garson, best actress; Teresa Wright, best supporting actress; William Wyler, best director; Arthur Wimperis, George Froeschel, James Hilton, and Claudine West, best written screenplay; and Joseph Ruttenberg, best cinematography.

Greer Garson faced a formidable array of actresses in her quest for the laurels in her class. Bette Davis had been nominated for "Now, Voyager," Katharine Hepburn for "Woman Of The Year," Rosalind Russell for "My Sister Eileen," and Teresa Wright for "The Pride Of The Yankees."

Walter Pidgeon garnered an acting nomination for his performance in "Mrs. Miniver," as did Ronald Colman for "Random Harvest," Gary Cooper for "The Pride Of The Yankees," and Monty Woolley for "The Pied Piper." But it was James Cagney, screen tough-guy de luxe, singing and dancing his way through the life story of George M. Cohan in "Yankee Doodle Dandy," who received the honors.

In "Johnny Eager," Robert Taylor played the title role of an unregenerate killer in the mold of an Edward G. Robinson or George Raft, and beautiful Lana Turner played the other half of the torrid romance. It was amazing that anyone even looked at Van Heflin, and yet it was he in the end who stole almost every scene. Heflin, for his portrait of Johnny's drunken but intellectual stooge, was named best supporting actor.

The short subject and documentary categories were dominated by films about the war, with "Beyond The Line Of Duty," "Kokoda Front Line," "Battle Of Midway," "Moscow Strikes Back," and "Prelude To War" winning in their classes.

Patriotism was evident even in the cartoon class, with Disney and Donald Duck bringing to the screen the classic "Der Fuehrer's Face."

"Mrs. Miniver" (best production) with Greer Garson (best actress) and Teresa Wright (best supporting actress). M-G-M

Greer Garson in "Mrs. Miniver,"
with Walter Pidgeon, above;
with Helmut Dantine, below. M-G-M

James Cagney (best actor), S. Z. Sakall, and Richard Whorf
in "Yankee Doodle Dandy." Warner Brothers

"This Above All"
(best art direction,
black and white)
with Joan Fontaine,
Tyrone Power,
and Nigel Bruce.
20th Century-Fox

"Der Fuehrer's Face"
(best cartoon).
Disney, RKO Radio

1943

The war thundered savagely and impersonally in the ears of the people, and Hollywood was quick to respond to the temper of the times with a series of films—dramas on the grand scale, showing heroism, bombings, flaming cities and invading armies. But it remained for "Casablanca," a film that dug deep behind the scenes of the war, to tell the intimate personal story of little people—Humphrey Bogart, an American; Paul Henried, a prisoner who escaped from a Nazi concentration camp; Ingrid Bergman, his wife; and Claude Rains, an unscrupulous policeman—to win the accolade as the best film of the year. Michael Curtiz' splendid direction garnered an Oscar as did the screenplay by Julius and Philip Epstein and Howard Koch.

A young, untried actress from Tulsa, Oklahoma, appearing in her first major role in a motion picture, was named best actress of the year. Jennifer Jones brought radiant beauty, touching simplicity, and honesty to the role of Bernadette, the peasant girl who glimpsed a holy vision in Lourdes, in "The Song Of Bernadette." What made the Award to Miss Jones even more extraordinary was the fact that four actresses of great stature and experience had also been nominated: Jean Arthur for "The More The Merrier," Ingrid Bergman for "For Whom The Bell Tolls," Joan Fontaine for "The Constant Nymph," and Greer Garson for "Madame Curie."

"The Song Of Bernadette," a story of simple faith, also won Awards for best cinematography, art direction, interior decoration, and musical score.

"Watch On The Rhine," Lillian Hellman's stark and gripping drama of Nazi indoctrination was translated to the film medium with accuracy and depth, and for his superb portrayal of the anti-Nazi, Paul Lukas won the Oscar as best actor. He was ably abetted by Bette Davis.

The wartime housing shortage in Washington, D.C., was the subject of the hilarious "The More The Merrier." Charles Coburn as a retired millionaire who rents half of Jean Arthur's apartment, and then proceeds to rent half of his half to Joel McCrea, was honored as best supporting actor.

Katina Paxinou won the female half of the Award for her stunning portrait of Pilar in Ernest Hemingway's "For Whom The Bell Tolls," with a brilliant cast including Gary Cooper, Ingrid Bergman, and Akim Tamiroff.

With Claude Rains as the love-crazed musician, "The Phantom Of The Opera," a remake of the Lon Chaney thriller, won three Awards in the color category: cinematography, art direction, and interior decoration.

Tyrone Power, Dana Andrews, and Anne Baxter starred in "Crash Dive," the story of the submarine service, which won the Award for special effects. Metro's patriotic cartoon "Yankee Doodle Mouse" marched away with the best cartoon Award.

Once again, wartime themes dominated the documentary Awards. "December 7th," produced by the U. S. Navy; and "Desert Victory," by the British Ministry of Information were selected.

AWARDS

Production: "Casablanca," Warner Brothers.

Actor: Paul Lukas in "Watch On The Rhine," Warner Brothers.

Actress: Jennifer Jones in "The Song Of Bernadette," 20th Century-Fox.

Supporting Actor: Charles Coburn in "The More The Merrier," Columbia.

Supporting Actress: Katina Paxinou in "For Whom The Bell Tolls," Paramount.

Direction: Michael Curtiz, "Casablanca."

Writing (original story): William Saroyan, "The Human Comedy," Metro-Goldwyn-Mayer.

Writing (original screenplay): Norman Krasna, "Princess O'Rourke," Warner Brothers.

Writing (best written screenplay): Julius J. Epstein, Philip G. Epstein, Howard Koch, "Casablanca."

Cinematography (black-and-white): Arthur Miller, "The Song Of Bernadette."

Cinematography (color): Hal Mohr, W. Howard Greene, "The Phantom Of The Opera," Universal.

Art Direction (black-and-white): James Basevi, William Darling, "The Song Of Bernadette."

Art Direction (color): Alexander Golitzen, John B. Goodman, "The Phantom Of The Opera."

Interior Decoration (black-and-white): Thomas Little, "The Song Of Bernadette."

Interior Decoration (color): R. A. Gausman, Ira Webb, "The Phantom Of The Opera."

Sound Recording: Stephen Dunn, "This Land Is Mine," RKO Radio.

Film Editing: George Amy, "Air Force," Warner Brothers.

Special Effects: Fred Sersen (photographic), Roger Heman (sound), "Crash Dive," 20th Century-Fox.

Music (scoring dramatic or comedy picture): Alfred Newman, "The Song Of Bernadette."

Music (scoring musical picture): Ray Heindorf, "This Is The Army," Warner Brothers.

Music (song): Mack Gordon (lyrics), Harry Warren (music), "You'll Never Know" from "Hello, Frisco, Hello," 20th Century-Fox.

Short Subjects (cartoon): "Yankee Doodle Mouse," Metro-Goldwyn-Mayer.

Short Subjects (1-reel): "Amphibious Fighters," Paramount.

Short Subjects (2-reel): "Heavenly Music," Metro-Goldwyn-Mayer.

Documentary (short subject): "December 7th," U. S. Navy.

Documentary (feature length): "Desert Victory," British Ministry of Information.

Irving G. Thalberg Memorial Award: Hal B. Wallis.

SPECIAL AWARD

George Pal, for the development of novel methods and techniques in the production of short subjects known as Puppetoons.

SCIENTIFIC AND TECHNICAL AWARDS

Farciot Edouart, Earle Morgan, Barton Thompson and the Paramount Studio Engineering and Transparency Departments, for the development and practical application to motion picture production of a method of duplicating and enlarging natural color photographs, transferring the image emulsions to glass plates and projecting these slides by especially designed stereopticon equipment.

Photo Products Department, E. I. duPont de Nemours and Co., Inc., for the development of fine-grain motion picture films.

Daniel J. Bloomberg and the Republic Studio Sound Department, for the design and development of an inexpensive method of converting Moviolas to Class B push-pull reproduction.

Charles Galloway Clarke and the 20th Century-Fox Studio Camera Department, for the development and practical application of a device for composing artificial clouds into motion picture scenes during production photography.

Farciot Edouart and the Paramount Studio Transparency Department, for an automatic electric transparency cueing timer.

Willard H. Turner and the RKO Radio Studio Sound Department, for the design and construction of the phono-cue starter.

"Casablanca" (best production)
with Humphrey Bogart and Ingrid Bergman. Warner Brothers

"The Song Of Bernadette" (best cinematography, black and white)
with Jennifer Jones, at right (best actress); Mary Anderson, Blanche Yurka,
Anne Revere and Ermadean Walters, left to right in foreground. 20th Century-Fox

Katina Paxinou (best supporting actress) in "For Whom The Bell Tolls." Paramount

Charles Coburn (best supporting actor) and Jean Arthur
in "The More The Merrier." Columbia

Paul Lukas (best actor), Janis Wilson, Eric Roberts,
and Donald Buka in "Watch On The Rhine." Warner Brothers

"The Phantom Of The Opera" (best cinematography, color)
with Claude Rains. Universal

AWARDS

Production: "Going My Way," Paramount.

Actor: Bing Crosby in "Going My Way."

Actress: Ingrid Bergman in "Gaslight," Metro-Goldwyn-Mayer

Supporting Actor: Barry Fitzgerald in "Going My Way."

Supporting Actress: Ethel Barrymore in "None But The Lonely Heart," RKO Radio.

Direction: Leo McCarey, "Going My Way."

Writing (original story): Leo McCarey, "Going My Way."

Writing (original screenplay): Lamar Trotti, "Wilson," 20th Century-Fox.

Writing (best written screenplay): Frank Butler, Frank Cavett, "Going My Way."

Cinematography (black-and-white): Joseph La Shelle, "Laura," 20th Century-Fox.

Cinematography (color): Leon Shamroy, "Wilson."

Art Direction (black-and-white): Cedric Gibbons, William Ferrari, "Gaslight."

Art Direction (color): Wiard Ihnen, "Wilson."

Interior Decoration (black-and-white): Edwin B. Willis, Paul Huldschinsky, "Gaslight."

Interior Decoration (color): Thomas Little, "Wilson."

Sound Recording: E. H. Hansen, "Wilson."

Film Editing: Barbara McLean, "Wilson."

Special Effects: A. Arnold Gillespie, Donald Jahraus, Warren Newcombe (photographic), Douglas Shearer (sound), "Thirty Seconds Over Tokyo," Metro-Goldwyn-Mayer.

Music (scoring dramatic or comedy picture): Max Steiner, "Since You Went Away," Selznick, United Artists.

Music (scoring musical picture): Morris Stoloff, Carmen Dragon, "Cover Girl," Columbia.

Music (song): Johnny Burke (lyrics), James Van Heusen (music), "Swinging On A Star" from "Going My Way."

Short Subjects (cartoon): "Mouse Trouble," Metro-Goldwyn-Mayer.

Short Subjects (1-reel): "Who's Who In Animal Land," Paramount.

Short Subjects (2-reel): "I Won't Play," Warner Brothers.

Documentary (short subject): "With The Marines At Tarawa," U.S. Marine Corps.

Documentary (feature length): "The Fighting Lady," U.S. Navy, 20th Century-Fox.

Irving G. Thalberg Memorial Award: Darryl F. Zanuck.

SPECIAL AWARDS

Margaret O'Brien, outstanding child actress of 1944.

Bob Hope, for his many services to the Academy, a Life Membership in the Academy of Motion Picture Arts and Sciences.

SCIENTIFIC AND TECHNICAL AWARDS

Stephen Dunn and the RKO Radio Studio Sound Department and Radio Corporation of America, for the design and development of the electronic compressor-limiter.

Linwood Dunn, Cecil Love and Acme Tool Manufacturing Co., for the design and construction of the Acme-Dunn Optical Printer.

Grover Laube and the 20th Century-Fox Studio Camera Department, for the development of a continuous loop projection device.

Western Electric Co., for the design and construction of the 1126A Limiting Amplifier for variable density sound recording.

Russell Brown, Ray Hinsdale and Joseph E. Robbins, for the development of the Paramount floating hydraulic boat rocker.

Gordon Jennings, for the design and construction of the Paramount nodal point tripod.

Radio Corporation of America and the RKO Radio Studio Sound Department, for the design and construction of the RKO reverberation chamber.

Daniel J. Bloomberg and the Republic Studio Sound Department, for the design and development of a multi-interlock selector switch.

Bernard B. Brown and John P. Livadary, for the design and engineering of a separate soloist and chorus recording room.

Paul Zeff, S. J. Twining and George Seid of the Columbia Studio Laboratory, for the formula and application to production of a simplified variable area sound negative developer.

Paul Lerpae, for the design and construction of the Paramount traveling matte projection and photographing device.

1944

"Wilson," "Double Indemnity," "Gaslight," and "Since You Went Away" were all nominated for best production honors. However, it was a deceptively simple film, exuding warmth, unashamed sentimentality, and good humor, "Going My Way," that was chosen for the honor by the Academy membership.

Leo McCarey, the producer, director, and author, artfully blended a series of episodes revolving around St. Dominic's parish—about a new young priest sent there to "Get the parish in shape." Father O'Malley was played with charm and understanding by Bing Crosby; and the older priest, set in his ways, was lovably portrayed by Barry Fitzgerald.

"Going My Way" won several Oscars: best production; Bing Crosby as best actor; Barry Fitzgerald as best supporting actor; Leo McCarey as best director; best original story; Frank Butler and Frank Cavett for best screenplay; and Johnny Burke and James Van Heusen for "Swinging On A Star," the best song.

But with all these Awards, the ultimate success of "Going My Way" must be laid at the feet of Crosby and Fitzgerald. Bing Crosby, best known as a singer, was playful, modern, and psychologically oriented as the young Father O'Malley, and he was placed in juxtaposition with Fitzgerald, the builder of the church, just a bit behind the times, but wise, nevertheless. The scenes between the two, as well as the scenes with the wayward youth of the parish were a joy to behold.

"Gaslight," adapted from the Broadway play "Angel Street" by John L. Bladerston, Walter Reisch, and John Van Druten, was a psychological melodrama: the story of a man trying to drive his wife insane. "Gaslight" was also honored for its art direction by Cedric Gibbons and William Ferrari, and for its interior decoration by Edwin B. Willis and Paul Huldschinsky. Ingrid Bergman was named best actress for her brilliant portrayal of the wife, slipping inexorably under the spell of her diabolical spouse, played incisively by Charles Boyer. The opposition in this category was formidable as Barbara Stanwyck was nominated for "Double Indemnity," Greer Garson for "Mrs. Parkington," Bette Davis for "Mr. Skeffington," and Claudette Colbert for "Since You Went Away."

For her performance with Cary Grant and Barry Fitzgerald in Clifford Odets' production of "None But The Lonely Heart," Ethel Barrymore was cited as best supporting actress.

Another film worthy of mention was "Wilson," in which Alexander Knox brought Woodrow Wilson to life on the screen. This fine film received six Awards: Lamar Trotti, original screenplay; Leon Shamroy, color cinematography; Wiard Ihnen, art direction; Thomas Little, interior decoration; E. H. Hansen, sound; and Barbara McLean, film editing.

Barry Fitzgerald (best supporting actor) in "Going My Way." Paramount

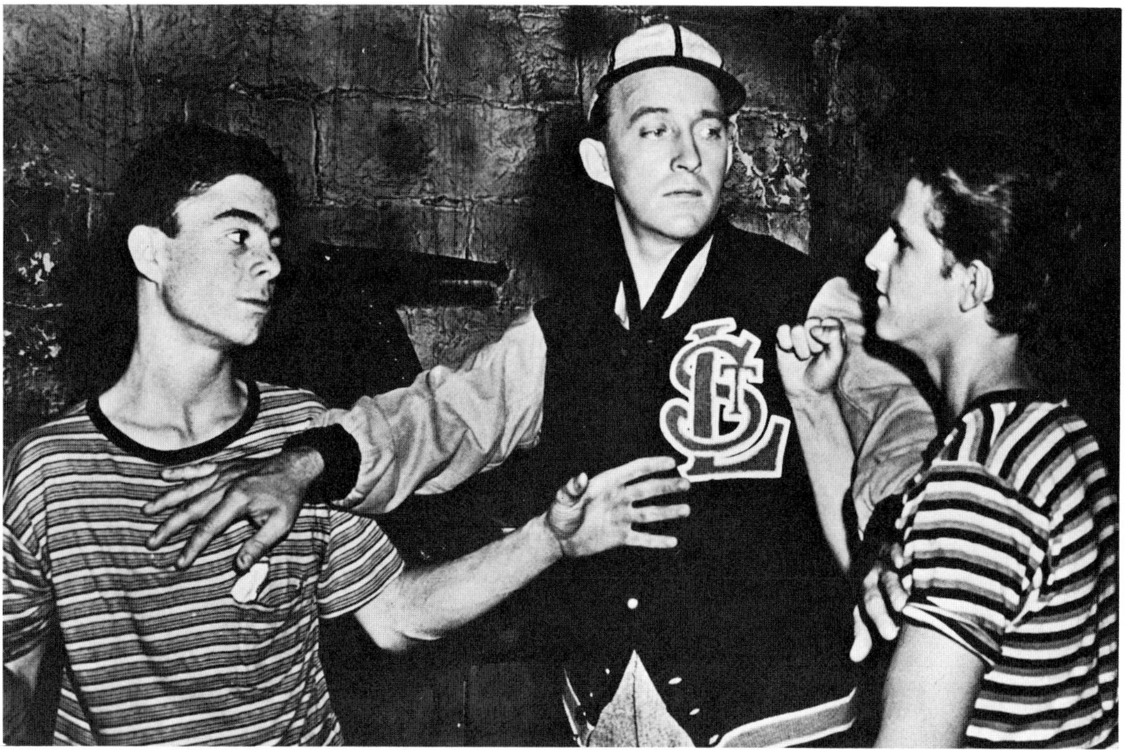

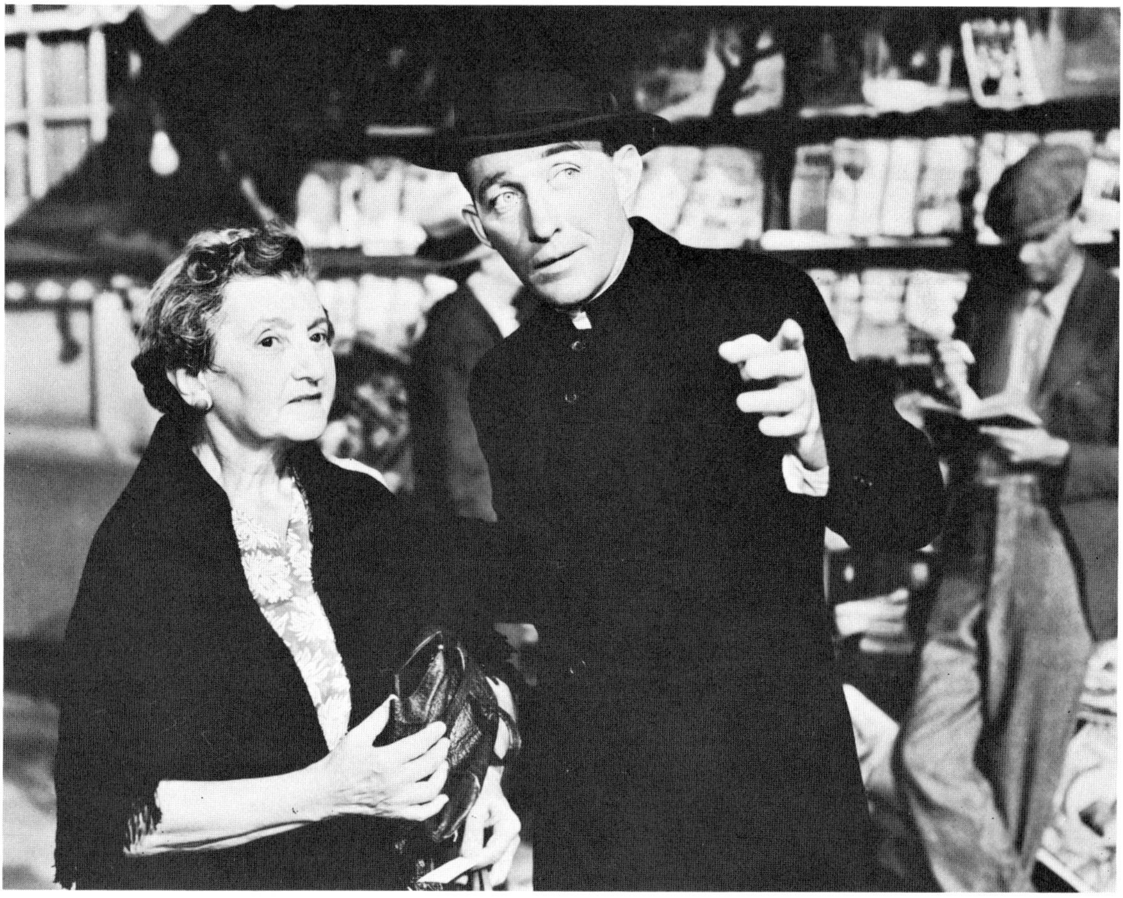

Ingrid Bergman (best actress) and Charles Boyer in "Gaslight." M-G-M

Ethel Barrymore (best supporting actress), Cary Grant,
and Barry Fitzgerald in "None But The Lonely Heart." RKO Radio

"Laura" (best cinematography, black and white) with
Clifton Webb and Dana Andrews. 20th Century-Fox

"Wilson" (best original screenplay) with Alexander Knox. 20th Century-Fox

1945

A question that had plagued Hollywood for years — should motion pictures be pure, 100 per cent entertainment, or should they make serious comments on social problems of the day? — was answered once and for all with the production of "The Lost Weekend." Here was a film that was neither entertaining nor amusing, but it was a box office bonanza as well as critically acclaimed.

This film adaptation of Charles Jackson's telling novel was a hard look at the alcoholic, and the torment of his desperate need for liquor. It was named best production of the year over such top films as "Spellbound," "Anchors Aweigh," "The Bells Of St. Mary's," and "Mildred Pierce." In "The Lost Weekend" there was no compromise with the reality of the fact that alcoholism was suicide, and many scenes were filled with stark terror.

Ray Milland, for years a romantic leading man and practitioner of the fine art of light comedy, came into his own as Don Birnam, the alcoholic. Milland, as Birnam, brought to the screen a fine performance of deep conviction and insight for which he was named best actor. Whether on a weekend binge or frantically searching for the drink he needed, Milland was always believable and moving. Billy Wilder was named best director for his deft handling of the controversial film, and he was also honored along with Charles Brackett for their screenplay.

The Academy membership had one of its most difficult tasks in selecting the best actress, as five splendid performers were nominated: Ingrid Bergman for "The Bells Of St. Mary's," Joan Crawford for "Mildred Pierce," Greer Garson for "The Valley Of Decision," Jennifer Jones for "Love Letters," and Gene Tierney for "Leave Her To Heaven."

Joan Crawford was selected to receive the Oscar for her restrained and sympathetic performance as the all-sacrificing mother in "Mildred Pierce," a film that had a little bit of everything in it: murder, a trace of larceny and blackmail, a dab of adultery, a short course in restaurant management, and some helpful hints on what not to do to raise a daughter.

The two Awards for supporting performances went to veteran players who appeared in frankly sentimental film dramas. James Dunn was honored for his fine performance as the vacillating, albeit wise father in the film adaptation of Betty Smith's best-selling novel, "A Tree Grows In Brooklyn." Anne Revere was named for her performance in "National Velvet."

Several excellent films which failed to take top honors did manage to garner a number of other Awards. "The House on 92nd Street," a thrilling story of spies on a mission to steal atomic secrets, was named as best original story. The cinematography Oscars went to "The Picture Of Dorian Gray," and "Blood On The Sun."

AWARDS

Production: "The Lost Weekend," Paramount.

Actor: Ray Milland in "The Lost Weekend."

Actress: Joan Crawford in "Mildred Pierce," Warner Brothers.

Supporting Actor: James Dunn in "A Tree Grows In Brooklyn," 20th Century-Fox.

Supporting Actress: Anne Revere in "National Velvet," Metro-Goldwyn-Mayer.

Direction: Billy Wilder, "The Lost Weekend."

Writing (original story): Charles G. Booth, "The House On 92nd Street," 20th Century-Fox.

Writing (original screenplay): Richard Schweizer, "Marie-Louise," Praesens Films.

Writing (best written screenplay): Charles Brackett, Billy Wilder, "The Lost Weekend."

Cinematography (black-and-white): Harry Stradling, "The Picture Of Dorian Gray," Metro-Goldwyn-Mayer.

Cinematography (color): Leon Shamroy, "Leave Her To Heaven," 20th Century-Fox.

Art Direction (black-and-white): Wiard Ihnen, "Blood On The Sun," Cagney, United Artists.

Art Direction (color): Hans Dreier, Ernst Fegte, "Frenchman's Creek," Paramount.

Interior Decoration (black-and-white): A. Roland Fields, "Blood On The Sun."

Interior Decoration (color): Sam Comer, "Frenchman's Creek."

Sound Recording: Stephen Dunn, "The Bells Of St. Mary's," Rainbow, RKO Radio.

Film Editing: Robert J. Kern, "National Velvet."

Special Effects: John Fulton (photographic), Arthur W. Johns (sound), "Wonder Man," Beverly Productions, RKO Radio.

Music (scoring dramatic or comedy picture): Miklos Rozsa, "Spellbound," Selznick, United Artists.

Music (scoring musical picture): Georgie Stoll, "Anchors Aweigh," Metro-Goldwyn-Mayer.

Music (song): Oscar Hammerstein II (lyrics), Richard Rodgers (music), "It Might As Well Be Spring" from "State Fair," 20th Century-Fox.

Short Subjects (cartoon): "Quiet, Please," Metro-Goldwyn-Mayer.

Short Subjects (1-reel): "Stairway To Light," Metro-Goldwyn-Mayer.

Short Subjects (2-reel): "Star In The Night," Warner Brothers.

Documentary (short subject): "Hitler Lives?," Warner Brothers.

Documentary (feature length): "The True Glory," Governments of Great Britain and the United States.

SPECIAL AWARDS

Walter Wanger, for his six years' service as President of the Academy Of Motion Picture Arts and Sciences.

Peggy Ann Garner, outstanding child actress of 1945.

"The House I Live In," tolerance short subject; produced by Frank Ross and Mervyn LeRoy; directed by Mervyn LeRoy; screenplay by Albert Maltz; song "The House I Live In," music by Earl Robinson, lyrics by Lewis Allen; starring Frank Sinatra; released by RKO Radio.

SCIENTIFIC AND TECHNICAL AWARDS

Loren L. Ryder, Charles R. Daily and the Paramount Studio Sound Department, for the design, construction and use of the first dial controlled step-by-step sound channel line-up and test circuit.

Michael S. Leshing, Benjamin C. Robinson, Arthur B. Chatelain and Robert C. Stevens of 20th Century-Fox Studio, and John G. Capstaff of Eastman Kodak Co., for the 20th Century-Fox film processing machine.

James Dunn (best supporting actor) and Peggy Ann Garner
in "A Tree Grows In Brooklyn." 20th Century-Fox

"The Lost Weekend" (best production)
with Ray Milland (best actor),
Philip Terry, and Jane Wyman.
Paramount

Joan Crawford (best actress) and Zachary Scott in "Mildred Pierce." Warner Brothers

"Leave Her To Heaven"
(best cinematography, color)
with Vincent Price,
Gene Tierney,
and Cornel Wilde.
20th Century-Fox

"The Picture Of Dorian Gray"
(best cinematography,
black and white)
with George Sanders
and Hurd Hatfield. M-G-M

"Hitler Lives?" (best documentary
short subject). Warner Brothers

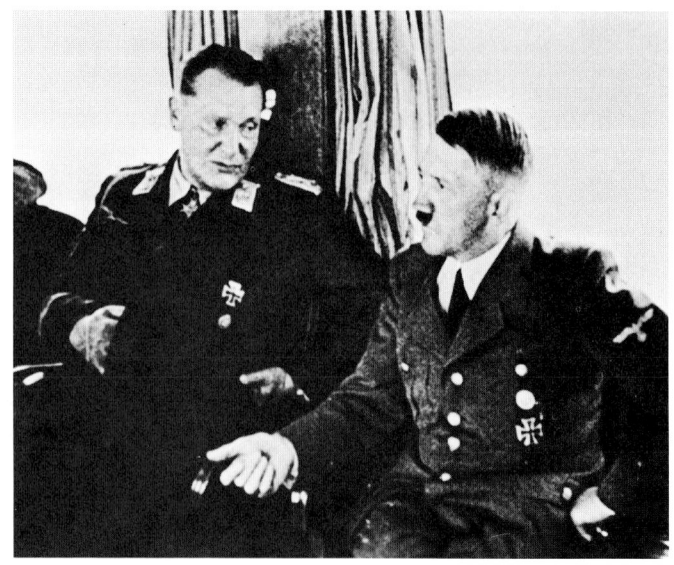

Anne Revere (best supporting actress)
and Elizabeth Taylor in "National Velvet." M-G-M

AWARDS

Production: "The Best Years Of Our Lives,"
Goldwyn, RKO Radio.

Actor: Fredric March in
"The Best Years Of Our Lives."

Actress: Olivia de Havilland in
"To Each His Own," Paramount.

Supporting Actor: Harold Russell in
"The Best Years Of Our Lives."

Supporting Actress: Anne Baxter in
"The Razor's Edge," 20th Century-Fox.

Direction: William Wyler,
"The Best Years Of Our Lives."

Writing (original story): Clemence Dane,
"Vacation From Marriage," London Films,
Metro-Goldwyn-Mayer.

Writing (original screenplay): Muriel Box,
Sydney Box, "The Seventh Veil," J. Arthur Rank,
Sydney Box, Ortus, Universal.

Writing (best written screenplay): Robert E.
Sherwood, "The Best Years Of Our Lives."

Cinematography (black-and-white): Arthur Miller,
"Anna And The King Of Siam," 20th Century-Fox.

Cinematography (color): Charles Rosher, Leonard
Smith, Arthur Arling, "The Yearling,"
Metro-Goldwyn-Mayer.

Art Direction (black-and-white): Lyle Wheeler,
William Darling, "Anna And The King Of Siam."

Art Direction (color): Cedric Gibbons,
Paul Groesse, "The Yearling."

Interior Decoration (black-and-white):
Thomas Little, Frank E. Hughes,
"Anna And The King Of Siam."

Interior Decoration (color): Edwin B. Willis,
"The Yearling."

Sound Recording: John Livadary,
"The Jolson Story," Columbia.

Film Editing: Daniel Mandell,
"The Best Years Of Our Lives."

Special Effects: Thomas Howard (photographic),
"Blithe Spirit," J. Arthur Rank, Noel Coward,
Cineguild, United Artists.

Music (scoring dramatic or comedy picture):
Hugo Friedhofer, "The Best Years Of Our Lives."

Music (scoring musical picture): Morris Stoloff,
"The Jolson Story."

Music (song): Johnny Mercer (lyrics),
Harry Warren (music), "On The Atchison,
Topeka And Santa Fe" from "The Harvey Girls,"
Metro-Goldwyn-Mayer.

Short Subjects (cartoon): "The Cat Concerto,"
Metro-Goldwyn-Mayer.

Short Subjects (1-reel): "Facing Your Danger,"
Warner Brothers.

Short Subjects (2-reel): "A Boy And His Dog,"
Warner Brothers.

Documentary (short subject): "Seeds Of Destiny,"
U.S. War Department.

Irving G. Thalberg Memorial Award:
Samuel Goldwyn.

SPECIAL AWARDS

Laurence Olivier, for his outstanding achievement
as actor, producer and director in bringing
"Henry V" to the screen.

Harold Russell, for bringing hope and courage
to his fellow veterans through his appearance
in "The Best Years Of Our Lives."

Ernst Lubitsch, for his distinguished contributions
to the art of the motion picture.

Claude Jarman, Jr., outstanding child actor of 1946.

SCIENTIFIC AND TECHNICAL AWARDS

Harlan L. Baumbach and Paramount, for an
improved method for the quantitative
determination of hydroquinone and metol in
photographic developing baths.

Herbert E. Britt, for the development and
application of formulas and equipment for
producing cloud and smoke effects.

Burton F. Miller and the Warner Bros. Studio
Sound and Electrical Departments, for the
design and construction of a motion picture arc
lighting generator filter.

Carl Faulkner of the 20th Century-Fox Studio
Sound Department, for the reversed bias
method, including a double bias method for
light valve and galvonometer density recording.

Mole-Richardson Co., for the Type 450 super high
intensity carbon arc lamp.

Arthur F. Blinn, Robert O. Cook, C. O. Slyfield and
the Walt Disney Studio, an audio finder and
track viewer for checking and locating noise
in sound tracks.

Burton F. Miller and Warner Bros., for an equalizer
to eliminate relative spectral energy distortion
in electronic compressors.

Marty Martin and Hal Adkins of RKO Radio, for
equipment providing visual bullet effects.

Harold Nye and the Warner Bros. Studio
Electrical Department, for the development of
the electronically controlled fire and
gaslight effect.

1946

"Last year it was kill Japs; this year it's make money." Here, in a single sentence, the words of one returning veteran, was the theme of "The Best Years Of Our Lives"—the realistic problem of thousands of men back from the war, who had to pick up the interrupted threads of their lives as civilians.

When a great motion picture like "The Best Years Of Our Lives" is produced, it is difficult, if not impossible, to single out individuals responsible for its greatness. Robert E. Sherwood's screenplay was a penetrating study of three veterans — a be-medaled Air Force captain who finds that his wife is a tramp; a middle-aged sergeant who discovers that his children have grown up in his absence; and a sailor who comes home to his family and fiancée with hooks instead of hands.

William Wyler directed the cast to stirring performances, and even though many were familiar faces—Dana Andrews, Fredric March, Myrna Loy, Virginia Mayo, and Teresa Wright—they all lost their star identities and became real people faced with real problems. Wyler's handling of Harold Russell, an amateur, in actuality a veteran who lost his hands in combat, was consummate in its artistry; and his overall telling of the story masterful, bringing out all the poignancy of the situation without slipping into the maudlin.

"The Best Years Of Our Lives" received seven Oscars: best production; William Wyler for best direction; Fredric March as best actor; Harold Russell as best supporting actor; Robert E. Sherwood for best screenplay; Daniel Mandell for best editing; and Hugo Friedhofer for best musical score.

Olivia de Havilland, nominated previously for her work in "Hold Back The Dawn," was chosen best actress of the year for her haunting portrait of an unwed mother in "To Each His Own." Her performance glowed with truth and simplicity as she showed the tragic necessity of giving up her child so that it would not face the stigma of illegitimacy.

An all-star cast including Tyrone Power, Gene Tierney, John Payne, Clifton Webb, Anne Baxter, and Herbert Marshall, was gathered for the filming of W. Somerset Maugham's "The Razor's Edge," but it was only Anne Baxter's performance as a wife who goes to pieces after the death of her husband and children, that shone through the vague plot. For this performance she was cited as best supporting actress.

There were several other important films made, and although they didn't receive any of the top Awards, they are worthy of mention. Among these were "Anna And The King Of Siam," starring Rex Harrison and Irene Dunne, named for best black-and-white cinematography, art direction, and interior decoration; and "The Yearling," which brought to the screen Claude Jarman, Jr., best child actor of the year.

Noel Coward's sly and charming tale of a jealous ghost, "Blithe Spirit," won a special effects Award for materializing that ghost at the drop of Coward's deft hand.

Fredric March (best actor)
in "The Best Years Of Our Lives"
(best production). Goldwyn, RKO Radio

"The Best Years Of Our Lives" (best production) with Dana Andrews, Myrna Loy,
Fredric March, Hoagy Carmichael, Harold Russell (best supporting actor).
Below, Harold Russell and Cathy O'Donnell. Goldwyn, RKO Radio

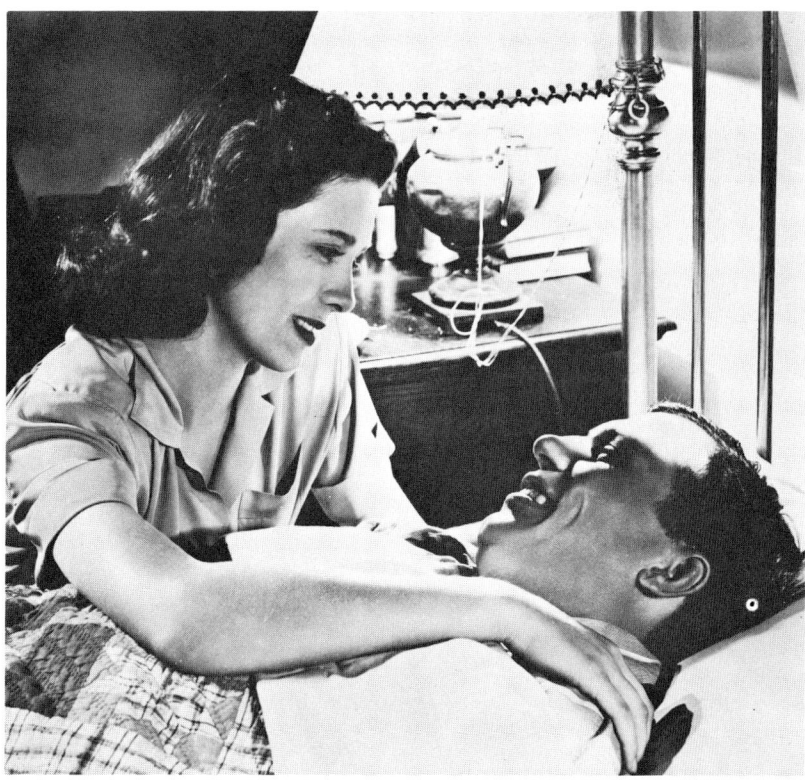

Olivia de Havilland (best actress)
and John Lund in "To Each His Own." Paramount

Anne Baxter
(best supporting actress)
and Tyrone Power
in "The Razor's Edge."
20th Century-Fox

"Blithe Spirit"
(best special effects)
with Kay Hammond,
Margaret Rutherford,
and Rex Harrison.
J. Arthur Rank

"Anna And The King Of Siam"
(best cinematography,
black and white)
with Irene Dunne
and Rex Harrison.
20th Century-Fox

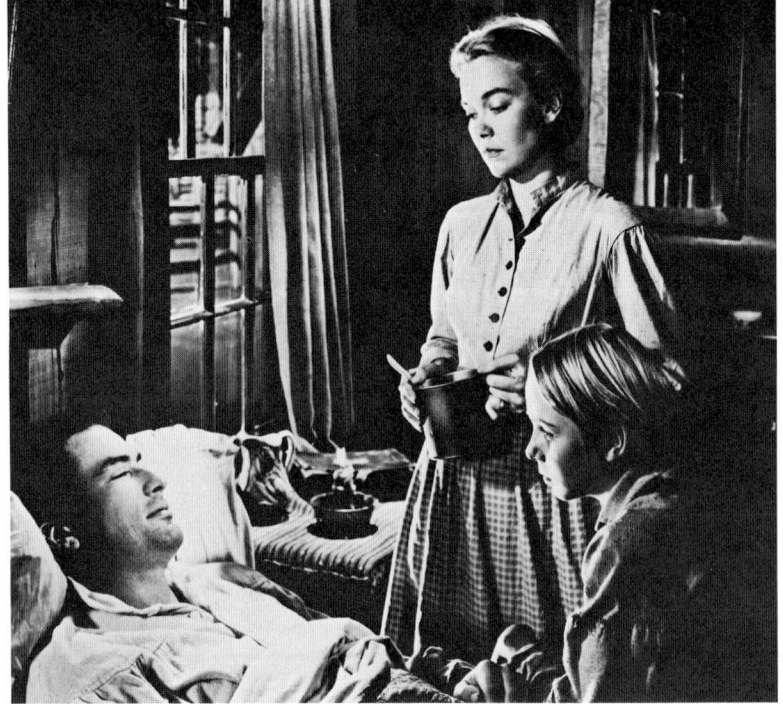

"The Yearling"
(best cinematograhy, color)
with Gregory Peck,
Jane Wyman,
and Claude Jarman, Jr.
(special award). M-G-M

1947

For the first time the Academy made a special Award to a foreign language film, and for this première garland, selected one of the finest films ever made, Vittorio De Sica's "Shoe Shine." Here was an Italian film, semi-documentary in nature, that told of the tragic effect of war's aftermath. With passion and deep understanding of the problems of his people, De Sica pictured a group of children of the street working in the black market, being used by gangsters, and going to prison. And yet there was no bitterness or editorialism in this production. Rather, it was the use of the film medium as an objective reporter's eye seeing all, telling all. With its predecessors "Open City" and "Paisan," this magnificent film ushered in a new world of film-making; a world populated by real people, trying to solve real problems.

By the same token, the film named best production of the year by the Academy membership, "Gentleman's Agreement," adapted from Laura Z. Hobson's novel, also tackled a very real problem, anti-Semitism. Starring Gregory Peck as a writer who posed as a Jew for six weeks to get the real story behind discrimination, with John Garfield, Celeste Holm, and Dorothy McGuire, "Gentleman's Agreement" brought this long-avoided subject to the screen. For his forthright direction, Elia Kazan was named best in his class and Celeste Holm was honored as best supporting actress.

Ronald Colman, who had already left his indelible mark on screen history for his brilliant, dramatic, and charmingly romantic performances in such films as "Arrowsmith," "A Tale Of Two Cities," "The Prisoner Of Zenda," "If I Were King," and "Random Harvest," was finally named best actor for his psychological study of a sensitive but insane actor in "A Double Life." His characterization was penetrating, and deserving of recognition.

Dorothy McGuire was nominated as best actress for her performance in "Gentleman's Agreement," as was Joan Crawford for "Possessed," Rosalind Russell for "Mourning Becomes Electra," Loretta Young for "The Farmer's Daughter," and Susan Hayward for "Smash Up." It was Loretta Young, however, who won the Oscar for her charming portrayal of the Swedish farm-girl who fumbled into a political career when she went to work for a congressman as a domestic. As improbable as the story was, its whimsey was infectious.

"Miracle On 34th Street" was honored with three Oscars: best original story by Valentine Davies, best written screenplay by George Seaton, and one for Edmund Gwenn as best supporting actor. Here was a sentimental story about an old man who got a job for Christmas playing Santa Claus at Macy's — and really believed that he was Santa. Gwenn, as Santa, proved that faith could perform miracles.

Two films produced in England by J. Arthur Rank, "Great Expectations" and "Black Narcissus," won a total of six Awards. Each won Oscars for cinematography, art direction, and set decoration; "Great Expectations" for black-and-white, and "Black Narcissus," for color.

AWARDS

Production: "Gentleman's Agreement,"
  20th Century-Fox.

Actor: Ronald Colman in "A Double Life,"
  Kanin Productions, Universal-International.

Actress: Loretta Young in
  "The Farmer's Daughter," RKO Radio.

Supporting Actor: Edmund Gwenn in
  "Miracle On 34th Street," 20th Century-Fox.

Supporting Actress: Celeste Holm in
  "Gentleman's Agreement."

Direction: Elia Kazan, "Gentleman's Agreement."

Writing (original story): Valentine Davies,
  "Miracle On 34th Street."

Writing (original screenplay): Sidney Sheldon,
  "The Bachelor And The Bobby-Soxer,"
  RKO Radio.

Writing (best written screenplay): George Seaton,
  "Miracle On 34th Street."

Cinematography (black-and-white): Guy Green,
  "Great Expectations," J. Arthur Rank,
  Universal-International.

Cinematography (color): Jack Cardiff,
  "Black Narcissus," J. Arthur Rank,
  Universal-International.

Art Direction (black-and-white): John Bryan,
  "Great Expectations."

Art Direction (color): Alfred Junge,
  "Black Narcissus."

Set Decoration (black-and-white):
  Wilfred Shingleton, "Great Expectations."

Set Decoration (color): Alfred Junge,
  "Black Narcissus."

Sound Recording: Gordon Sawyer, "The Bishop's
  Wife," Goldwyn, RKO Radio.

Film Editing: Francis Lyon, Robert Parrish,
  "Body And Soul," Enterprise Productions,
  United Artists.

Special Effects: A. Arnold Gillespie, Warren
  Newcombe (visual), Douglas Shearer, Michael
  Steinore (audible), "Green Dolphin Street,"
  Metro-Goldwyn-Mayer.

Music (scoring dramatic or comedy picture):
  Dr. Miklos Rozsa, "A Double Life."

Music (scoring musical picture): Alfred Newman,
  "Mother Wore Tights," 20th Century-Fox.

Music (song): Ray Gilbert (lyrics), Allie Wrubel
  (music), "Zip-A-Dee-Doo-Dah" from
  "Song Of The South," Disney, RKO Radio.

Short Subjects (cartoon): "Tweetie Pie,"
  Warner Brothers.

Short Subjects (1-reel): "Goodbye Miss Turlock,"
  Metro-Goldwyn-Mayer.

Short Subjects (2-reel): "Climbing The
  Matterhorn," Monogram.

Documentary (short subject): "First Steps,"
  United Nations Division of Films and
  Visual Information.

Documentary (feature length):
  "Design For Death," RKO Radio.

SPECIAL AWARDS

James Baskette, for his able and heart-warming
  characterization of Uncle Remus in "Song Of
  The South," friend and story teller to the
  children of the world.

"Bill And Cook," in which artistry and patience
  medium of motion pictures.

"Shoe Shine," for the high quality of this film.

Colonel William N. Selig, Albert E. Smith,
  Thomas Armat and George K. Spoor,
  film pioneers.

SCIENTIFIC AND TECHNICAL AWARDS

C. C. Davis and Electrical Research Products,
  Division of Western Electric Co., for the
  development and application of an improved
  film drive filter mechanism.

C. R. Daily and the Paramount Studio Film
  Laboratory, Still and Engineering Departments,
  for the development and first practical
  application to motion picture and still
  photography of a method of increasing film
  speed as first suggested to the industry by
  E. I. duPont de Nemours & Co.

Nathan Levinson and the Warner Bros. Studio
  Sound Department, for the design and
  construction of a constant-speed sound
  editing machine.

Farciot Edouart, C. R. Daily, Hal Corl,
  H. G. Cartwright and the Paramount Studio
  Transparency and Engineering Departments,
  for the first application of a special
  anti-solarizing glass to high intensity
  background and spot arc projectors.

Fred Ponedel of Warner Bros. Studio, for
  pioneering the fabrication and practical
  application to motion picture color photography
  of large translucent photographic backgrounds.

Kurt Singer and the RCA-Victor Division of the
  Radio Corporation of America, for the design
  and development of a continuously variable
  band elimination filter.

James Gibbons of Warner Bros. Studio, for the
  development and production of large dyed
  plastic filters for motion picture photography.

Ronald Colman (best actor) and Shelley Winters in "A Double Life." Kanin, Universal-International

"Gentleman's Agreement" (best production) with Celeste Holm (best supporting actress) and Gregory Peck, above; Dorothy McGuire, Gregory Peck, and John Garfield, opposite. 20th Century-Fox

"Black Narcissus"
(best cinematography,
color) with Deborah Kerr
and Nancy Roberts.
J. Arthur Rank,
Universal-International

"Great Expectations" (best
cinematography, black and white)
with Finlay Currie
and Anthony Wager.
J. Arthur Rank,
Universal-International

"Shoe Shine" (best foreign
language film). Italy

Loretta Young (best actress) and Joseph Cotten in "The Farmer's Daughter." RKO Radio

Edmund Gwenn (best supporting actor) and Natalie Wood in "Miracle on 34th Street" (best screenplay). 20th Century-Fox

AWARDS

Production: "Hamlet," J. Arthur Rank, Two Cities, Universal-International.

Actor: Laurence Olivier in "Hamlet."

Actress: Jane Wyman in "Johnny Belinda," Warner Brothers.

Supporting Actor: Walter Huston in "The Treasure Of The Sierra Madre," Warner Brothers.

Supporting Actress: Claire Trevor in "Key Largo," Warner Brothers.

Direction: John Huston, "The Treasure Of The Sierra Madre."

Writing (motion picture story): Richard Schweizer, David Wechsler, "The Search," Praesens Film, Metro-Goldwyn-Mayer.

Writing (best written screenplay): John Huston, "The Treasure Of The Sierra Madre."

Cinematography (black-and-white): William Daniels, "The Naked City," Mark Hellinger Productions, Universal-International.

Cinematography (color): Joseph Valentine, William V. Skall, Winton Hoch, "Joan Of Arc," Sierra Pictures, RKO Radio.

Art Direction (black-and-white): Roger K. Furse, "Hamlet."

Art Direction (color): Hein Heckroth, "The Red Shoes," J. Arthur Rank, Archers, Eagle-Lion.

Set Decoration (black-and-white): Carmen Dillon, "Hamlet."

Set Decoration (color): Arthur Lawson, "The Red Shoes."

Costume Design (black-and-white): Roger K. Furse, "Hamlet."

Costume Design (color): Dorothy Jeakins, Karinska, "Joan Of Arc."

Sound Recording: Thomas T. Moulton, "The Snake Pit," 20th Century-Fox.

Film Editing: Paul Weatherwax, "The Naked City."

Special Effects: Paul Eagler, J. McMillan Johnson, Russell Shearman, Clarence Slifer (visual), Charles Freeman, James G. Stewart (audible), "Portrait Of Jennie," The Selznick Studio.

Music (scoring dramatic or comedy picture): Brian Easdale, "The Red Shoes."

Music (scoring musical picture): Johnny Green, Roger Edens, "Easter Parade," Metro-Goldwyn-Mayer.

Music (song): Jay Livingston, Ray Evans (lyrics and music), "Buttons And Bows" from "The Paleface," Paramount.

Short Subjects (cartoon): "The Little Orphan," Metro-Goldwyn-Mayer.

Short Subjects (1-reel): "Symphony Of A City," 20th Century-Fox.

Short Subjects (2-reel): "Seal Island," Disney, RKO Radio.

Documentary (short subject): "Toward Independence," U.S. Army.

Documentary (feature length): "The Secret Land," U.S. Navy, Metro-Goldwyn-Mayer.

Irving G. Thalberg Memorial Award: Jerry Wald.

SPECIAL AWARDS

"Monsieur Vincent," (French), voted by the Academy Board of Governors as the most outstanding foreign language film released in the United States during 1948. Brandon.

Ivan Jandl, for the outstanding juvenile performance of 1948 in "The Search."

Sid Grauman, master showman, who raised the standard of exhibition of motion pictures.

Adolph Zukor, a man who has been called the father of the feature film in America, for his services to the industry over a period of forty years.

Walter Wanger, for distinguished service to the industry in adding to its moral stature in the world community by his production of the picture "Joan Of Arc."

SCIENTIFIC AND TECHNICAL AWARDS

Victor Caccialanza, Maurice Ayers and the Paramount Studio Set Construction Department, for the development and application of "Paralite," a new lightweight plaster process for set construction.

Nick Kalten, Louis J. Witti and the 20th Century-Fox Studio Mechanical Effects Department, for a process of preserving and flame-proofing foliage.

Marty Martin, Jack Lannon, Russell Shearman and the RKO Radio Studio Special Effects Department, for the development of a new method of simulating falling snow on motion picture sets.

A. J. Moran and the Warner Bros. Studio Electrical Department, for a method of remote control for shutters on motion picture arc lighting equipment.

1948

Although several English films, notably "Great Expectations" and "Henry V," had been nominated in the past for the Academy's highest Award, it was not until Laurence Olivier's "Hamlet" was presented that one garnered the best production laurels. And, it was named in a year that saw such top-notch American films as "Johnny Belinda," "The Snake Pit," and "The Treasure Of The Sierra Madre" in contention.

In bringing Shakespeare's classic drama to the screen, a play called by many the greatest ever written in the English language, Olivier, playing the title role himself, brought together a powerful cast, well versed in the Shakespearean tradition. The production was mounted brilliantly, every detail drawn with painstaking care. In Olivier's "Hamlet," extraordinary use was made of the close-up, especially in the soliloquies, so that there was a new clarity and directness in the well-known lines.

Olivier was a masterful Hamlet, and for his exceptionally intricate interpretation of the brooding Dane, he was named best actor. "Hamlet" was also honored for Roger K. Furse's art direction and costume design, and Carmen Dillon's set decoration.

It might seem that the role of a deaf-mute could not possibly offer an actress the opportunity to turn in an Award-winning performance, particularly in competition with Barbara Stanwyck, nominated for "Sorry, Wrong Number"; Ingrid Bergman for "Joan Of Arc"; Olivia de Havilland for "The Snake Pit"; and Irene Dunne for "I Remember Mama." But, in precisely that role, Jane Wyman was named best actress of the year. Her portrayal of a young girl unable to speak was memorable in "Johnny Belinda." With Lew Ayres, Charles Bickford, Agnes Moorehead, and Stephen McNally, she played the part with touching skill and sensitivity.

An adventure story of the he-man variety, John Huston's "The Treasure Of The Sierra Madre," proved to be a field-day for the actors involved. Walter Huston as the prototype of the "old prospector" did everything he could to safeguard his two new friends, Humphrey Bogart and Tim Holt, on the burro-trail to fortunes in gold. But, Bogart, as mean and ugly as the infamous Duke Mantee of "Petrified Forest" fame, ruined everything. For his deft portrait of the prospector, Walter Huston was cited as best supporting actor, while John Huston, his son, was named for his direction and screenplay.

Claire Trevor was in good company in the gangster film, "Key Largo." Lauren Bacall, Humphrey Bogart, Edward G. Robinson, and Lionel Barrymore appeared in the film with her, but it was Miss Trevor who won the Oscar as best supporting actress.

"Hamlet" (best production) with Laurence Olivier (best actor) and Basil Sydney, right;
Laurence Olivier, Basil Sydney, Eileen Herlie, and Jean Simmons, below.
J. Arthur Rank, Two Cities, Universal-International

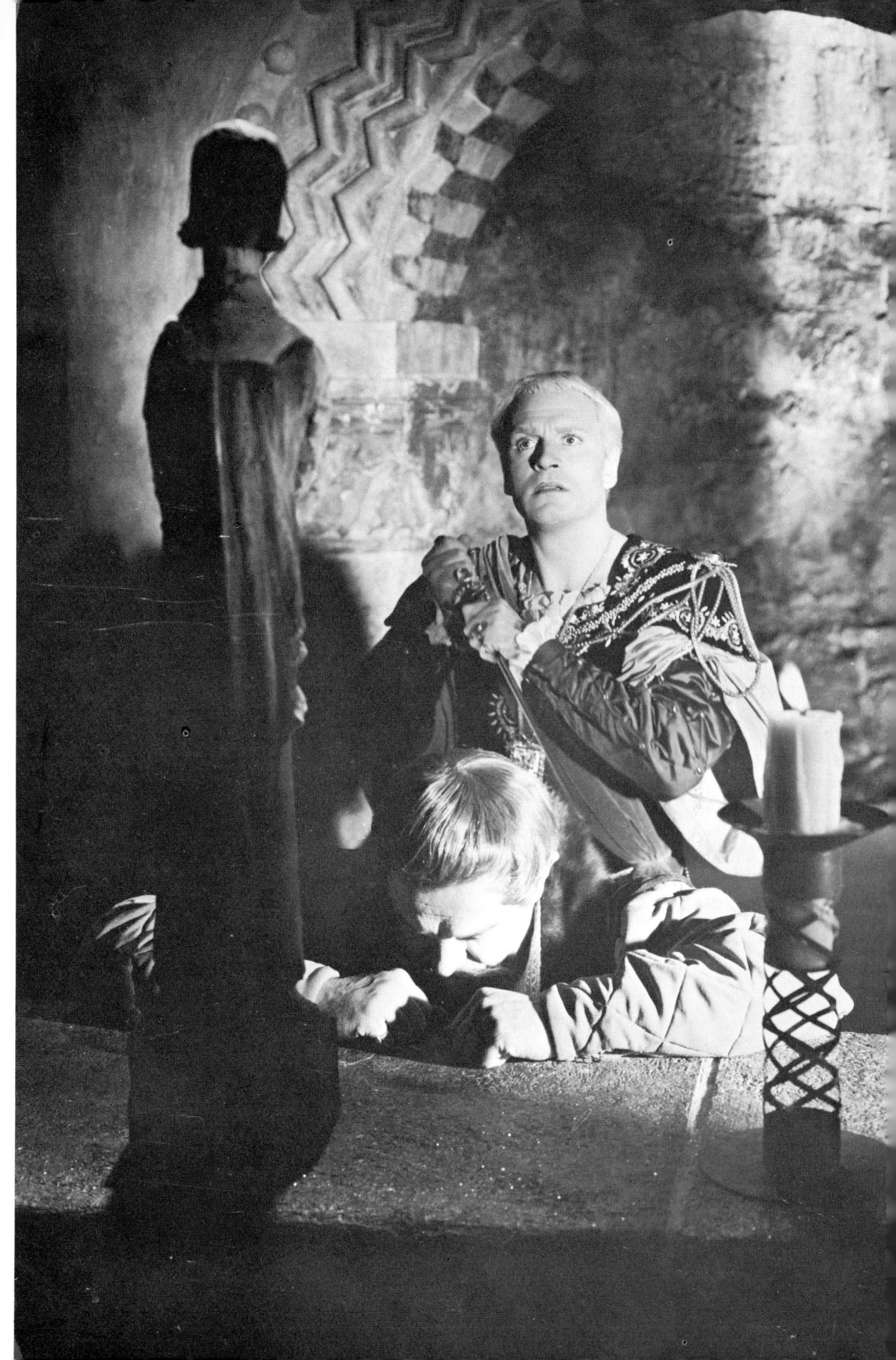

Jane Wyman (best actress) and Lew Ayres
in "Johnny Belinda." Warner Brothers

Walter Huston (best supporting actor)
in "The Treasure Of The Sierra Madre"
(best direction). Warner Brothers

"The Naked City"
(best cinematography,
black and white)
with Barry Fitzgerald.
Hellinger,
Universal-International

"Portrait Of Jenny"
(best special effects)
with Jennifer Jones
and Joseph Cotten.
Selznick

"Monsieur Vincent" (best foreign language film). France, Brandon

1949

The frightening story of the meteoric rise and the sudden disastrous downfall of American dictator Willie Stark, and how his own personal brand of fascism thrived in a supposedly democratic state was the subject matter of "All The King's Men." Adapted from Robert Penn Warren's compelling novel, and paralleling the life and times of Louisiana's Huey Long, this realistic film won the Oscar as best production of the year.

From the first scenes with Willie as a backwoods lawyer in an unnamed Southern state; through his election as governor, his violent and ruthless cutting down of all opposition, his seizure of totalitarian power, his fierce desire to seek national office; to his ultimate downfall, cut down by an assassin's bullet, "All The King's Men" never compromised with truth.

Broderick Crawford's portrait of Willie was a towering achievement, and he was named best actor; with Mercedes McCambridge, as a newspaperwoman reporting the scene, cited as best supporting actress.

Five superior actresses were nominated for top acting honors: Jeanne Crain for "Pinky," Olivia de Havilland for "The Heiress," Susan Hayward for "My Foolish Heart," Deborah Kerr for "Edward, My Son," and Loretta Young for "Come To The Stable." Olivia de Havilland took the Oscar, her second, for her beautiful characterization of the tragic, plain girl forced by an embittered father to give up her only chance for love.

The Award for best supporting actor went to Dean Jagger for his performance in "Twelve O'Clock High," the saga of the Air Force in war which starred Gregory Peck and Gary Merrill.

A comedy aimed at the sophisticated, adult audience, "A Letter To Three Wives," with an all-star cast including Kirk Douglas, Jeanne Crain, Linda Darnell, Ann Sothern, and Paul Douglas, brought a pair of Awards to Joseph L. Mankiewicz: best director and best screenplay.

The story of the historic Battle of the Bulge in World War II, and the heroic role of the 101st Airborne Division in that battle, "Battleground," won two Oscars: one for its story and screenplay by Robert Pirosh, and one for black-and-white cinematography by Paul C. Vogel.

For the second consecutive year the Board of Governors of the Academy honored an Italian film with a special Award, and again, Vittorio De Sica was the director. The film, "The Bicycle Thief," was a simple story that dug deep into its characters and found their hopes, their fears, their frustrations, their intimate relationships with each other, and especially the relationship between a father and his seven-year-old son. It was an eloquent statement, humorous and tragic at the same time. Here was a vivid portrait brought to the screen with complete honesty.

AWARDS

Production: "All The King's Men," A Robert Rossen Production, Columbia.

Actor: Broderick Crawford in "All The King's Men."

Actress: Olivia de Havilland in "The Heiress," Paramount.

Supporting Actor: Dean Jagger in "Twelve O'Clock High," 20th Century-Fox.

Supporting Actress: Mercedes McCambridge in "All The King's Men."

Direction: Joseph L. Mankiewicz, "A Letter To Three Wives," 20th Century-Fox.

Writing (motion picture story): Douglas Morrow, "The Stratton Story," Metro-Goldwyn-Mayer.

Writing (best written screenplay): Joseph L. Mankiewicz, "A Letter To Three Wives."

Writing (story and screenplay): Robert Pirosh, "Battleground," Metro-Goldwyn-Mayer.

Cinematography (black-and-white): Paul C. Vogel, "Battleground."

Cinematography (color): Winton Hoch, "She Wore A Yellow Ribbon," Argosy Pictures Corporation, RKO Radio.

Art Direction (black-and-white): Harry Horner, John Meehan, "The Heiress."

Art Direction (color): Cedric Gibbons, Paule Groesse, "Little Women," Metro-Goldwyn-Mayer.

Set Decoration (black-and-white): Emile Kuri, "The Heiress."

Set Decoration (color): Edwin B. Willis, Jack D. Moore, "Little Women."

Costume Design (black-and-white): Edith Head, Gile Steele, "The Heiress."

Costume Design (color): Leah Rhodes, Travilla, Marjorie Best, "Adventures Of Don Juan," Warner Brothers.

Sound Recording: Thomas T. Moulton, "Twelve O'Clock High."

Film Editing: Harry Gerstad, "Champion," Screen Plays Corporation, United Artists.

Special Effects: "Mighty Joe Young," ARKO Productions, RKO Radio.

Music (scoring dramatic or comedy picture): Aaron Copland, "The Heiress."

Music (scoring musical picture): Roger Edens, Lennie Hayton, "On The Town," Metro-Goldwyn-Mayer.

Music (song): Frank Loesser (lyrics and music), "Baby, It's Cold Outside" from "Neptune's Daughter," Metro-Goldwyn-Mayer.

Short Subjects (cartoon): "For Scent-Imental Reasons," Warner Brothers.

Short Subjects (1-reel): "Aquatic House-Party," Paramount.

Short Subjects (2-reel): "Van Gogh," Cinema Distributors.

Documentary (short subject): "A Chance To Live," March of Time, 20th Century-Fox. "So Much For So Little," Warner Brothers Cartoons, Inc.

Documentary (feature length): "Daybreak In Udi," British Information Services.

SPECIAL AWARDS

"The Bicycle Thief" (Italian), voted by the Academy Board of Governors as the most outstanding foreign language film released in the United States during 1949. Burstyn.

Bobby Driscoll, as the outstanding juvenile actor of 1949.

Fred Astaire, for his unique artistry and his contributions to the technique of musical pictures.

Cecil B. De Mille, distinguished motion picture pioneer, for 37 years of brilliant showmanship.

Jean Hersholt, for distinguished service to the Motion Picture Industry.

SCIENTIFIC AND TECHNICAL AWARDS

Eastman Kodak Co., for the development and introduction of an improved safety base motion picture film.

Loren L. Ryder, Bruce H. Denney, Robert Carr and the Paramount Studio Sound Department, for the development and application of the supersonic playback and public address system.

M. B. Paul, for the first successful large-area seamless translucent backgrounds.

Herbert Britt, for the development and application of formulas and equipment producing artificial snow and ice for dressing motion picture sets.

Andre Coutant and Jacques Mathot, for the design of the Eclair Camerette.

Charles R. Daily, Steve Csillag and the Paramount Studio Engineering, Editorial and Music Departments, for a new precision method of computing variable tempo-click tracks.

International Projector Corp., for a simplified and self-adjusting take-up device for projection machines.

Alexander Velcoff, for the application to production of the infra-red photographic evaluator.

Olivia de Havilland (best actress) and Montgomery Clift in "The Heiress." Paramount

"All The King's Men" (best production)
with Broderick Crawford (best actor),
Mercedes McCambridge (best supporting actress),
and John Ireland. Columbia

"A Letter To Three Wives" (best direction) with Jeanne Crain, Paul Douglas, foreground, Linda Darnell, Ralph Brooks, background. 20th Century-Fox

Dean Jagger (best supporting actor) and Gregory Peck in "Twelve O'Clock High." 20th Century-Fox

AWARDS

Production: "All About Eve," 20th Century-Fox.

Actor: Jose Ferrer in "Cyrano de Bergerac," A Stanley Kramer Production, United Artists.

Actress: Judy Holliday in "Born Yesterday," Columbia.

Supporting Actor: George Sanders in "All About Eve."

Supporting Actress: Josephine Hull in "Harvey," Universal-International.

Direction: Joseph L. Mankiewicz, "All About Eve."

Writing (motion picture story): Edna and Edward Anhalt, "Panic In The Streets," 20th Century-Fox.

Writing (screenplay): Joseph L. Mankiewicz, "All About Eve."

Writing (story and screenplay): Charles Brackett, Billy Wilder, D. M. Marshman, Jr., "Sunset Boulevard," Paramount.

Cinematography (black-and-white): Robert Krasker, "The Third Man," Selznick Enterprises in association with London Films, Ltd., Selznick Releasing Organization, Inc.

Cinematography (color): Robert Surtees, "King Solomon's Mines," Metro-Goldwyn-Mayer.

Art Direction (black-and-white): Hans Dreier, John Meehan, "Sunset Boulevard."

Art Direction (color): Hans Dreier, Walter Tyler "Samson And Delilah," Cecil B. De Mille, Paramount.

Set Decoration (black-and-white): Sam Comer, Ray Moyer, "Sunset Boulevard."

Set Direction (color): Sam Comer, Ray Moyer, "Samson And Delilah."

Costume Design (black-and-white): Edith Head, Charles LeMaire, "All About Eve."

Costume Design (color): Edith Head, Dorothy Jeakins, Eloise Jenssen, Gile Steel, Gwen Wakeling, "Samson And Delilah."

Sound Recording: "All About Eve," 20th Century-Fox Sound Department.

Film Editing: Ralph E. Winters, Conrad A. Nervig, "King Solomon's Mines."

Special Effects: "Destination Moon," George Pal Productions, Eagle Lion Classics.

Music (music score of a dramatic or comedy picture): Franz Waxman, "Sunset Boulevard."

Music (scoring musical picture): Adolph Deutsch, Roger Edens, "Annie Get Your Gun," Metro-Goldwyn-Mayer.

Music (song): Ray Evans, Jay Livingston (lyrics and music), "Mona Lisa" from "Captain Carey, USA," Paramount.

Short Subjects (cartoon): "Gerald McBoing-Boing," United Productions of America, Columbia.

Short Subjects (1-reel): "Grandad Of Races," Warner Brothers.

Short Subjects (2-reel): "In Beaver Valley," Disney, RKO Radio.

Documentary (short subject): "Why Korea?," 20th Century-Fox, Movietone.

Documentary (feature length): "The Titan: Story Of Michelangelo," Michelangelo Company, Classics Pictures, Inc.

Irving G. Thalberg Memorial Award: Darryl F. Zanuck.

SPECIAL AWARDS

"The Walls Of Malapaga" (Franco-Italian), voted by the Board of Governors as the most outstanding foreign language film released in the United States in 1950.

George Murphy, for his services in interpreting the film industry to the country at large.

Louis B. Mayer, for distinguished service to the motion picture industry.

SCIENTIFIC AND TECHNICAL AWARDS

James B. Gordon and the 20th Century-Fox Studio Camera Department, for the design and development of a multiple image film viewer.

John Paul Livadary, Floyd Campbell, L. W. Russell and the Columbia Studio Sound Department, for the development of a multi-track magnetic re-recording system.

Loren L. Ryder and the Paramount Studio Sound Department, for the first studio-wide application of magnetic sound recording to motion picture production.

1950

"All About Eve" was a film which pierced the hard shell of Broadway's armor and laid bare the pulse and heartbeat of the people who inhabit the world of the theatre. The penetrating story of an older actress near the end of her fabulous career, doing battle with a calculating and treacherous newcomer, is really the age-old story of every woman's dread of an adversary who has the advantage of being fresher and younger. With perception, wit, and unfailing candor, "All About Eve" showed what part vaulting ambition played in the success of an actress.

With a star-studded cast—Bette Davis, Anne Baxter, Gary Merrill, Hugh Marlowe, George Sanders, Celeste Holm, and Marilyn Monroe in a bit role—"All About Eve" was named best production of the year. Again, Joseph L. Mankiewicz was doubly honored as best director and for best screenplay. George Sanders took the Oscar for best supporting actor.

Two performers straight from the boards of Broadway walked away with Hollywood's top acting honors. Recreating the role that brought her stardom on Broadway in "Born Yesterday," Judy Holliday was named best actress. Her droll and witty impersonation of Billie Dawn, the classic "dumb blonde," brought the level of this satirical comedy, co-starring Broderick Crawford and William Holden, to a high plane.

Jose Ferrer's characterization of Rostand's dashing, big-hearted, big-nosed hero, Cyrano, in "Cyrano de Bergerac" was a tour de force. Although much of the nineteenth-century play was hopelessly outdated, and the characters little more than caricatures, Ferrer's inspired performance was all that was necessary to make "Cyrano de Bergerac" an outstanding film. Several other fine performers were nominated for best actor: Louis Calhern for "The Magnificent Yankee," William Holden for "Sunset Boulevard," Spencer Tracy for "Father Of The Bride," and James Stewart for "Harvey." But the swashbuckling, fencing, eloquent Ferrer was more than a match for any of them.

"Harvey," adapted from Mary Chase's hit play about a six-foot-three invisible rabbit, was the vehicle for one Award-winning performance. Even though James Stewart did not make the grade, Josephine Hull was named best supporting actress for her hilarious contribution to the proceedings.

"Sunset Boulevard" did not win any of the major Awards, although it was nominated in almost every category. Bringing Gloria Swanson and Erich von Stroheim together again, "Sunset Boulevard," a brilliant film, was named for best story and screenplay, best art direction and set decoration, and best musical score.

"All About Eve" (best production)
with Celeste Holm, Hugh Marlowe, Bette Davis, and Anne Baxter, above.
Opposite, above, Anne Baxter, George Sanders (best supporting actor),
Marilyn Monroe, Bette Davis, Hugh Marlowe.
Opposite, below, George Sanders and Anne Baxter. 20th Century-Fox

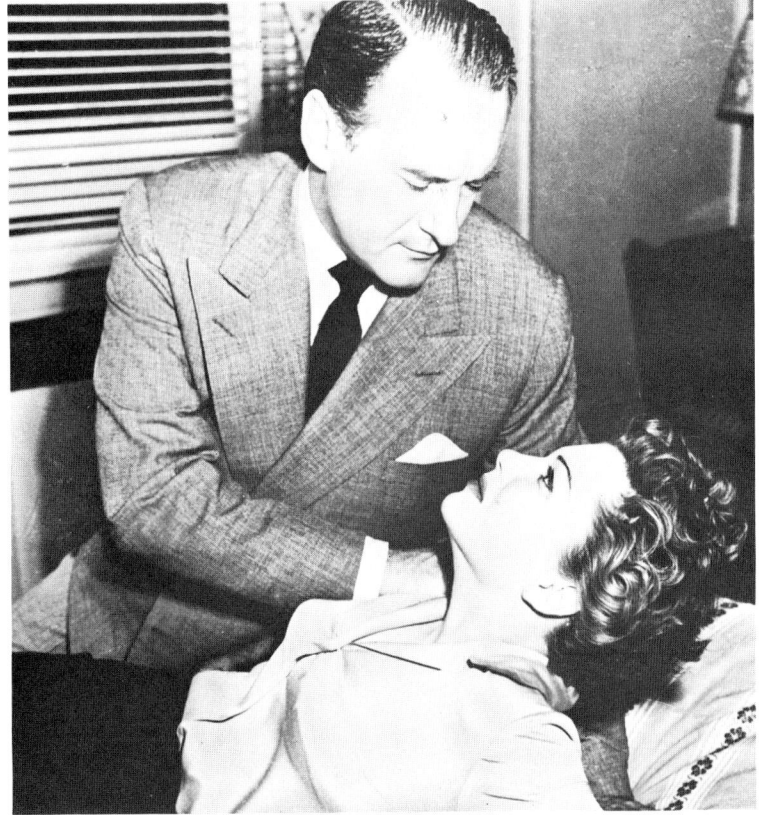

Judy Holliday (best actress) and William Holden in "Born Yesterday." Columbia

Josephine Hull (best supporting actress)
and James Stewart in "Harvey." Universal-International

"The Walls Of Malapaga" (best foreign language film) with Jean Gabin. Italy, France

1951

For the first time in fifteen years, since the great success of "The Great Ziegfeld," the membership of the Academy voted their highest accolade, best production, to a film musical, the dazzling production "An American In Paris." Under the stylish and imaginative direction of Vincente Minnelli, this extravaganza had everything: a fine cast starring Gene Kelly, Leslie Caron, Nina Foch, and Oscar Levant; brilliant Technicolor; a captivating Gershwin score; dancing in the inimitable Kelly style; all tied together with a charming, amusing script. And most of all, this fine film had Paris with its life, gaiety, the Left Bank, Toulouse-Lautrec posters, flower sellers, and bohemians in beards and berets.

The colorful fantasy of song, dance, and romance won eight Oscars in all: best production; best story and screenplay; best color cinematography, art direction, set decoration and costume design; best musical score; and a special Award to Gene Kelly for his brilliant choreography.

Three of the four acting Awards went to members of the cast of Elia Kazan's production of "A Streetcar Named Desire." Adapted from Tennessee Williams' powerful play, "Streetcar" was in reality a series of character studies. Vivien Leigh was named best actress for her stirring portrait of the shabby, genteel Blanche Dubois, the psychological study of the complete degeneration of a once-proud beauty to a harlot. Kim Hunter, as her wholesome sister, was best supporting actress, and young character man Karl Malden, as Blanche's suitor, was best supporting actor.

Marlon Brando was nominated for best actor Award, for his brooding, animal-like performance in "A Streetcar Named Desire," as was Fredric March for "Death Of A Salesman," Arthur Kennedy for "Bright Victory," and Montgomery Clift for "A Place In The Sun," but it was Humphrey Bogart who was acclaimed. Bogart, as the timid braggart and dissolute riverboat captain in "The African Queen" was nothing short of superb. Just watching him caught in the radiant love scenes (written with humor by James Agee) with the missionary lady Katharine Hepburn, was a joy.

"Rashomon," directed by Japan's internationally famous Akira Kurosawa, was named best foreign language film. The story was based on a crime of passion, that of a brigand who, desiring the wife of a samurai, kills the husband and violates the woman. It revolved around different versions of the crime as told by eye-witnesses. So fluid was the action that the dialogue and subtitles flowed together to make a continuously emotional experience, highlighted by magnificent photography, haunting music, and fine performances by Toshiro Mifune and Machiko Kyo.

AWARDS

Production: "An American In Paris,"
Metro-Goldwyn-Mayer.

Actor: Humphrey Bogart in "The African Queen,"
Horizon, United Artists.

Actress: Vivien Leigh in "A Streetcar Named
Desire," Feldman, Warner Brothers.

Supporting Actor: Karl Malden in
"A Streetcar Named Desire."

Supporting Actress: Kim Hunter in
"A Streetcar Named Desire."

Direction: George Stevens, "A Place In The Sun,"
Paramount.

Writing (motion picture story): Paul Dehn,
James Bernard, "Seven Days To Noon,"
Boulting Brothers, Mayer, Kingsley,
Distinguished Films.

Writing (screenplay): Michael Wilson, Harry Brown,
"A Place In The Sun."

Writing (story and screenplay): Alan Jay Lerner,
"An American In Paris."

Cinematography (black-and-white): William C.
Mellor, "A Place In The Sun."

Cinematography (color): Alfred Gilks, John Alton,
"An American In Paris."

Art Direction (black-and-white): Richard Day,
"A Streetcar Named Desire."

Art Direction (color): Cedric Gibbons,
Preston Ames, "An American In Paris."

Set Decoration (black-and-white): George James
Hopkins, "A Streetcar Named Desire."

Set Decoration (color): Edwin B. Willis,
Keogh Gleason, "An American In Paris."

Costume Design (black-and-white): Edith Head,
"A Place In The Sun."

Costume Design (color): Orry-Kelly, Walter
Plunkett, Irene Sharaff, "An American In Paris."

Sound Recording: "The Great Caruso,"
Metro-Goldwyn-Mayer Sound Department,
Douglas Shearer, Sound Director.

Film Editing: William Hornbeck,
"A Place In The Sun."

Special Effects: "When Worlds Collide,"
Paramount.

**Music (music score of a dramatic or
comedy picture):** Franz Waxman,
"A Place In The Sun."

Music (scoring musical picture): Johnny Green,
Saul Chaplin, "An American In Paris."

Music (song): Johnny Mercer (lyrics),
Hoagy Carmichael (music), "In The Cool, Cool,
Cool Of The Evening" from "Here Comes
The Groom," Paramount.

Short Subjects (cartoon): "Two Mouseketeers,"
Metro-Goldwyn-Mayer.

Short Subjects (1-reel): "World Of Kids,"
Warner Brothers.

Short Subjects (2-reel): "Nature's Half Acre,"
Disney, RKO Radio.

Documentary (short subject): "Benjy,"
Paramount.

Documentary (feature length): "Kon-Tiki,"
Artfilm, RKO Radio.

Irving G. Thalberg Memorial Award: Arthur Freed.

SPECIAL AWARDS

"Rashomon" (Japanese), voted by the Board of
Governors as the most outstanding foreign
language film released in the United States
during 1951. Harrison.

Gene Kelly, in appreciation of his versatility
as an actor, singer, director and dancer, and
specifically for his brilliant achievements
in the art of choreography on film.

SCIENTIFIC AND TECHNICAL AWARDS

Gordon Jennings, S. L. Stancliffe and the
Paramount Studio Special Photographic
and Engineering Departments, for the design,
construction and application of a servo-operated
recording and repeating device.

Olin L. Dupy of Metro-Goldwyn-Mayer Studio,
for the design, construction and application
of a motion picture reproducing system.

Radio Corporation of America, Victor Division,
for pioneering direct positive recording with
anticipatory noise reduction.

Richard M. Haff, Frank P. Herrnfeld, Garland C.
Misener and the Ansco Film Division of
General Aniline and Film Corp., for the
development of the Ansco color scene tester.

Fred Ponedel, Ralph Ayres and George Brown
of Warner Bros. Studio, for an air-driven
water motor to provide flow, wake and
white water for marine sequences in
motion pictures.

Glen Robinson and the Metro-Goldwyn-Mayer
Studio Construction Department, for the
development of a new music wire
and cable cutter.

Jack Gaylord and the Metro-Goldwyn-Mayer
Studio Construction Department, for the
development of balsa falling snow.

Carlos Rivas of Metro-Goldwyn-Mayer Studio,
for the development of an automatic
magnetic film splicer.

"An American In Paris" (best production)
with Gene Kelly (honorary award), below;
with Leslie Caron, opposite. M-G-M

"A Streetcar Named Desire" with Karl Malden (best supporting actor)
and Vivien Leigh (best actress) opposite.
Below, Kim Hunter (best supporting actress). Feldman, Warner Brothers

Humphrey Bogart (best actor)
and Katharine Hepburn
in "The African Queen."
Horizon, United Artists

"Rashomon" (best foreign language film)
with Toshiro Mifune and Machiko Kyo. Japan, Harrison

AWARDS

Production: "The Greatest Show On Earth," Cecil B. De Mille, Paramount.

Actor: Gary Cooper in "High Noon," Kramer, United Artists.

Actress: Shirley Booth in "Come Back, Little Sheba," Hal Wallis, Paramount.

Supporting Actor: Anthony Quinn in "Viva Zapata!," 20th Century-Fox.

Supporting Actress: Gloria Grahame in "The Bad And The Beautiful," Metro-Goldwyn-Mayer.

Direction: John Ford, "The Quiet Man," Argosy Pictures, Republic.

Writing (motion picture story): Fredric M. Frank, Theodore St. John, Frank Cavett, "The Greatest Show On Earth."

Writing (screenplay): Charles Schnee, "The Bad And The Beautiful."

Writing (story and screenplay): T. E. B. Clarke, "The Lavender Hill Mob," J. Arthur Rank, Ealing Studios, Universal-International.

Cinematography (black-and-white): Robert Surtees, "The Bad And The Beautiful."

Cinematography (color): Winton C. Hoch, Archie Stout, "The Quiet Man."

Art Direction (black-and-white): Cedric Gibbons, Edward Carfagno, "The Bad And The Beautiful."

Art Direction (color): Paul Sheriff, "Moulin Rouge," Romulus Films, United Artists.

Set Decoration (black-and-white): Edwin B. Willis, Keogh Gleason, "The Bad And The Beautiful."

Set Decoration (color): Marcel Vertes, "Moulin Rouge."

Costume Design (black-and-white): Helen Rose, "The Bad And The Beautiful."

Costume Design (color): Marcel Vertes, "Moulin Rouge."

Sound Recording: "Breaking The Sound Barrier," London Films, United Artists.

Film Editing: Elmo Williams, Harry Gerstad, "High Noon."

Special Effects: "Plymouth Adventure," Metro-Goldwyn-Mayer.

Music (music score of a dramatic or comedy picture): Dimitri Tiomkin, "High Noon."

Music (scoring musical picture): Alfred Newman, "With A Song In My Heart," 20th Century-Fox.

Music (song): Ned Washington (lyrics), Dimitri Tiomkin (music), "High Noon" from "High Noon."

Short Subjects (cartoon): "Johann Mouse," Metro-Goldwyn-Mayer.

Short Subjects (1-reel): "Light In The Window," Art Films, 20th Century-Fox.

Short Subjects (2-reel): "Water Birds," Disney, RKO Radio.

Documentary (short subject): "Neighbours," National Film Board of Canada, Mayer-Kingsly.

Documentary (feature length): "The Sea Around Us," RKO Radio.

Irving G. Thalberg Memorial Award: Cecil B. De Mille.

SPECIAL AWARDS

"Forbidden Games" (French), best foreign language film first released in the United States during 1952. Times.

George Alfred Mitchell, for the design and development of the camera which bears his name and for his continued and dominant presence in the field of cinematography.

Joseph M. Schenck for long and distinguished service to the Motion Picture Industry.

Merian C. Cooper, for his many innovations and contributions to the art of motion pictures.

Harold Lloyd, master comedian and good citizen.

Bob Hope, for his contribution to the laughter of the world.

SCIENTIFIC AND TECHNICAL AWARDS

Eastman Kodak Co., for the introduction of Eastman color negative and Eastman color print film.

Ansco Division, General Aniline and Film Corp., for the introduction of Ansco color negative and Ansco color print film.

Technicolor Motion Picture Corp., for an improved method of color motion picture photography under incandescent light.

The Projection, Still Photographic and Development Engineering Departments of Metro-Goldwyn-Mayer Studio, for an improved method of projecting photographic backgrounds.

John G. Frayne and R. R. Scoville and Westrex Corp., for a method of measuring distortion in sound reproduction.

Photo Research Corp., for creating the Spectra color temperature meter.

Gustav Jirouch, for the design of the Robot automatic film splicer.

Carlos Rivas of Metro-Goldwyn-Mayer Studio, for the development of a sound reproducer for magnetic film.

1952

Once in a great while an actress gives a performance so brilliant, so intelligent, so poignant and sensitive, that its image is burned indelibly into the memory of all who see it. This was the case with Shirley Booth's splendid characterization in "Come Back, Little Sheba," for which she was named best actress of the year. Her portrait of the hopelessly disheveled, loving but ignorant wife was real and true. In her rumpled bathrobe, she was a constant reminder to her husband of his lost opportunities and frustrations—the fact that he had to marry her when she became pregnant and thereby lost his opportunity to go to medical school. Her efforts in this film, adapted from William Inge's hit play were aided immeasurably by the support of Burt Lancaster, as the husband driven to drink.

Cecil B. De Mille made his first film in 1914, a western called "The Squaw Man," and at seventy, the acknowledged king of spectacular motion pictures, produced "The Greatest Show On Earth." Here was the story of the Big Top, the Ringling Brothers, Barnum & Bailey Circus, caught in all its kaleidoscopic color and excitement that brings joy to children and adults of all ages. Here was a three-ring circus on film; the clowns, the trapeze artists, the wild animal acts, the elephants, plus romance and intrigue. "The Greatest Show On Earth" had a cast of thousands including Betty Hutton, Charlton Heston, Cornel Wilde, Gloria Grahame, and Dorothy Lamour. It was named best production and was also honored for best motion picture story.

"High Noon," a tension-filled and absorbing western, directed by Fred Zinnemann, was also nominated in the best production category, and although it did not win the top Award, Gary Cooper, its star, was named best actor for his graphic performance. "High Noon" was not the usual "Cowboys and Indians" thriller, but rather a drama of depth and keen insight into men. Its overall telling quality was heightened by the excellence of its Award-winning musical score by Dimitri Tiomkin.

John Ford won his fourth Award as best director for his broadly comic, sentimental film, "The Quiet Man," which benefited from the amusing performances of John Wayne, Barry Fitzgerald, Maureen O'Hara, and Victor McLaglen.

"The Bad And The Beautiful" was never in contention for the big prize, but it was honored in a number of other categories. Gloria Grahame was named best supporting actress, and the film captured black-and-white Awards for cinematography, art direction, and set decoration. Charles Schnee was cited for his fine screenplay.

In John Steinbeck's historical film, "Viva Zapata!" Anthony Quinn won the trophy for best supporting actor, for his portrait of the brother of the Mexican dictator, Emiliano Zapata.

Gary Cooper (best actor) in "High Noon." Kramer, United Artists

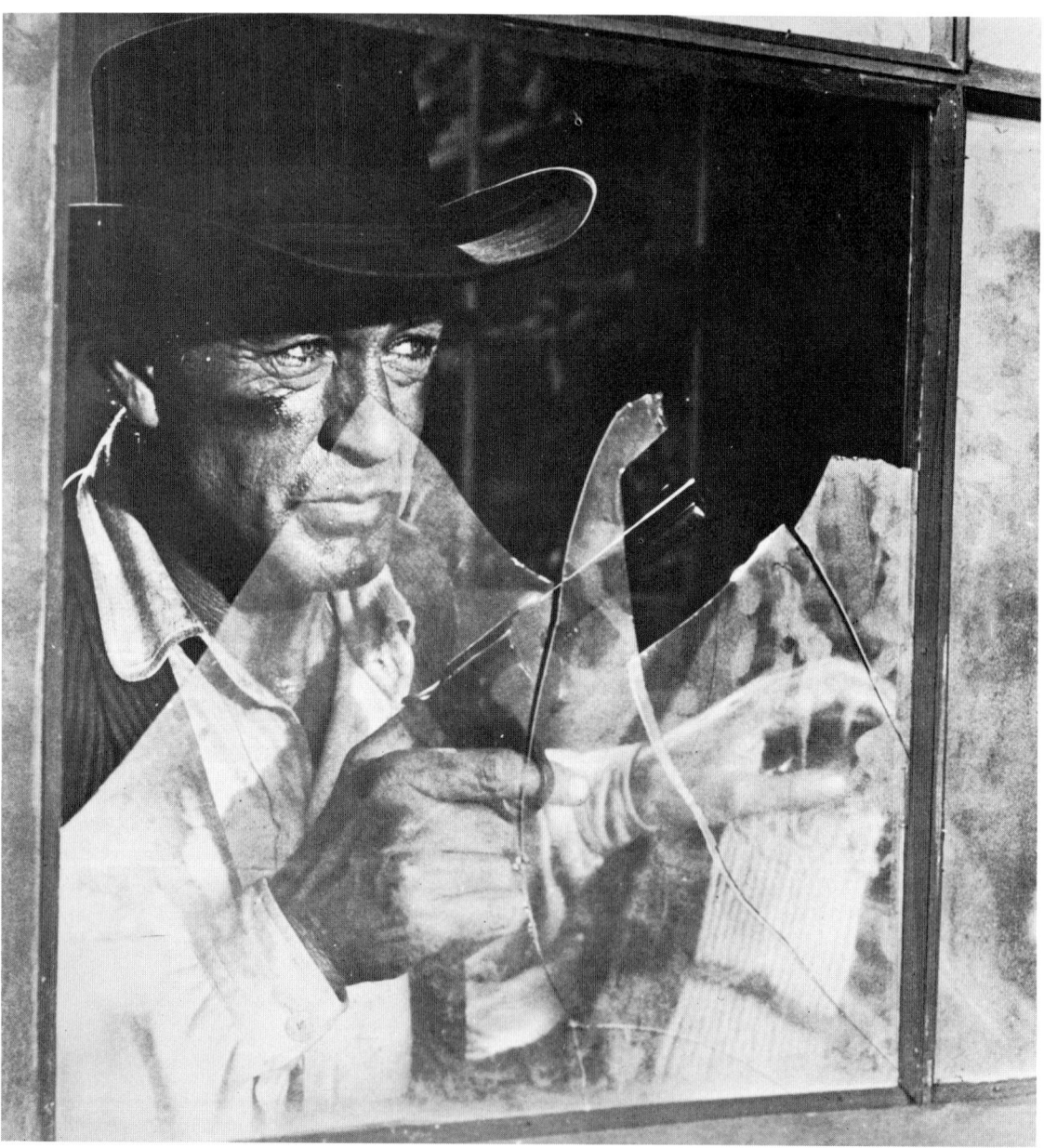

Shirley Booth (best actress) and Burt Lancaster in "Come Back Little Sheba," Wallis, Paramount

"The Bad And The Beautiful" (best cinematography, black and white)
with Gloria Grahame (best supporting actress) and Dick Powell, above,
Kirk Douglas and Lana Turner, below. M-G-M

"The Greatest Show On Earth"
(best production)
with Charlton Heston and Betty Hutton.
De Mille, Paramount

"Forbidden Games" (best foreign language film). France, Times

"The Quiet Man" (best direction) with Maureen O'Hara and John Wayne. Argosy, Republic

"Plymouth Adventure" (best special effects). M-G-M

1953

From the pages of James Jones' tumultuous, bawdy, and best-selling novel of army life prior to World War II, came a tough, brawling, but at the same time, tenderly moving and vivid motion picture, "From Here To Eternity." Director Fred Zinnemann, at the height of his immense powers, moved his players in an unswerving line toward truth, reality, and the complete understanding of the complex nature of the characters they portrayed.

"From Here To Eternity" won the Award as best production as well as a host of other trophies. Although Daniel Taradash's prize screenplay removed the four-letter words, changed the New Congress Club from a brothel to a bar, played down a good deal of the brutality and sex, it did not diminish one bit of the film's value or impact. It heightened the effect and power of the story by concentrating the action around the characters themselves.

Both supporting Awards went to members of the fine cast. Frank Sinatra as Maggio, the tough little Italian-American soldier, was brilliant in a moving performance that proved once and for all that he was more than just a singer, much more. As Alma, a "hostess" at the New Congress Club, Donna Reed was also honored.

Montgomery Clift, ideally cast as the tough, pigheaded Southern boy Prewitt, and Burt Lancaster, as the sympathetic Sergeant Warden, were both nominated for best acting laurels, as were Richard Burton for "The Robe," William Holden for "Stalag 17," and Marlon Brando for "Julius Caesar."

Holden, as a POW who got a raw deal from his fellow prisoners in "Stalag 17," a German POW camp, was totally convincing, and for this powerful performance was named best actor.

A charming, romantic and amusing film, "Roman Holiday," gave radiantly lovely Audrey Hepburn the chance to become a star, and at the same time waltz away with the Award as best actress of the year. As the young princess of an unnamed country, on a good-will tour of Europe, badly unnerved by the protocol, and eager to see Rome, Audrey Hepburn was a singular combination of guilelessness, refinement, and savoir-faire. Under the skillful direction of William Wyler, both Miss Hepburn and Gregory Peck, as a correspondent and her guide to the wonders of the eternal city, gave performances that sparkled.

Walt Disney took four different Oscars: best cartoon "Toot, Whistle, Plunk and Boom"; best 2-reel short subject for "Bear Country"; and both documentary Awards for "The Living Desert" and "The Alaskan Eskimo." A science fiction thriller, "The War Of The Worlds," was named for its astounding special effects.

AWARDS

Production: "From Here To Eternity," Columbia.

Actor: William Holden in "Stalag 17," Paramount.

Actress: Audrey Hepburn in "Roman Holiday," Paramount.

Supporting Actor: Frank Sinatra in "From Here To Eternity."

Supporting Actress: Donna Reed in "From Here To Eternity."

Direction: Fred Zinnemann, "From Here To Eternity."

Writing (motion picture story): Ian McLellan Hunter, "Roman Holiday."

Writing (screenplay): Daniel Taradash, "From Here To Eternity."

Writing (story and screenplay): Charles Brackett, Walter Reisch, Richard Breen, "Titanic," 20th Century-Fox.

Cinematography (black-and-white): Burnett Guffey, "From Here To Eternity."

Cinematography (color): Loyal Griggs, "Shane," Paramount.

Art Direction (black-and-white): Cedric Gibbons, Edward Carfagno, "Julius Caesar," Metro-Goldwyn-Mayer.

Art Direction (color): Lyle Wheeler, George W. Davis, "The Robe," 20th Century-Fox.

Set Decoration (black-and-white): Edwin B. Willis, Hugh Hunt, "Julius Caesar."

Set Decoration (color): Walter M. Scott, Paul S. Fox, "The Robe."

Costume Design (black-and-white): Edith Head, "Roman Holiday."

Costume Design (color): Charles Le Maire, Emile Santiago, "The Robe."

Sound Recording: "From Here To Eternity," Columbia Studio Sound Department, John P. Livadary, Sound Director.

Film Editing: William Lyon, "From Here To Eternity."

Special Effects: "The War Of The Worlds," Paramount.

Music (music score of a dramatic or comedy picture): Bronislau Kaper, "Lili," Metro-Goldwyn-Mayer.

Music (scoring musical picture): Alfred Newman, "Call Me Madam," 20th Century-Fox.

Music (song): Paul Francis Webster (lyrics), Sammy Fain (music), "Secret Love" from "Calamity Jane," Warner Brothers.

Short Subjects (cartoon): "Toot, Whistle, Plunk And Boom," Disney, Buena Vista.

Short Subjects (1-reel): "The Merry Wives Of Windsor Overture," Metro-Goldwyn-Mayer.

Short Subjects (2-reel): "Bear Country," Disney, RKO Radio.

Documentary (short subject): "The Alaskan Eskimo," Disney, RKO Radio.

Documentary (feature length): "The Living Desert," Disney, Buena Vista.

Irving G. Thalberg Memorial Award: George Stevens.

SPECIAL AWARDS

Pete Smith, for his witty and pungent observations on the American scene in the series of "Pete Smith Specialties."

The 20th Century-Fox Film Corporation, in recognition of their imagination, showmanship and foresight in introducing the revolutionary process known as CinemaScope.

Joseph I. Breen, for his conscientious, open-minded and dignified management of the Motion Picture Production Code.

Bell and Howell Company, for their pioneering and basic achievements in the advancement of the Motion Picture Industry.

SCIENTIFIC AND TECHNICAL AWARDS

Professor Henri Chretien and Earl Sponable, Sol Halprin, Lorin Grignon, Herbert Bragg and Carl Faulkner of 20th Century-Fox Studios, for creating, developing and engineering the equipment, processes and techniques known as CinemaScope.

Fred Waller, for designing and developing the multiple photographic and projection systems which culminated in Cinerama.

Reeves Soundcraft Corp., for their development of a process of applying stripes of magnetic oxide to motion picture film for sound recording and reproduction.

Westrex Corp., for the design and construction of a new film editing machine.

"The Living Desert"
(best documentary feature).
Disney, Buena Vista

"Toot, Whistle, Plunk And Boom"
(best cartoon). Disney

"From Here To Eternity" (best production) with Montgomery Clift
and Donna Reed (best supporting actress), above;
Deborah Kerr, Burt Lancaster, opposite, above;
Ernest Borgnine, Burt Lancaster and
Frank Sinatra (best supporting actor), opposite, below. Columbia

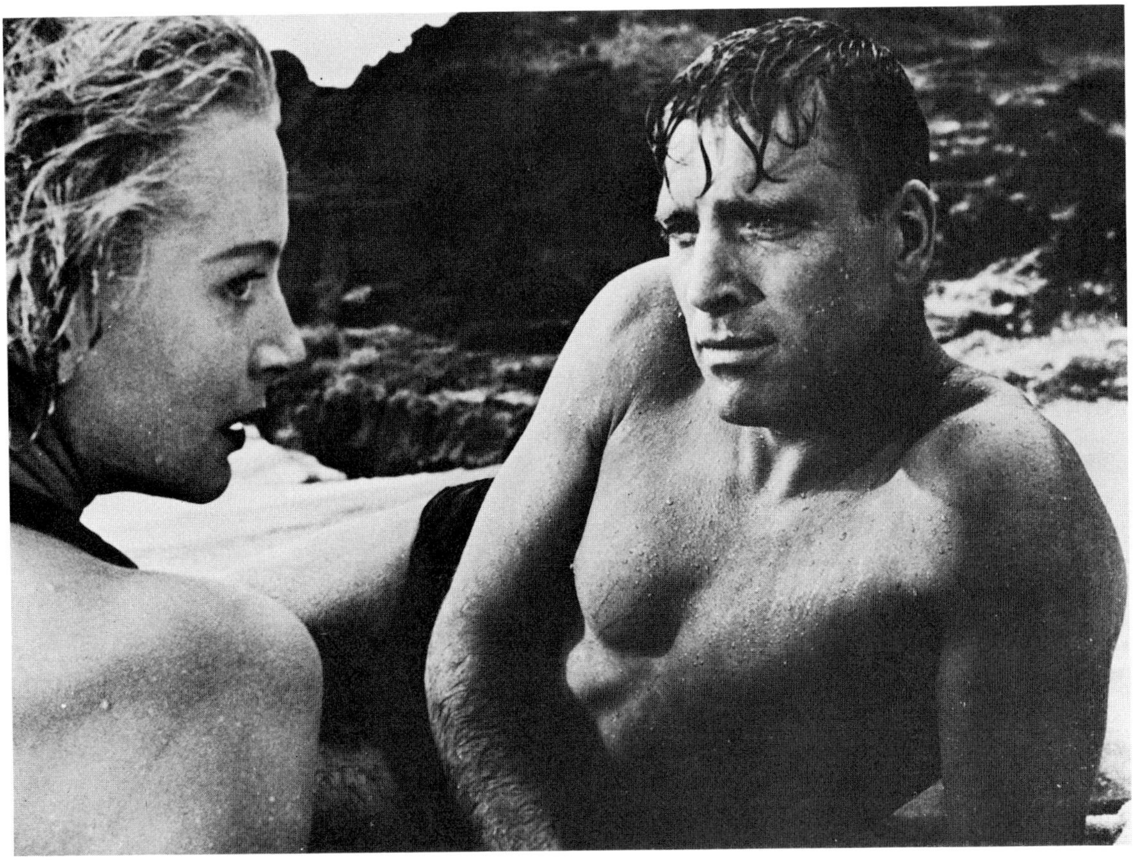

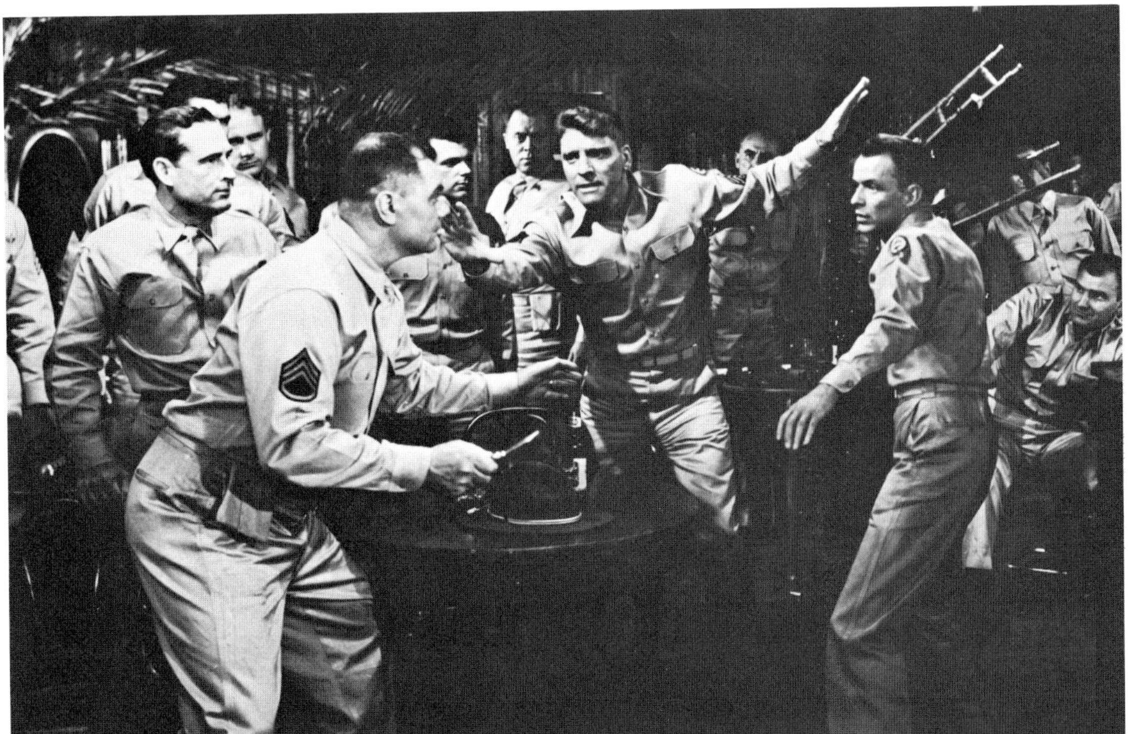

William Holden (best actor) and Sig Ruman in "Stalag 17." Paramount

"Shane" (best cinematography, color)
with Alan Ladd and Brandon De Wilde, above;
Jack Palance, opposite. Paramount

AWARDS

Production: "On The Waterfront,"
Horizon-American, Columbia.

Actor: Marlon Brando in "On The Waterfront."

Actress: Grace Kelly in "The Country Girl,"
Perlberg-Seaton, Paramount.

Supporting Actor: Edmond O'Brien in
"The Barefoot Contessa," Figaro, United Artists.

Supporting Actress: Eva Marie Saint in
"On The Waterfront."

Direction: Elia Kazan, "On The Waterfront."

Writing (motion picture story): Philip Yordan,
"Broken Lance," 20th Century-Fox.

Writing (screenplay): George Seaton,
"The Country Girl."

Writing (story and screenplay): Bud Schulberg,
"On The Waterfront."

Cinematography (black-and-white): Boris Kaufman,
"On The Waterfront."

Cinematography (color): Milton Krasner,
"Three Coins In The Fountain," 20th Century-Fox.

Art Direction (black-and-white): Richard Day,
"On The Waterfront."

Art Direction (color): John Meehan,
"20,000 Leagues Under The Sea,"
Disney, Buena Vista.

Set Decoration (color): Emile Kuri,
"20,000 Leagues Under The Sea."

Costume Design (black-and-white): Edith Head,
"Sabrina," Paramount.

Costume Design (color): Sanzo Wada,
"Gate Of Hell," Daiei, Harrison.

Sound Recording: "The Glenn Miller Story,"
Universal-International Sound Department,
Leslie I. Carey, Sound Director.

Film Editing: Gene Milford, "On The Waterfront."

Special Effects: "20,000 Leagues Under The Sea."

**Music (music score of a dramatic or
comedy picture):** Dimitri Tiomkin,
"The High And The Mighty," Wayne-Fellows,
Warner Brothers.

Music (scoring musical picture): Adolph Deutsch,
Saul Chaplin, "Seven Brides For
Seven Brothers," Metro-Goldwyn-Mayer.

Music (song): Sammy Cahn (lyrics), Jule Styne
(music), "Three Coins In The Fountain" from
"Three Coins In The Fountain."

Short Subjects (cartoon): "When Magoo Flew,"
United Productions of America, Columbia.

Short Subjects (1-reel): "This Mechanical Age,"
Warner Brothers.

Short Subjects (2-reel): "A Time Out Of War,"
Carnival Productions.

Documentary (short subject): "Thursday's
Children," British Information Services,
World Wide-Morse.

Documentary (feature length): "The Vanishing
Prairie," Disney, Buena Vista.

SPECIAL AWARDS

"Gate Of Hell" (Japanese), best foreign language
film of 1954.

Bausch and Lomb Optical Company, for their
contributions to the advancement of the
motion picture industry.

Kemp R. Niver, for the development of the
Renovare Process.

Greta Garbo, for unforgettable performances.

Danny Kaye, for his unique talents, his service
to the Academy, the motion picture industry,
and the American people.

Jon Whitely, for his outstanding juvenile
performance in "The Little Kidnappers."

Vincent Winter, for his outstanding juvenile
performance in "The Little Kidnappers."

SCIENTIFIC AND TECHNICAL AWARDS

Paramount Pictures, Inc., Loren L. Ryder, John R.
Bishop, for VistaVision.

David S. Horsley and Universal-International,
for a portable remote control device for process
projectors.

Karl Freund and Frank Crandell of Photo Research
Corp., for the design and development of a
direct reading brightness meter.

Wesley C. Miller, J. W. Stafford, K. M. Frierson,
and M-G-M, for an electronic sound printing
comparison device.

John P. Livadary, Lloyd Russell and Columbia,
for an improved limiting amplifier as applied to
sound level comparison devices.

Roland Miller and Max Goeppinger of Magnascope
Corp., for the design and development of a
cathode ray magnetic sound track viewer.

Carlos Rivas, G. M. Sprague and M-G-M, for the
design of a magnetic sound editing machine.

Fred Wilson of Goldwyn Studio, for a variable
multiple-band equalizer.

P. C. Young of the Metro-Goldwyn-Mayer Studio
Projection Department, for the practical
application of a variable focal length
attachment to motion picture projector lenses.

Fred Knoth and Orien Ernest of the
Universal-International Studio Technical
Department, for the development of a hand
portable, electric, dry oil-fog machine.

1954

After the end of World War II, Hollywood productions got bigger and bigger. Screens became so large that new theatres had to be built to house them. During the same period, European film makers had moved in a different direction—toward films which caught the lives and problems of the working people, filmed on location in actual houses and bars, and in the streets. Reality was the key word.

"On The Waterfront," a film absolutely explosive in its impact on the emotions and on the motion picture as an art form, brought reality to the American screen. And if "On The Waterfront" was not an event for this reason, it would have been one because of the Oscar-winning performance of Marlon Brando, one of the finest ever on the screen.

The story is a brutal one. Terry, played by Brando, has become the errand boy for a crooked labor leader and his hoodlums. He is little more than a mascot, tolerated only because his brother happens to be the labor leader's lawyer. Terry's search for truth in life, and his ultimate bloody beating, provided the springboard for Brando's superb performance.

It was a piece of genuine artistry, projecting a wonderfully absorbing image of a semi-stupid, stubborn, inner-sweet young man.

Perhaps the greatest scene ever filmed in America—between Brando and Rod Steiger, his brother, in the back seat of a taxi—is never to be forgotten. "It was you made me a bum, Charlie," says the fighter, and Brando's reading of this line was matchless. "I coulda had class. I coulda been a contender."

Elia Kazan, director of "On The Waterfront," received the directorial accolade, and Eva Marie Saint, a television actress making her film debut, got the nod as best supporting actress. "On The Waterfront" also won Awards for best art direction, cinematography, film editing, and screenplay.

Grace Kelly, in the role of the loving, struggling wife of a down-and-out actor, Bing Crosby, in "The Country Girl," won the trophy as best actress. Edmond O'Brien took the honors as best supporting actor opposite Ava Gardner in "The Barefoot Contessa."

"Three Coins In The Fountain," a light, romantic color film set in Rome with Dorothy McGuire and Clifton Webb, was named for its cinematography.

Walt Disney added to his many Awards by taking two: one in the documentary class for "The Vanishing Prairie," and one for the special effects in "20,000 Leagues Under The Sea."

"Gate Of Hell," with perhaps the most magnificent color photography ever seen on the screen, and much the same quality as a Japanese painting—the story of palace intrigue and lost love in ancient Japan—won the special Award as best foreign language film of the year. It is interesting that although "Gate Of Hell" won the Oscar as well as the Grand Prize at the International Cannes Film Festival, it was not considered exceptional or extraordinary in its homeland. It was not named on a single Japanese critic's best film list.

"On The Waterfront" (best production)
with Eva Marie Saint (best supporting actress)
and Marlon Brando (best actor).
Horizon-American, Columbia

Grace Kelly (best actress), Bing Crosby, and William Holden
in "The Country Girl." Perlberg-Seaton, Paramount

Edmond O'Brien (best supporting actor) and Ava Gardner
in "The Barefoot Contessa." Figaro, United Artists

"Three Coins In The Fountain" (best cinematography, color)
with Clifton Webb and Dorothy McGuire, 20th Century-Fox

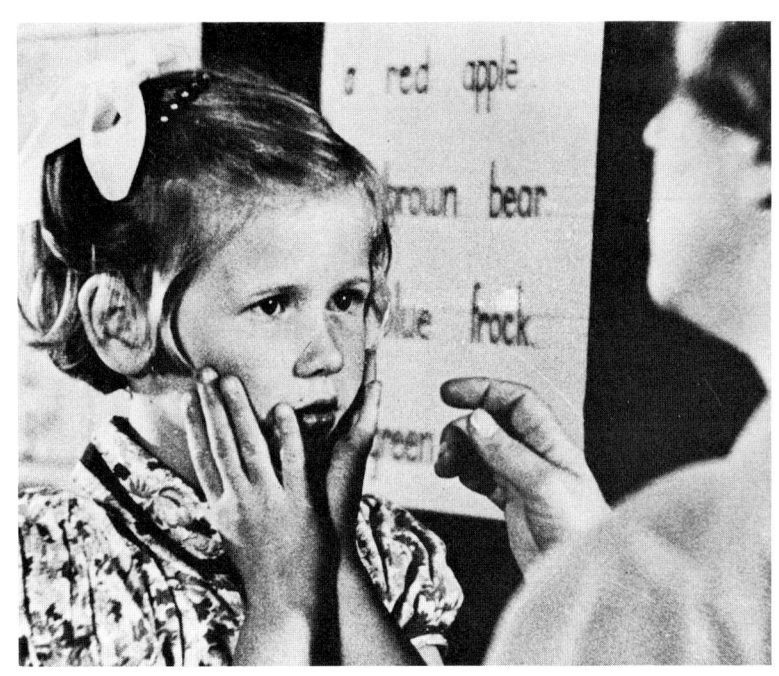

"Thursday's Children"
(best documentary short subject).
British Information Services

"When Magoo Flew"
(best cartoon).
UPA, Columbia

"Gate Of Hell" (best foreign language film)
with Kazuo Hasegawa and Machiko Kyo. Japan, Harrison

1955

For years Hollywood turned out a never-ending series of romantic films; some light and fluffy as air, some heavily steeped in dramatic cliches. They all had one thing in common—they had nothing whatever to do with life or reality. But, with the production of "Marty," a touching, muted film adapted by Paddy Chayefsky from his television play, the lives of two lonely and love-starved people were captured on film, and the idea that romance was only for the handsome, the beautiful and the well-bred, was turned aside, at least for the time being.

The hero and heroine of this tender love story were an over-thirty butcher from the Bronx and a husbandless schoolteacher. Under Delbert Mann's subtle and discerning direction, Ernest Borgnine and Betsy Blair caught all the poignancy of loneliness in the big city. "Marty" was named best picture and Delbert Mann, best director. Paddy Chayefsky's screenplay was also honored with an Oscar.

Borgnine etched an unforgettable portrait as the unsettled, obliging bachelor who was averse to breaking away from his old friends and possibly hurting his mother. He was named best actor for this performance, so different from his past villainous portrayals in "From Here To Eternity" and "Bad Day At Black Rock."

And Borgnine's performance was not the only outstanding one of the year: James Cagney was nominated for "Love Me Or Leave Me," James Dean for "East Of Eden," Spencer Tracy for "Bad Day At Black Rock," and Frank Sinatra for "The Man With The Golden Arm."

Anna Magnani, with her ability to move an audience from tears of anguish to gales of hilarious laughter at a change of her mobile face, won acclaim for her virtuoso performance in Tennessee Williams' "The Rose Tattoo."

Even with her fine performance, Anna Magnani did not have an easy time winning the Award, as it was a year for top female performances. Susan Hayward had been nominated for "I'll Cry Tomorrow," Katharine Hepburn for "Summertime," Jennifer Jones for "Love Is A Many-Splendored Thing," and Eleanor Parker for "Interrupted Melody."

The best supporting actor Award went to Jack Lemmon for his broadly comic performance in "Mister Roberts." He swung through the role of Laundry and Morale Officer Pulver, the erstwhile plotter of the Captain's downfall, with energy and spirit, and was the perfect comic relief in this tale of Navy men caught in the backwash of the war.

Although James Dean received star billing in "East Of Eden," and was nominated for acting honors, it was another member of the cast of the modern Cain and Abel story that walked away with a prize. Jo Van Fleet was judged best supporting actress of the year for her illuminating character study of a mother who abandoned her children and became a brothel-keeper.

AWARDS

Best Picture: "Marty," Steven, United Artists.

Actor: Ernest Borgnine in "Marty."

Actress: Anna Magnani in "The Rose Tattoo," Hal Wallis, Paramount.

Supporting Actor: Jack Lemmon in "Mister Roberts," Orange, Warner Brothers.

Supporting Actress: Jo Van Fleet in "East of Eden," Warner Brothers.

Direction: Delbert Mann, "Marty."

Writing (motion picture story): Daniel Fuchs, "Love Me Or Leave Me," Metro-Goldwyn-Mayer.

Writing (screenplay): Paddy Chayefsky, "Marty."

Writing (story and screenplay): William Ludwig, Sonya Levien, "Interrupted Melody," Metro-Goldwyn-Mayer.

Cinematography (black-and-white): James Wong Howe, "The Rose Tattoo."

Cinematography (color): Robert Burks, "To Catch A Thief," Paramount.

Art Direction (black-and-white): Hal Pereira, Tambi Larsen, "The Rose Tattoo."

Art Direction (color): William Flannery, Jo Mielziner, "Picnic," Columbia.

Set Decoration (black-and-white): Sam Comer, Arthur Krams, "The Rose Tattoo."

Set Decoration (color): Robert Priestly, "Picnic."

Costume Design (black-and-white): Helen Rose, "I'll Cry Tomorrow," Metro-Goldwyn-Mayer.

Costume Design (color): Charles Le Maire, "Love Is A Many-Splendored Thing," 20th Century-Fox.

Sound Recording: "Oklahoma!" Todd-AO Sound Department, Fred Hynes, Sound Director.

Film Editing: Charles Nelson, William A. Lyon, "Picnic."

Music (music score of a dramatic or comedy picture): Alfred Newman, "Love Is A Many-Splendored Thing" from "Love Is A Many-Splendored Thing."

Music (scoring musical picture): Robert Russell Bennett, Jay Blackton, Adolph Deutsch, "Oklahoma!" Rodgers and Hammerstein, Magna.

Music (song): Paul Francis Webster (lyrics), Sammy Fain (music), "Love Is A Many-Splendored Thing."

Short Subjects (cartoon): "Speedy Gonzales," Warner Brothers.

Short Subjects (1-reel): "Survival City," 20th Century-Fox.

Short Subjects (2-reel): "The Face Of Lincoln," University of Southern California, Cavalcade.

Documentary (short subject): "Men Against The Arctic," Disney, Buena Vista.

Documentary (feature length): "Helen Keller In Her Story," Hamilton.

SPECIAL AWARD

"Samurai" (Japanese), best foreign language film of 1955. Toho.

SCIENTIFIC AND TECHNICAL AWARDS

National Carbon Co., for the development and production of a high efficiency yellow flame carbon for motion picture color photography.

Eastman Kodak Co., for Eastman Tri-X panchromatic negative film.

Farciot Edouart, Hal Corl and the Paramount Studio Transparency Department, for the engineering and development of a double-frame, triple-head background projector.

20th Century-Fox Studio and Bausch & Lomb Co., for the new combination lenses for CinemaScope photography.

Walter Jolley, Maurice Larson and R. H. Spies of 20th Century-Fox Studio, for a spraying process which creates simulated metallic surfaces.

Steve Krilanovich, for an improved camera dolly incorporating multi-directional steering.

Dave Anderson of 20th Century-Fox Studio, for an improved spotlight capable of maintaining a fixed circle of light at constant intensity over varied distances.

Loren L. Ryder, Charles West, Henry Fracker and Paramount Studio, for a projection film index to establish proper framing for various aspect ratios.

Farciot Edouart, Hal Corl and the Paramount Studio Transparency Department, for an improved dual stereopticon background projector.

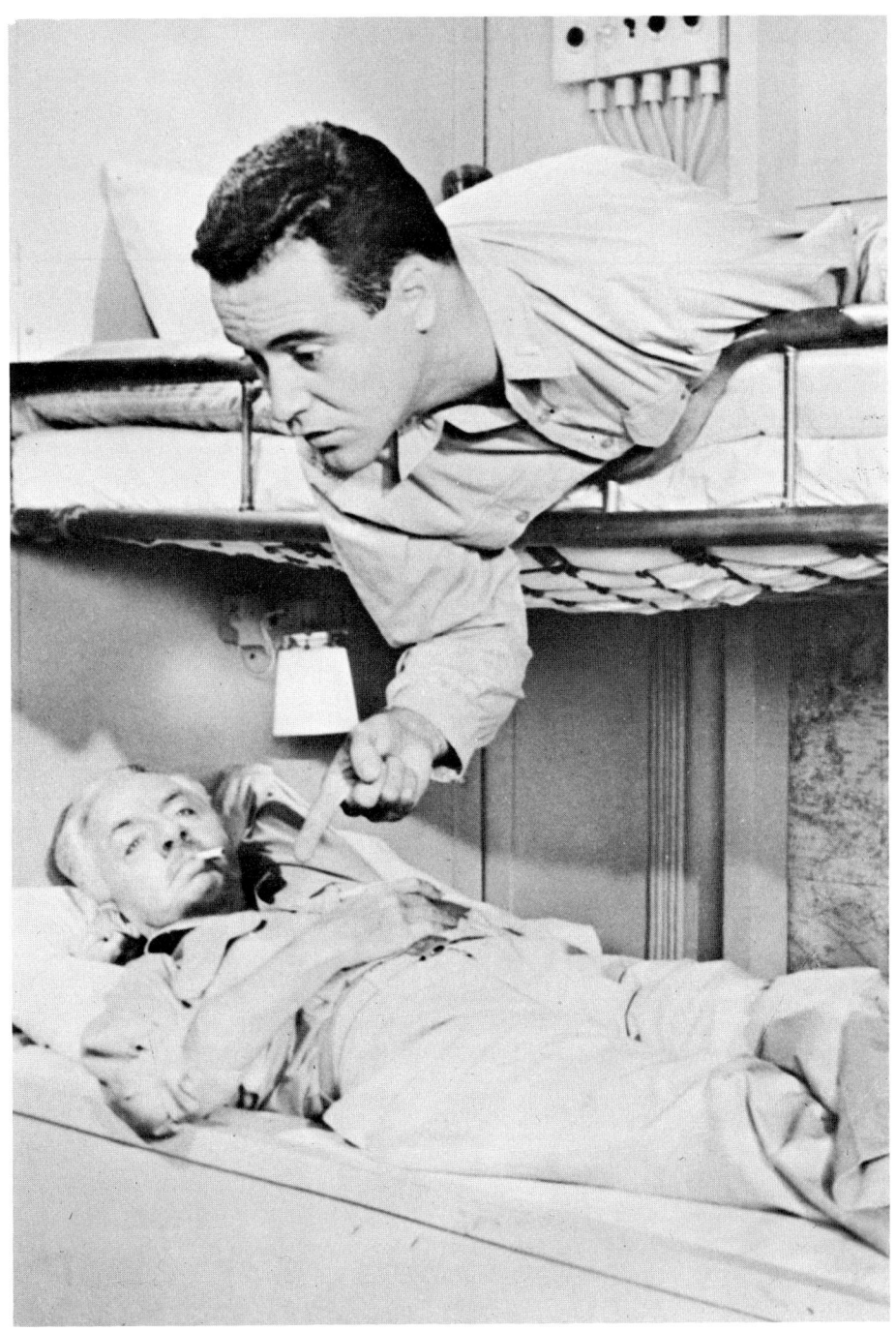

Jack Lemmon (best supporting actor)
and William Powell in "Mister Roberts."
Orange, Warner Brothers

"Marty" (best picture) with Ernest Borgnine (best actor) and Esther Minciotti, opposite;
Ernest Borgnine and Betsy Blair, below. Steven, United Artists

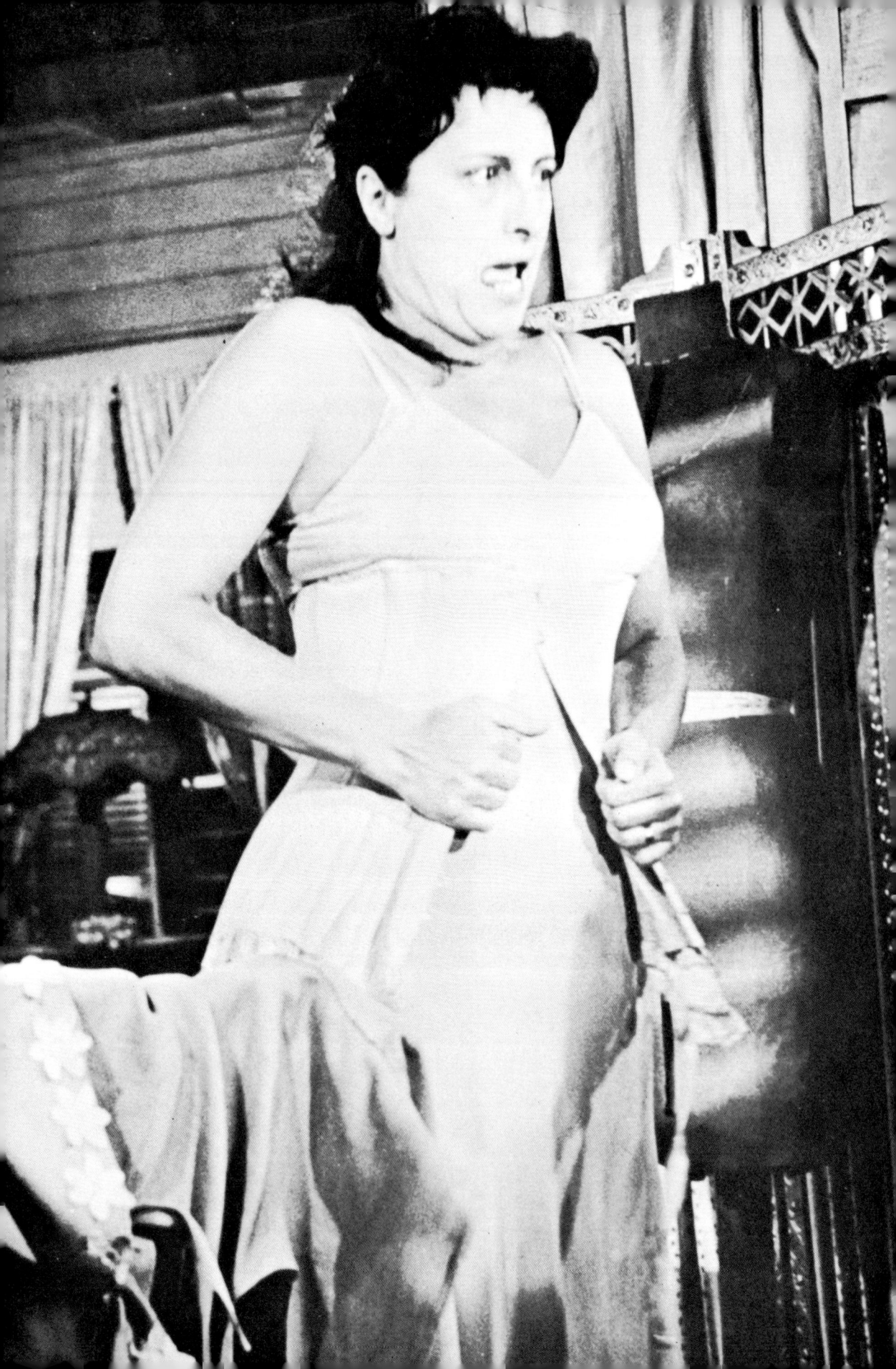

Anna Magnani (best actress) Marisa Pavan, and Burt Lancaster
in "The Rose Tattoo" (best cinematography, black and white). Wallis, Paramount

Jo Van Fleet (best supporting actress)
and James Dean in "East Of Eden."
Warner Brothers

"Samurai"
(best foreign
language film)
with Takashi Shimura
and Toshiro Mifune.
Japan, Toho

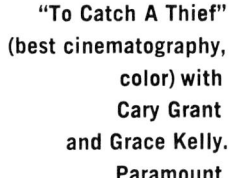

"To Catch A Thief"
(best cinematography,
color) with
Cary Grant
and Grace Kelly.
Paramount

AWARDS

Best Picture: "Around The World In 80 Days,"
Todd, United Artists.

Actor: Yul Brynner in "The King And I,"
20th Century-Fox.

Actress: Ingrid Bergman in "Anastasia,"
20th Century-Fox.

Supporting Actor: Anthony Quinn in
"Lust For Life," Metro-Goldwyn-Mayer.

Supporting Actress: Dorothy Malone in
"Written On The Wind," Universal-International.

Direction: George Stevens, "Giant," Productions,
Warner Brothers.

Foreign Language Film Award: "La Strada,"
Ponti-De Laurentiis, Trans-Lux.

Writing (motion picture story): Robert Rich
(Dalton Trumbo), "The Brave One,"
King Brothers, RKO Radio.

Writing (screenplay-adapted): James Poe, John
Farrow, S. J. Perelman, "Around The World
In 80 Days."

Writing (screenplay-original): Albert Lamorisse,
"The Red Balloon," Films Montsouris, Lopert.

Cinematography (black-and-white): Joseph
Ruttenberg, "Somebody Up There Likes Me,"
Metro-Goldwyn-Mayer.

Cinematography (color): Lionel Lindon,
"Around The World In 80 Days."

Art Direction (black-and-white): "Somebody Up
There Likes Me," Cedric Gibbons, Malcolm F.
Brown (art direction), Edwin B. Willis, F. Keogh
Gleason (set decoration).

Art Direction (color): "The King And I," Lyle R.
Wheeler, John DeCuir (art direction), Walter M.
Scott, Paul S. Fox (set decoration).

Costume Design (black-and-white): Jean Louis,
"The Solid Gold Cadillac," Columbia.

Costume Design (color): Irene Sharaff,
"The King And I."

Sound Recording: "The King And I,"
20th Century-Fox Sound Department.

Film Editing: Gene Ruggiero, Paul Weatherwax,
"Around The World In 80 Days."

Special Effects: John Fulton, "The Ten
Commandments," Motion Picture Associates,
Paramount.

**Music (music score of a dramatic or comedy
picture):** Victor Young, "Around The World
In 80 Days."

Music (scoring musical picture): Alfred Newman,
Ken Darby, "The King And I."

Music (song): Ray Evans, Jay Livingston (lyrics and
music), "Whatever Will Be, Will Be" (Que Sera,
Sera) from "The Man Who Knew Too Much,"
Filwite, Paramount.

Short Subjects (cartoon): "Mister Magoo's Puddle
Jumper," UPA, Columbia.

Short Subjects (1-reel): "Crashing The Water
Barrier," Warner Brothers.

Short Subjects (2-reel): "The Bespoke Overcoat,"
Romulus.

Documentary (short subject): "The True Story
Of The Civil War," Camera Eye.

Documentary (feature length): "The Silent World,"
Filmad-F.S.J.Y.C., Columbia.

Irving G. Thalberg Memorial Award: Buddy Adler.

Jean Hersholt Humanitarian Award:
Y. Frank Freeman.

SPECIAL AWARD

Eddie Cantor, for distinguished service to the
film industry.

SCIENTIFIC AND TECHNICAL AWARDS

Richard H. Ranger of Rangertone, Inc., for a
synchronous recording and reproducing system
for quarter-inch magnetic tape.

Ted Hirsch, Carl Hauge and Edward Reichard of
Consolidated Film Industries, for an automatic
scene counter for laboratory projection rooms.

The Technical Departments of Paramount Pictures
Corp., for the engineering and development
of the Paramount Light-weight
horizontal-movement VistaVision camera.

Roy C. Stewart and Sons of Stewart-Trans Lux
Corp., Dr. C. R. Daily and the Transparency
Department of Paramount Pictures Corp., for
the engineering and development of the
HiTrans and Para-HiTrans rear projection
screens.

The Construction Department of
Metro-Goldwyn-Mayer Studio, for a new
hand-portable fog machine.

Daniel J. Bloomberg, John Pond, William Wade
and the Engineering and Camera Departments
of Republic Studio, for the Naturama adaptation
to the Mitchell camera.

1956

Jules Verne undoubtedly would have been pleased with Mike Todd's glistening film adaptation of his novel, "Around The World In 80 Days," named best picture of the year. This film was many things, all of them good. First and foremost it was a jubilant frolic with David Niven as Phileas Fogg and Cantinflas as his "man" Passepartout, chasing around the world determined to win their bet. It was a beautiful travelog and also a sensational thriller with adventures and misadventures in London, Paris, Spain, India, Hong Kong, Japan, through the United States, and back once again to London. A tremendous supporting cast: Frank Sinatra, Fernandel, Peter Lorre, Gilbert Roland, Charles Boyer, Marlene Dietrich, George Raft, Buster Keaton, and a host of other luminaries in "cameo" roles popped up in unexpected places as unlikely characters—a pianist, a saloon entertainer, a steward, a "sporting lady," a train conductor—added to the hilarity. From the opening, right through to the highly imaginative titles in the epilogue, "Around The World In 80 Days" was a delight to both eye and ear.

Yul Brynner made the transition from stage to screen with ease, and won the best acting trophy for his ingenious performance as the King in "The King And I." Brynner played the complex monarch perfectly, showing at every turn the dual nature of the King's personality: power and weakness, finesse and candor, and most of all, supreme egotism. Brynner had to be superb in order to win out over such performers as Laurence Olivier in "Richard III," Kirk Douglas in "Lust For Life," Rock Hudson and James Dean in "Giant."

The distaff side of the acting honors went to Ingrid Bergman for her illuminating portrait of a hopeless, lonely girl, molded into a passable replica of a czar's daughter in "Anastasia." The transformation was miraculous as Miss Bergman emerged from the cocoon of poverty as a glorious butterfly.

The Awards for supporting players went to Anthony Quinn for his characterization of Gauguin, opposite Kirk Douglas' Van Gogh in "Lust For Life," and Dorothy Malone for her acid portrayal of a nymphomaniac in "Written On The Wind."

After nine years, the Award for best foreign language film was taken out of the honorary class and made a regular Oscar. The Academy membership chose Federico Fellini's masterpiece, "La Strada," starring Anthony Quinn, Giulietta Masina and Richard Basehart.

"Around The World In 80 Days" (best picture) with Shirley MacLaine,
David Niven, Cantinflas, and Buster Keaton. Todd

Cantinflas, David Niven, Marlene Dietrich, and Frank Sinatra
in "Around The World In 80 Days." Todd

Yul Brynner (best actor) in "The King And I." 20th Century-Fox

Ingrid Bergman (best actress)
and Helen Hayes in "Anastasia."
20th Century-Fox

Anthony Quinn (best supporting actor)
and Kirk Douglas in "Lust For Life." M-G-M

Dorothy Malone (best supporting actress), Robert Stack, and Rock Hudson in "Written On The Wind." Universal-International

"The Bespoke Overcoat" (best short subject, 2-reel) with Alfie Bass. Romulus

"The Ten Commandments"
(best special effects)
with Edward G. Robinson
and Charlton Heston. Paramount

"Mister Magoo's Puddle Jumper"
(best cartoon). UPA, Columbia

"La Strada" (best foreign language film)
with Giulietta Masina and Anthony Quinn.
Italy, Ponti-De Laurentiis, Trans-Lux

1957

A distinguished and unusual film, "The Bridge On The River Kwai" garnered the Oscar as best picture of the year as well as six other Awards for outstanding achievement. It had a rare combination of elements, which, taken together, formed an almost perfect motion picture. First there was the brilliant and powerful screenplay which Pierre Boulle adapted from his own novel, which built to an unbelievably suspenseful climax. There was the imaginative direction of David Lean, whose ability to develop characters in film was unquestionably great. Alec Guinness, as a British colonel led a first-rate cast, including William Holden, Jack Hawkins, Sessue Hayakawa, and Geoffrey Horne. The vivid cinematography of Jack Hildyard and the haunting martial music of Malcolm Arnold heightened the impact of the film. Here was a war movie, and yet it dispensed with the usual tremendous battle scenes to concentrate the focus and attention of the audience on the psychological battles raging within the characters.

Other excellent films, "Twelve Angry Men," "Peyton Place," "Sayonara," and "Witness For The Prosecution," had also been nominated, but the overall excellence of "The Bridge On The River Kwai" could not be denied.

A motion picture drawn from an actual psychiatric case of split personality, "The Three Faces Of Eve" afforded a comparative newcomer to the screen, Joanne Woodward, with the opportunity to give an outstanding performance and win the Oscar as the best actress of the year. Her triple characterization as Eve White, a dull, uninteresting housewife; Eve Black, a passionate, mercurial strumpet; and Jane, a nice young woman, was a tour de force.

Joanne Woodward went into the contest for best actress a distinct underdog, since Deborah Kerr had been nominated for "Heaven Knows, Mr. Allison," Lana Turner for "Peyton Place," Elizabeth Taylor for "Raintree County," and Anna Magnani for "Wild Is The Wind."

Both Awards for best supporting players went to members of the cast of "Sayonara." Under the skillful direction of veteran Josh Logan, Red Buttons was honored for his first attempt at a serious acting role, as an airman who defied regulations to marry his Japanese sweetheart, only to face the despair of having to leave her to return home. With warmth and passion Buttons captured the pathos of the character with unerring accuracy. As his girl, Miyoshi Umeki gave a wonderfully charming performance and won the distaff side of this honor.

"Nights Of Cabiria," directed by Federico Fellini and starring Giulietta Masina won the accolade as best foreign language picture of the year. Here was a film that was an emotional experience, full of humor and pathos—as gay and tragic as life itself. Miss Masina, in reality, Mrs. Fellini, was brilliant as the bitter-sweet prostitute.

AWARDS

Best Picture: "The Bridge On The River Kwai," Horizon, Columbia.

Actor: Alec Guinness in "The Bridge On The River Kwai."

Actress: Joanne Woodward in "The Three Faces Of Eve," 20th Century-Fox.

Supporting Actor: Red Buttons in "Sayonara," Goetz, Warner Brothers.

Supporting Actress: Miyoshi Umeki in "Sayonara."

Direction: David Lean, "The Bridge On The River Kwai."

Foreign Language Film Award: "The Nights Of Cabiria," De Laurentiis, Lopert Films.

Writing (screenplay based on material from another medium): Pierre Boulle, "The Bridge On The River Kwai."

Writing (story and screenplay written directly for the screen): George Wells, "Designing Woman," Metro-Goldwyn-Mayer.

Cinematography: Jack Hildyard, "The Bridge On The River Kwai."

Art Direction: "Sayonara," Ted Haworth (art direction), Robert Priestley (set decoration).

Costume Design: Orry-Kelly, "Les Girls," Siegel, Metro-Goldwyn-Mayer.

Sound Recording: "Sayonara," Warner Brothers Studio Sound Department, George R. Groves, Sound Director.

Film Editing: Peter Taylor, "The Bridge On The River Kwai."

Special Effects: Walter Rossi, "The Enemy Below," 20th Century-Fox.

Music (scoring): Malcolm Arnold, "The Bridge On The River Kwai."

Music (song): Sammy Cahn (lyrics), James Van Heusen (music), "All The Way" from "The Joker Is Wild," A.M.B.L., Paramount.

Short Subjects (cartoon): "Birds Anonymous," Warner Brothers.

Short Subjects (live action): "The Wetback Hound," Disney, Buena Vista.

Documentary (feature length): "Albert Schweitzer," Hill and Anderson, de Rochemont.

Jean Hersholt Humanitarian Award: Samuel Goldwyn.

SPECIAL AWARDS

Charles Brackett, for outstanding service to the Academy.

B. B. Kahane, for distinguished service to the Motion Picture Industry.

Gilbert M. ("Broncho Billy") Anderson, motion picture pioneer, for his contributions to the development of motion pictures as entertainment.

The Society of Motion Picture and Television Engineers, for their contributions to the advancement of the Motion Picture Industry.

SCIENTIFIC AND TECHNICAL AWARDS

The Todd-AO Corp. and Westrex Corp., for developing a method of producing and exhibiting wide-film motion pictures known as the Todd-AO System.

The Motion Picture Research Council, for the design and development of a high efficiency projection screen for drive-in theatres.

The Societe D'Optique et de Mechanique de Haute Precision, for the development of a high speed vari-focal photographic lens.

Harlan L. Baumbach, Lorand Wargo, Howard M. Little and the Unicorn Engineering Corp., for the development of an automatic printer light selector.

Charles E. Sutter, William B. Smith, Paramount Pictures Corp. and General Cable Corp., for the engineering and application to studio use of aluminum lightweight electrical cable and connectors.

Joanne Woodward (best actress)
and Vincent Edwards in
"The Three Faces Of Eve."
20th Century-Fox

Red Buttons (best supporting actor) and Miyoshi Umeki
(best supporting actress) in "Sayonara." Goetz, Warner Brothers

"The Nights of Cabiria" (best foreign language film)
with Giulietta Masina. Italy, De Laurentiis, Lopert

"The Bridge On The River Kwai" (best picture) with Alec Guinness (best actor), William Holden, and Jack Hawkins. Horizon, Columbia

AWARDS

Best Picture: "Gigi," Freed, Metro-Goldwyn-Mayer.

Actor: David Niven in "Separate Tables," Clifton, United Artists.

Actress: Susan Hayward in "I Want To Live," Figaro, United Artists.

Supporting Actor: Burl Ives in "The Big Country," Anthony-Worldwide, United Artists.

Supporting Actress: Wendy Hiller in "Separate Tables."

Direction: Vincente Minnelli, "Gigi."

Foreign Language Film Award: "My Uncle," Specta-Gray-Alter, Films del Centaure, Continental.

Writing (screenplay based on material from another medium): Alan Jay Lerner, "Gigi."

Writing (story and screenplay written directly for the screen): Nathan E. Douglas, Harold Jacob Smith, "The Defiant Ones," Kramer, United Artists.

Cinematography (black-and-white): Sam Leavitt, "The Defiant Ones."

Cinematography (color): Joseph Ruttenberg, "Gigi."

Art Direction: William A. Horning, Preston Ames (art direction), Henry Grace, Keogh Gleason (set decoration), "Gigi."

Costume Design: Cecil Beaton, "Gigi."

Sound: "South Pacific," Todd-AO Sound Department, Fred Hynes, Sound Director.

Film Editing: Adrienne Fazan, "Gigi."

Special Effects: Tom Howard, "tom thumb," George Pal, Metro-Goldwyn-Mayer.

Music (music score of a dramatic or comedy picture): Dimitri Tiomkin, "The Old Man And The Sea," Hayward, Warner Brothers.

Music (scoring musical picture): Andre Previn, "Gigi."

Music (song): Alan Jay Lerner (lyrics), Frederick Loewe (music), "Gigi" from "Gigi."

Short Subjects (cartoon): "Knighty Knight Bugs," Warner Brothers.

Short Subjects (live action): "Grand Canyon," Disney, Buena Vista.

Documentary (short subject): "AMA Girls," Disney, Buena Vista.

Documentary (feature length): "White Wilderness," Disney, Buena Vista.

Irving G. Thalberg Memorial Award: Jack L. Warner.

SPECIAL AWARD

Maurice Chevalier, for his contributions to the world of entertainment for more than half a century.

SCIENTIFIC AND TECHNICAL AWARDS

Don W. Prideaux, Leroy G. Leighton and the Lamp Division of General Electric Co., for an improved 10 kilowatt lamp for motion picture set lighting.

Panavision, Inc., for the design and development of the Auto Panatar anamorphic photographic lens for 35mm CinemaScope photography.

Willy Borberg of the General Precision Laboratory, Inc., for the development of a high speed intermittent movement for 35mm motion picture theatre projection equipment.

Fred Ponedel, George Brown and Conrad Boye of the Warner Bros. Special Effects Department, for the design and fabrication of a new rapid fire marble gun.

1958

The magic of Alan Jay Lerner and Frederick Loewe that held audiences captivated in theatres during the run of their "My Fair Lady," struck pure gold again with their delightful "Gigi." Here was one of the most honored films of all time, walking away with nine Oscars.

The delightfully saucy story, set in turn-of-the-century Paris, was adapted from the story by Colette, and concerned a charming and exhilarating French youngster who outwitted her elders who wanted to train her to be a mistress instead of a wife. Vincente Minnelli, who had been nominated for his splendid musical, "An American In Paris," handled the superlative cast of "Gigi" with a light touch, and was named best director. Leslie Caron, Louis Jourdan, and Maurice Chevalier sang, danced, and romanced, and their performances seemed almost effortless.

The Academy honored Maurice Chevalier with a special Award for his outstanding film contributions over half a century. His performance in "Gigi," as the old friend of the family with a twinkle in his eye, and an eye for femininity, was a jewel. Susan Hayward, in one of the most unsympathetic roles of her career, was named best actress for her performance in "I Want To Live." As Barbara Graham, a B-girl convicted of murder and sent to the gas chamber, Susan Hayward painted a subtle portrait of a prostitute without a heart of gold, a woman with utter disdain for the law, a liar and perjurer.

The members of the Academy had a most difficult choice to make in awarding best acting honors, as many fine performances had been nominated. Spencer Tracy in Ernest Hemingway's "The Old Man And The Sea" was unforgettable. Both Tony Curtis and Sidney Poitier as escaped convicts, one white and one black, chained together at the wrist but torn apart by racial prejudice and bigotry, were brilliant in "The Defiant Ones." Paul Newman in Tennessee Williams' "Cat On A Hot Tin Roof" was completely convincing in a difficult role.

However, David Niven, as a lonely, aging, shamed British major afraid of sex and life, and unable to communicate, was named best actor for "Separate Tables." Wendy Hiller, as the understanding and wise hotel manager in the same film was honored as best supporting actress.

Burl Ives was named best supporting actor, for his portrayal of a violent, feuding rancher in "The Big Country," which starred Gregory Peck, Carroll Baker, Charles Bickford, and Charlton Heston.

"My Uncle," with Jacques Tati as star, producer, director, and co-author, was named best foreign language film. It was a laugh-filled production; pure slapstick in its highest form, with Tati playing Mr. Hulot, the universal man faced with the problems of modern times.

"Gigi" (best picture) with Hermione Gingold,
Louis Jourdan, Leslie Caron, below;
Maurice Chevalier and Lydia Stevens, opposite. Freed, M-G-M

David Niven (best actor) and Deborah Kerr, below;
Wendy Hiller (best supporting actress)
and Burt Lancaster, opposite, in "Separate Tables."
Clifton, United Artists

243

Susan Hayward (best actress)
in "I Want To Live."
Figaro, United Artists

Burl Ives (best supporting actor) and Gregory Peck in "The Big Country."
Anthony-Worldwide, United Artists

"The Defiant Ones" (best cinematography, black and white)
with Sidney Poitier and Tony Curtis. Kramer, United Artists

"My Uncle" (best foreign language film) with Jacques Tati.
France, Specta-Gray-Alter, Films del Centaure, Continental

1959

"Ben-Hur," adapted from General Lew Wallace's antique novel of 1880, was brought to the screen in super-spectacular fashion by a highly skilled team of film makers led by director William Wyler, script writers Karl Tunberg and Christopher Fry, actors Charlton Heston and Hugh Griffith, cinematographer Robert Surtees, and Miklos Rozsa, whose dramatic musical score was an important adjunct to the overall powerful effect of the film. When Award time rolled around, the members of the Academy voted it no less than eleven Oscars.

The motion picture itself was impressive in size, scope, and color, with magnificent sea battles and, of course, the famous chariot race, but under Wyler's inspired direction, "Ben-Hur" never for a moment forgot that it was the story of a man—the intensely personal portrait of a Jewish Prince, Judah Ben-Hur. It was selected best picture over such fine films as "Anatomy Of A Murder," "The Diary Of Anne Frank," "The Nun's Story," and "Room At The Top," which had also been nominated.

Charlton Heston was named best actor for his stirring performance as Judah, a man who spoke his mind against his captors and who never lost sight of his convictions and his ideals. Heston's performance brought the most important single factor in Ben-Hur's character, a basic human dignity, into sharp focus. Hugh Griffith as the crafty Arab who sponsored Ben-Hur's chariot race against Messala, was outstanding and won the Oscar for best supporting actor.

Simone Signoret's perceptive and sensitive delineation of the character of Alice, opposite Laurence Harvey's Joe, was an unbelievably accurate portrait, in the British film "Room At The Top." Although French, she was honored as the best actress even though nominations went to such American stars as Elizabeth Taylor and Katharine Hepburn for "Suddenly, Last Summer," Doris Day for "Pillow Talk," and Audrey Hepburn for "The Nun's Story."

A moving film, "The Diary Of Anne Frank," based on an actual heart-rending story of a Jewish girl and her family forced to hide from the Nazis, was triply honored. Shelley Winters took the laurels as best supporting actress, and the beautiful film was named for its brilliant cinematography and art direction.

A modern version of the Orpheus and Eurydice legend, "Black Orpheus," garnered the Oscar as best foreign language film of the year. Set in Rio de Janeiro at carnival time, and excellently played by an all-Negro cast, this splendid film wove a magic spell which captured the ancient story in purely modern terms.

AWARDS

Best Picture: "Ben-Hur," Metro-Goldwyn-Mayer.

Actor: Charlton Heston in "Ben-Hur."

Actress: Simone Signoret in "Room At The Top," Romulus, Continental.

Supporting Actor: Hugh Griffith in "Ben-Hur."

Supporting Actress: Shelley Winters in "The Diary Of Anne Frank," 20th Century-Fox.

Direction: William Wyler, "Ben-Hur."

Foreign Language Film Award: "Black Orpheus," Dispatfilm & Gemme Cinematografica, United Artists.

Writing (screenplay based on material from another medium): Neil Paterson, "Room At The Top."

Writing (story and screenplay written directly for the screen): Russell Rouse, Clarence Greene (story), Stanley Shapiro, Maurice Richlin (screenplay), "Pillow Talk," Arwin, Universal-International.

Cinematography (black-and-white): William C. Mellor, "The Diary Of Anne Frank."

Cinematography (color): Robert L. Surtees, "Ben-Hur."

Art Direction (black-and-white): "The Diary Of Anne Frank," Lyle R. Wheeler, George W. Davis (art direction), Walter M. Scott, Stuart A. Reiss (set decoration).

Art Direction (color): "Ben-Hur," William A. Horning, Edward Carfagno (art direction), Hugh Hunt (set decoration).

Costume Design (black-and-white): Orry-Kelly, "Some Like It Hot," Ashton, Mirisch, United Artists.

Costume Design (color): Elizabeth Haffenden, "Ben-Hur."

Sound: "Ben-Hur," Metro-Goldwyn-Mayer Studio Sound Department, Franklin E. Milton, Sound Director.

Film Editing: Ralph E. Winters, John D. Dunning, "Ben-Hur."

Sound Effects: "Ben-Hur," A. Arnold Gillespie, Robert MacDonald (visual effects), Milo Lory (audible effects).

Music (music score of a dramatic or comedy picture): Miklos Rozsa, "Ben-Hur."

Music (scoring musical picture): Andre Previn, Ken Darby, "Porgy And Bess," Goldwyn, Columbia.

Music (song): Sammy Cahn (lyrics), James Van Heusen (music), "High Hopes" from "A Hole In The Head," Sincap, United Artists.

Short Subjects (cartoon): "Moonbirds," Storyboard, Harrison.

Short Subjects (live action): "The Golden Fish," Les Requins, Columbia.

Documentary (short subject): "Glass," Netherlands Government, Arthur-Go.

Documentary (feature length): "Serengeti Shall Not Die," Okapia-Film, Transocean-Film.

Jean Hersholt Humanitarian Award: Bob Hope.

SPECIAL AWARDS

Lee de Forest, for his pioneering inventions which brought sound to motion pictures.

Buster Keaton, for his unique talents which brought immortal comedies to the screen.

SCIENTIFIC AND TECHNICAL AWARDS

Douglas Shearer of Metro-Goldwyn-Mayer, Inc., and Robert E. Gottschalk and John R. Moore of Panavision, Inc., for the development of a system of producing and exhibiting wide-film motion pictures known as Camera 65.

Wadsworth E. Pohl, William Evans, Werner Hopf, S. E. Howse, Thomas P. Dixon, Stanford Research Institute and Technicolor Corp., for the design and development of the Technicolor electronic printing timer.

Wadsworth E. Pohl, Jack Alford, Henry Imus, Joseph Schmit, Paul Fassnacht, Al Lofquist and Technicolor Corp., for the development and practical application of equipment for wet printing.

Dr. Howard S. Coleman, Dr. A. Francis Turner, Harold H. Schroeder, James R. Benford and Harold E. Rosenberger of the Bausch & Lomb Optical Co., for the design and development of the Balcold projection mirror.

Robert P. Gutterman of General Kinetics, Inc., and the Lipsner-Smith Corp., for the design and development of the CF-2 Ultra-sonic Film Cleaner.

Ub Iwerks of Walt Disney Prods., for the design of an improved optical printer for special effects and matte shots.

E. L. Stones, Glen Robinson, Winfield Hubbard and Luther Newman of the M-G-M Construction Department, for the design of a multiple cable remote controlled winch.

Hugh Griffith (best supporting actor), seated center, and Stephen Boyd, seated right, in "Ben-Hur." M-G-M

"Ben-Hur" (best picture). Charlton Heston (best actor)
with Jack Hawkins, opposite; with Stephen Boyd, above. M-G-M

Shelley Winters (best supporting actress),
Lou Jacobi, Diane Baker, Ed Wynn,
Joseph Schildkraut, Gusti Huber, Richard Beymer,
and Millie Perkins in "The Diary Of Anne Frank"
(best cinematography, black and white).
20th Century-Fox

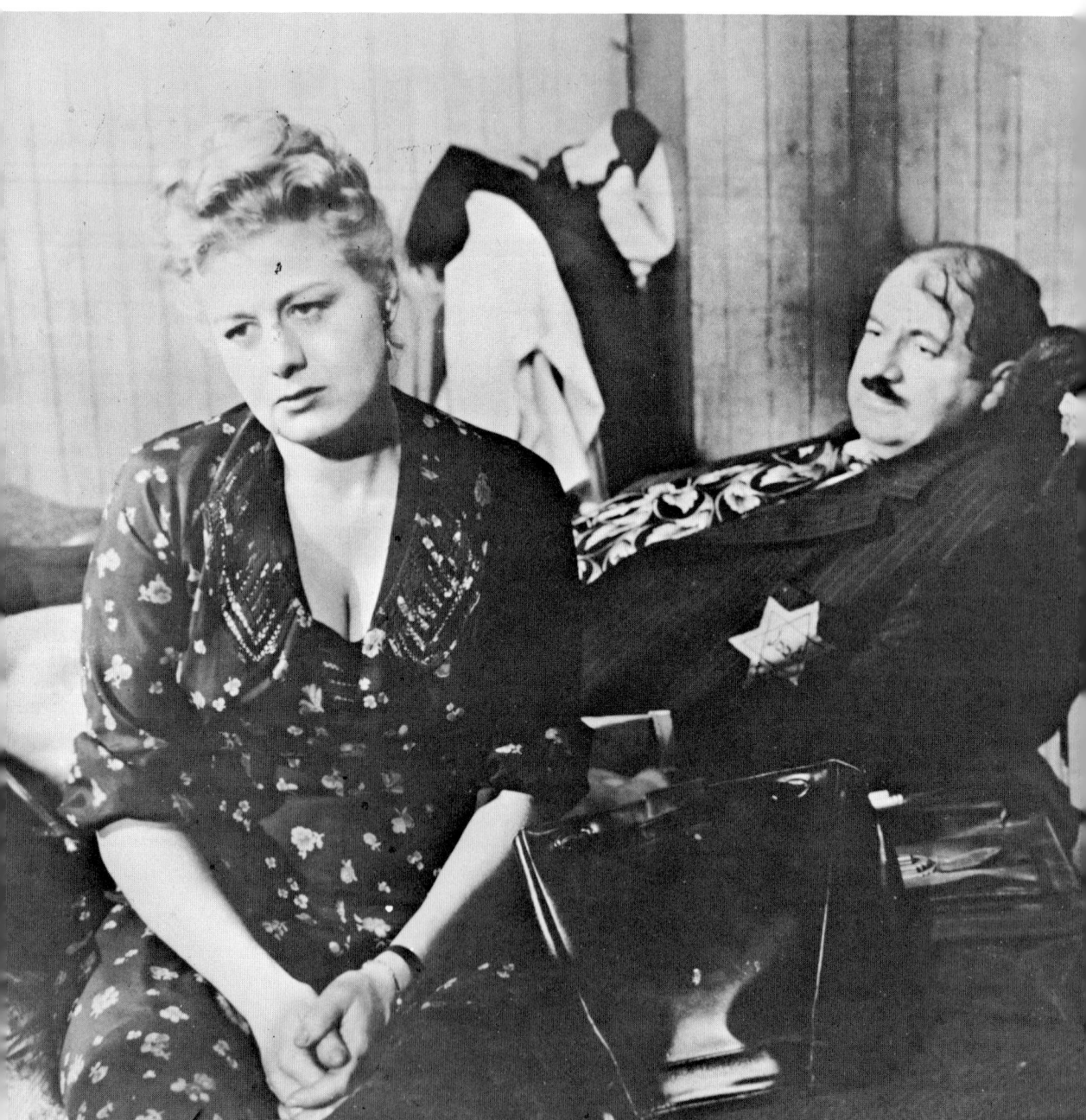

"Black Orpheus" (best foreign language film) with Breno Mello.
France, Dispatfilm, Gemma, United Artists

Simone Signoret (best actress) with Laurence Harvey
in "Room At The Top." Romulus, Continental

AWARDS

Best Picture: "The Apartment," Mirisch, United Artists.

Actor: Burt Lancaster in "Elmer Gantry," Lancaster-Brooks, United Artists.

Actress: Elizabeth Taylor in "Butterfield 8," Afton-Linebrook, Metro-Goldwyn-Mayer.

Supporting Actor: Peter Ustinov in "Spartacus," Bryna, Universal-International.

Supporting Actress: Shirley Jones in "Elmer Gantry."

Direction: Billy Wilder, "The Apartment."

Foreign Language Film Award: "The Virgin Spring," Svensk Filmindustri, Janus.

Writing (screenplay based on material from another medium): Richard Brooks, "Elmer Gantry."

Writing (story and screenplay written directly for the screen): Billy Wilder, I.A.L. Diamond, "The Apartment."

Cinematography (black-and-white): Freddie Francis, "Sons And Lovers," Company of Artists, 20th Century-Fox.

Cinematography (color): Russell Metty, "Spartacus."

Art Direction (black-and-white): "The Apartment," Alexander Trauner (art direction), Edward G. Boyle (set decoration).

Art Direction (color): "Spartacus," Alexander Golitzen, Eric Orbom (art direction), Russell A. Gausman, Julia Heron (set decoration).

Costume Design (black-and-white): Edith Head, Edward Stevenson, "The Facts Of Life," Panama & Frank, United Artists.

Costume Design (color): Valles and Bill Thomas, "Spartacus."

Sound: "The Alamo," Samuel Goldwyn Studio Sound Department, Gordon E. Sawyer, Sound Director; Todd-AO Sound Department, Fred Hynes, Sound Director.

Film Editing: Daniel Mandell, "The Apartment."

Special Effects: "The Time Machine," Gene Warren, Tim Baar (visual effects), Galaxy, Metro-Goldwyn-Mayer.

Music (music score of a dramatic or comedy picture): Ernest Gold, "Exodus," Carlyle-Alpina, United Artists.

Music (scoring musical picture): Morris Stoloff, Harry Sukman, "Song Without End (The Story Of Franz Liszt)," Goetz-Vidor, Columbia.

Music (song): Manos Hadjidakis (lyrics and music), "Never On Sunday" from "Never On Sunday," Melinafilm, Lopert.

Short Subjects (cartoon): "Munro," Rembrandt, Film Representations.

Short Subjects (live action): "Day Of The Painter," Little Movies, Kingsley-Union.

Documentary (short subject): "Giuseppina," Hill, Schoenfeld.

Documentary (feature length): "The Horse With The Flying Tail," Disney, Buena Vista.

Jean Hersholt Humanitarian Award: Sol Lesser.

SPECIAL AWARDS

Gary Cooper, for his many memorable screen performances and the international recognition he, as an individual, has gained for the motion picture industry.

Stan Laurel, for his creative pioneering in the field of cinema comedy.

Hayley Mills, for "Pollyanna," the most outstanding juvenile performance during 1960.

SCIENTIFIC AND TECHNICAL AWARDS

Ampex Professional Products Co., for the production of a well-engineered multi-purpose sound system combining high standards of quality with convenience of control, dependable operation and simplified emergency provisions.

Arthur Holcomb, Petro Vlahos and Columbia Studio Camera Department, for a camera flicker indicating device.

Anthony Paglia and the 20th Century-Fox Studio Mechanical Effects Department, for the design and construction of a miniature flak gun and ammunition.

Carl Hauge, Robert Grubel and Edward Reichard of Consolidated Film Industries, for the development of an automatic developer replenisher system.

1960

"The Apartment" was a comedy, but that description only skims the surface of the film's intent. It also contained pathos, near-tragedy, satire, and a wealth of observations on life. It was a biting view of deed and action in the aspirin age, with emphasis on the hot pursuit of money and sex. This fine film won five Oscars in all, including the top honor as best picture of the year.

The plot revolved around a young man, brilliantly portrayed by Jack Lemmon, an ambitious IBM operator in a large New York insurance company, who endeavored to advance himself in an ingenious manner. To ingratiate himself with the officials who could help him, he made his bachelor apartment available to them for their romantic trysts. He even provided refreshments for those who inconvenienced him on cold and rainy nights.

Under Wilder's adroit direction, Jack Lemmon, Shirley Mac-Laine as the girl betrayed by her married lover and driven to suicide, and Fred MacMurray, turned in superior performances. They moved from the comic to the near-tragic with finesse.

Jack Lemmon was nominated as best actor along with Trevor Howard for "Sons And Lovers," Laurence Olivier for "The Entertainer," Spencer Tracy for "Inherit The Wind," and Burt Lancaster for "Elmer Gantry."

Although each of these performances was admirable in its own way, Lancaster's luminous, full-blown portrait of the power-mad evangelist was a burning, intense characterization, for which he was selected as best actor. As a prostitute who blackmails Gantry, Shirley Jones gave a performance that caught all the caustic quality of the character. She was given the Oscar as best supporting actress.

Elizabeth Taylor, who had been nominated for top acting honors in 1957 for "Raintree County," in 1958 for "Cat On A Hot Tin Roof," and in 1959 for "Suddenly, Last Summer," finally garnered the Award for her superb characterization of a nymphomaniac in "Butterfield 8." Miss Taylor's portrait of the glamorous Gloria Wandrous was extraordinary in its authenticity and unerring in its realism.

"Spartacus" was a super-spectacular film, but as directed by Stanley Kubrick it was more than pure spectacle. It was the heroic story of the struggle for freedom by the Roman slaves. Peter Ustinov was chosen as best supporting actor for his performance as a Roman slaveholder. "Spartacus" won three other Oscars, for color cinematography, art direction, and costume design.

"The Virgin Spring," a classic film from Sweden, written and directed by the brilliant Ingmar Bergman, was named best foreign language film of the year.

Elizabeth Taylor (best actress)
and Laurence Harvey in "Butterfield 8."
Clifton-Linebrook, M-G-M

"The Apartment" (best picture)
with Jack Lemmon and Shirley MacLaine.
Mirisch, United Artists

Burt Lancaster (best actor) above,
and Shirley Jones (best supporting actress),
opposite, in "Elmer Gantry."
Lancaster-Brooks, United Artists

Peter Ustinov
(best supporting actor)
and Jean Simmons, left;
Kirk Douglas and
Woody Strode, below,
in "Spartacus" (best
cinematography, color).
Bryna, Universal-International

"Sons And Lovers" (best cinematography, black and white)
with Wendy Hiller, Dean Stockwell, Trevor Howard. 20th Century-Fox

"The Virigin Spring" (best foreign language film)
with Max von Sydow, above;
Birgitta Pettersson, Axel Duberg, Tor Isedal, Ove Porath, opposite above;
Max von Sydow, Birgitta Valberg, Birgitta Pettersson, opposite below.
Sweden, Svensk Filmindustri, Janus

"The Time Machine" (best special effects) with Rod Taylor. Galaxy, M-G-M

1961

From the opening helicopter shots of New York's soaring sky-line, gradually moving closer and closer to the threatening finger snapping of a juvenile street gang lounging against a fence, through the sometimes violent, sometimes bitter-sweet story of two New York gangs, told in terms of "Romeo and Juliet," "West Side Story" was a work of art. It is most unusual when a work of art also captures the popular imagination, but in the case of this drama-musical-ballet, popularity and art danced arm in arm through the teeming city streets, the gymnasium, the tenements. In all, "West Side Story" won ten Oscars, including the laurel for the best picture of the year.

George Chakiris, in his first important role, was named best supporting actor for his performance as Bernardo, leader of the Puerto Rican gang. He combined grace with authority, power with tenderness in his portrayal.

The distaff side of the supporting Awards went to Rita Moreno who was nothing less than superb as Bernardo's girl friend.

"West Side Story" had a rare sense of dedication and refused to compromise in order to please certain people. Much of this dedication came from the brilliant direction of Robert Wise and Jerome Robbins. This fine film also won accolades for best art direction, color cinematography, costume design, music, sound, and film editing.

For the first time in the history of the Awards an actress appearing in a non-English speaking role was chosen as best actress, as Sophia Loren earned the trophy for her moving performance in "Two Women." Another foreign actor won the blue ribbon in the male division as Swiss-born Maximilian Schell was named best actor for "Judgment At Nuremberg," the story of the war crimes trials after World War II.

Two excellent films which failed to take top honors, "The Hustler" and "The Guns Of Navarone," did however win several lesser Awards. In "The Hustler," Paul Newman, Jackie Gleason, and George C. Scott brought life and passion to the story of a deteriorating gambler, and the film won the Award for best black-and-white cinematography. "The Guns Of Navarone" was cited for its massive special effects.

For the second consecutive year Ingmar Bergman, perhaps, along with Fellini, the most important and influential director in Europe, won the Award for best foreign language film with "Through A Glass Darkly." This poignant film starred two of Bergman's so-called repertory company, Max von Sydow and Harriet Andersson.

AWARDS

Best Picture: "West Side Story," Mirisch, B & P, United Artists.

Actor: Maximilian Schell in "Judgment At Nuremberg," Kramer, United Artists.

Actress: Sophia Loren in "Two Women," Champion-Les Films Marceau-Cocinor, Societe Generale De Cinematographic, Embassy.

Supporting Actor: George Chakiris in "West Side Story."

Supporting Actress: Rita Moreno in "West Side Story."

Direction: Robert Wise, Jerome Robbins, "West Side Story."

Foreign Language Film Award: "Through A Glass Darkly," Svensk Filmindustri, Janus.

Writing (screenplay based on material from another medium): Abby Mann, "Judgment At Nuremberg."

Writing (story and screenplay written directly for the screen): William Inge, "Splendor In The Grass," NBI, Warner Brothers.

Cinematography (black-and-white): Eugen Shuftan, "The Hustler," Robert Rossen, 20th Century-Fox.

Cinematography (color): Daniel L. Fapp, "West Side Story."

Art Direction (black-and-white): "The Hustler," Harry Horner (art direction), Gene Callahan (set decoration).

Art Direction (color): "West Side Story," Boris Leven (art direction), Victor A. Gangelin (set decoration).

Costume Design (black-and-white): Piero Gherardi, "La Dolce Vita," Riama, Astor.

Costume Design (color): Irene Sharaff, "West Side Story."

Sound: "West Side Story," Todd-AO Sound Department, Fred Hynes, Sound Director; Samuel Goldwyn Sound Department, Gordon E. Sawyer, Sound Director.

Film Editing: Thomas Stanford, "West Side Story."

Special Effects: "The Guns Of Navarone," Bill Warrington (visual effects), Vivian C. Greenham (audible effects), Foreman, Columbia.

Music (music score of a dramatic or comedy picture): Henry Mancini, "Breakfast At Tiffany's," Jurow-Shepherd, Paramount.

Music (scoring musical picture): Saul Chaplin, Johnny Green, Sid Ramin, Irwin Kostal, "West Side Story."

Music (song): Johnny Mercer (lyrics), Henry Mancini (music), "Moon River" from "Breakfast At Tiffany's."

Short Subjects (cartoon): "Ersatz," Zagreb, Herts-Lion International.

Short Subjects (live action): "Seawards The Great Ships," Templar, Schoenfeld.

Documentary (short subjects): "Project Hope," MacManus, John & Adams, Ex-Cell-O, Klaeger.

Documentary (feature length): "Le Ciel Et La Boue" (Sky Above And Mud Beneath), Ardennes, J. Arthur Rank.

Irving G. Thalberg Memorial Award: Stanley Kramer.

SPECIAL AWARDS

William L. Hendricks, for his outstanding patriotic service in the conception, writing and production of the Marine Corps Film, "A Force In Readiness," which has brought honor to the Academy and the motion picture industry.

Jerome Robbins, for his brilliant achievements in the art of choreography on film in "West Side Story."

Fred L. Metzler, for his dedication and outstanding service to the Academy of Motion Picture Arts and Sciences.

SCIENTIFIC AND TECHNICAL AWARDS

Sylvania Electric Products, Inc., for the development of a hand held high-power photographic lighting unit known as the Sun Gun Professional.

James Dale, S. Wilson, H. E. Rice, John Rude, Laurie Atkin, Wadsworth E. Pohl, H. Peasgood and Technicolor Corp., for a process of automatic selective printing.

20th Century-Fox Research Department, under the direction of E. I. Sponable and Herbert E. Bragg, and Deluxe Laboratories, Inc., with the assistance of F. D. Leslie, R. D. Whitmore, A. A. Alden, Endel Pool and James B. Gordon, for a system of decompressing and recomposing CinemaScope pictures for conventional aspect ratios.

Hurletron, Inc., Electric Eye Equipment Division, for an automatic light changing system for motion picture printers.

Wadsworth E. Pohl and Technicolor Corp., for an integrated sound and picture transfer process.

Rita Moreno (best supporting actress), above;
George Chakiris (best supporting actor), center below,
with Natalie Wood and Richard Beymer in "West Side Story."
Mirsich, United Artists

Sophia Loren (best actress)
and Eleanora Brown in "Two Women." Embassy

"The Hustler" (best cinematography, black and white)
with Paul Newman, Myron McCormick, and Jackie Gleason.
Rossen, 20th Century-Fox.

"Splendor In The Grass"
(best story and screenplay)
with Natalie Wood and Audrey Christie.
NBI, Warner Brothers

Maximilian Schell (best actor) and Richard Widmark
in "Judgment At Nuremberg." Kramer, United Artists

"Through A Glass Darkly" (best foreign language film)
with Harriet Andersson and Max von Sydow.
Sweden, Svensk Filmindustri, Janus

AWARDS

Best Picture: "Lawrence Of Arabia," Horizon, Spiegel, Lean, Columbia.

Actor: Gregory Peck in "To Kill A Mockingbird," Universal-International, Pakula-Mulligan, Brentwood.

Actress: Anne Bancroft in "The Miracle Worker," Playfilms, United Artists.

Supporting Actor: Ed Begley in "Sweet Bird Of Youth," Roxbury, Metro-Goldwyn-Mayer.

Supporting Actress: Patty Duke in "The Miracle Worker."

Direction: David Lean, "Lawrence Of Arabia."

Foreign Language Film Award: "Sundays And Cybele," Terra-Fides-Orsay, Trocadero, Columbia.

Writing (screenplay based on material from another medium): Horton Foote, "To Kill A Mockingbird."

Writing (story and screenplay written directly for the screen): Ennio De Concini, Alfredo Giannetti, Pietro Germi, "Divorce—Italian Style," Lux-Vides-Galatea, Embassy.

Cinematography (black-and-white): Jean Bourgoin, Walter Wottitz, "The Longest Day," Zanuck, 20th Century-Fox.

Cinematography (color): Fred A. Young, "Lawrence Of Arabia."

Art Direction (black-and-white): "To Kill A Mockingbird," Alexander Golitzen, Henry Bumstead (art direction), Oliver Emert (set decoration).

Art Direction (color): "Lawrence Of Arabia," John Box, John Stoll (art direction), Dario Simoni (set decoration).

Costume Design (black-and-white): Norma Koch, "What Ever Happened To Baby Jane?" Seven Arts, Aldrich, Warner Brothers.

Costume Design (color): Mary Wills, "The Wonderful World Of The Brothers Grimm," Metro-Goldwyn-Mayer, Cinerama.

Sound: "Lawrence Of Arabia," Shepperton Studio Sound Department, John Cox, Sound Director.

Film Editing: Anne Coates, "Lawrence Of Arabia."

Special Effects: "The Longest Day," Robert MacDonald (visual effects), Jacques Maumont (audible effects).

Music (score—substantially original): Maurice Jarre, "Lawrence Of Arabia."

Music (score—adaptation or treatment): Ray Heindorf, Meredith Willson's "The Music Man," Warner Brothers.

Music (song): Johnny Mercer (lyrics), Henry Mancini (music), "Days Of Wine And Roses" from "Days Of Wine And Roses," Manulis-Jalem, Warner Brothers.

Short Subjects (cartoon): "The Hole," Storyboard, Brandon.

Short Subjects (live action): "Heureux Anniversaire" (Happy Anniversary), CAPAC, Atlantic.

Documentary (short subject): "Dylan Thomas," TWW, Janus.

Documentary (feature length): "Black Fox," Image, Heritage.

Jean Hersholt Humanitarian Award: Steve Broidy.

SCIENTIFIC AND TECHNICAL AWARDS

Ralph Chapman, for the design and development of an advanced motion picture camera crane.

Albert S. Pratt, James L. Wassell and Hans C. Wohlrab of the Professional Division, Bell and Howell Co., for the design and development of a new and improved automatic motion picture additive color printer.

North American Philips Co., Inc., for the design and engineering of the Norelco Universal 70/35mm motion picture projector.

Charles E. Sutter, William Bryson Smith and Louis C. Kennell of Paramount Pictures Corp., for the engineering and application to motion picture production of a new system of electric power distribution.

Electro-Voice, Inc., for a highly directional dynamic line microphone.

Louis G. Mackenzie, for a selective sound effects repeater.

1962

The questions that had puzzled historians and psychologists through the years about the enigmatic T. E. Lawrence were not answered in Sam Spiegel's superb production "Lawrence Of Arabia," voted the best picture of the year. For "Lawrence" was not a deep and penetrating study or an analysis of character. Rather, it was an adventure story of the highest order, told in total cinematic terms; faultlessly directed, brilliantly photographed, forcefully written, and acted to perfection down to the smallest role.

David Lean, already the recipient of one Oscar for his direction of "The Bridge On The River Kwai," and nominated on three other occasions, showed his skill and versatility by keeping the excitement going full tilt for the almost four hours of the film, from the opening sequences of Lawrence's motorcycle death, through the flash-backs of his rise to fame and legend.

Each member of the cast added a telling portrait to this outstanding film. Peter O'Toole, as the flamboyant and sensitive Lawrence; Jack Hawkins as General Allenby; Claude Rains as his advisor; Arthur Kennedy as an American correspondent; Alec Guinness; Anthony Quinn; Omar Sharif; and Jose Ferrer.

"The Miracle Worker," transplanted from the Broadway stage to the sound stages of Hollywood, lost none of the power and intensity of the compelling story of Annie Sullivan's struggle to help the deaf and blind Helen Keller. Recreating their original roles, Anne Bancroft and Patty Duke were selected for Oscars as best actress and best supporting actress.

The race for honors in the best actor category was the closest in years. Burt Lancaster was nominated for "Bird Man Of Alcatraz," Jack Lemmon for "Days Of Wine And Roses," Peter O'Toole for "Lawrence Of Arabia," Marcello Mastroianni for "Divorce-Italian Style," and Gregory Peck for "To Kill A Mockingbird."

Peck, after failing to take the honors in four previous attempts for his performances in "The Keys Of The Kingdom," "The Yearling," "Twelve O'Clock High," and "Gentleman's Agreement," finally was named best actor for his performance in "To Kill A Mockingbird." As Atticus Finch, a smalltown Southern lawyer, defending a Negro accused of rape, Peck brought quiet strength and integrity to this man of principle. His beautifully controlled relationship with the three children was a masterpiece of understatement.

The Oscar for the best foreign language film went to "Sundays And Cybele," one of the most poignant and touching films ever made. The idyllic relationship between a young man, the victim of amnesia, and a motherless twelve-year-old girl, wise beyond her years, was explored in depth by French director Serge Bourguignon, with gemlike purity. It was a film that will live as long as films are seen.

"Lawrence Of Arabia" (best picture) with Anthony Quinn, below;
Peter O'Toole, opposite. Horizon, Spiegel, Lean, Columbia

Ed Begley (best supporting actor)
and Rip Torn in "Sweet Bird Of Youth."
Roxbury, M-G-M

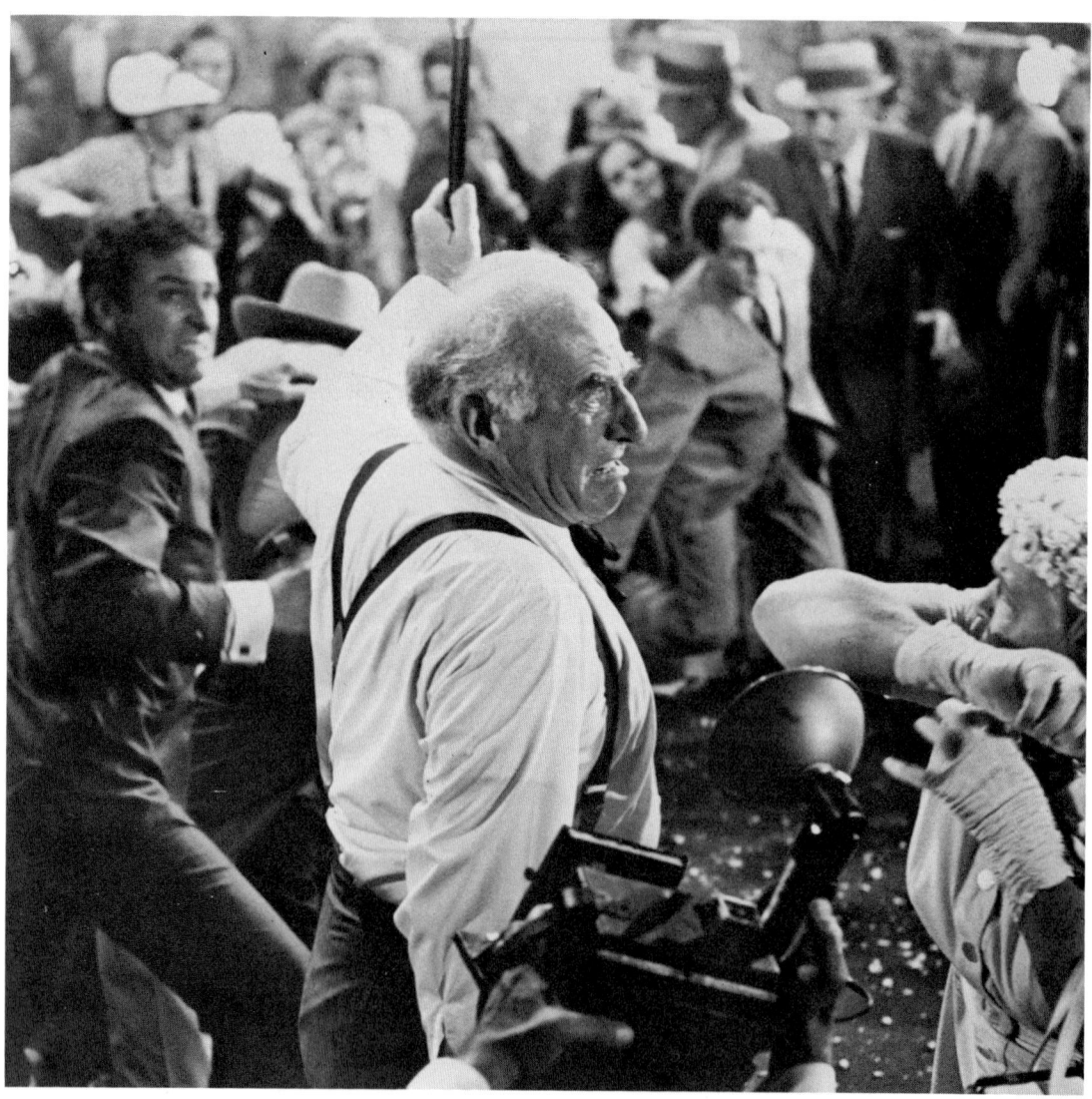

Gregory Peck (best actor),
Collin Wilcox, and Paul Fix
in "To Kill A Mockingbird."
Universal-International

"Sundays And Cybele"
(best foreign language film)
with Patricia Gozzi
and Hardy Kruger.
France, Terra-Fides-Orsay,
Trocadero, Columbia

"Divorce—Italian Style"
(best story and screenplay)
with Marcello Mastroianni.
Lux-Vides-Galatea, Embassy

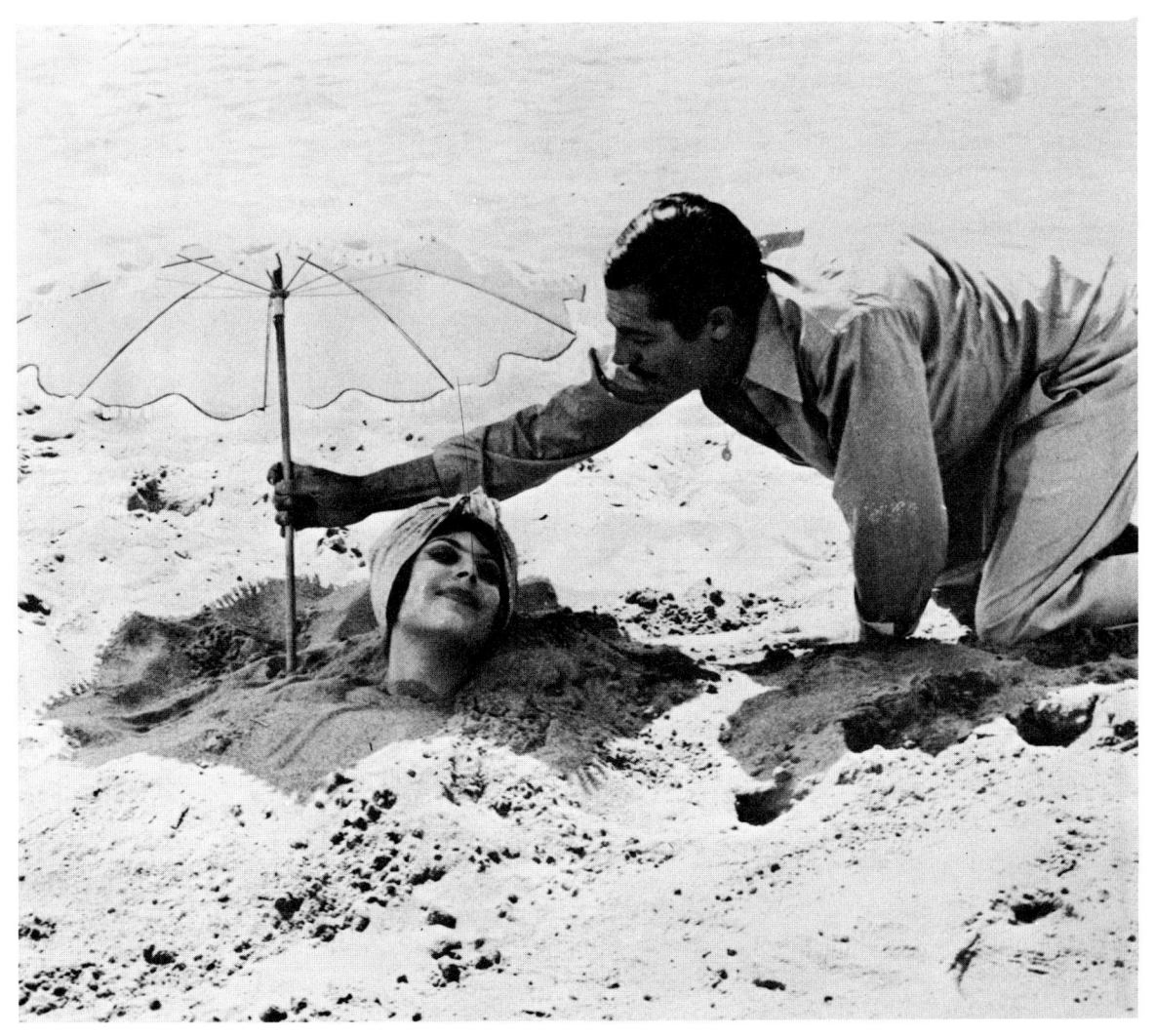

"What Ever Happened To Baby Jane?" (best costume design, black and white)
with Joan Crawford and Bette Davis. Seven Arts, Warner Brothers

1963

The lush, green countryside of eighteenth-century England where eating, loving, and hunting were a way of life, and the raucous, vibrant streets and drawing rooms of London provide the backgrounds for "Tom Jones," the gay and lusty film named best picture of the year. It was the first time since "Hamlet" in 1948 that a British film was named best picture. Such top American films as "Cleopatra," "How The West Was Won," "Lilies Of The Field," and "America, America" had also been nominated.

For producer-director Tony Richardson, it was a complete change of pace, coming on the heels of two grim, realistic film studies of big-city life, "Look Back In Anger" and "A Taste Of Honey."

Under Richardson's flawless direction the entire cast romped through John Osborne's fun-filled and mischievous screenplay at a merry pace, and an unprecedented five members of the cast were nominated for Oscars. Albert Finney was nominated for the best actor Award for his charming portrayal of the handsome and earthy Tom; Hugh Griffith for best supporting actor as the short-tempered Squire Western; and Joyce Redman, Diane Cilento, and Dame Edith Evans, all nominated as best supporting actress. But, it was a year of great performances in many films, and not one of the acting nominees in "Tom Jones" won an Oscar.

Sidney Poitier was acclaimed best actor for his beguiling performance as a foot-loose, Southern G.I. in "Lilies Of The Field." Poitier's portrait was full of life and vitality as he met and "adopted" five bewildered refugee nuns, and helped them build a chapel and a new life—and in the process built a new life for himself.

"Hud," a grim, outspoken film about the independent, tough cattlemen of modern Texas provided the vehicle that two stars rode to Oscar victories. Patricia Neal gave a poignant portrayal of Alma, a kind, understanding, earthy woman frayed by a drab life and hurt by men. She was selected for the best actress Oscar. Melvyn Douglas was named best supporting actor. As Homer Bannon, Paul Newman's father, Douglas played an aging rancher, rapidly failing in mind and body in the face of economic adversity and bitter conflict with his selfish son.

Margaret Rutherford was delightful as usual in "The V.I.P.s," and was chosen best supporting actress.

Federico Fellini, one of the world's great directors, an artist in the realm of motion picture improvisation, presented his "8½" to American audiences, and it walked away with the honors as best foreign language film and best black-and-white costume design.

"Cleopatra," the most expensive film ever made, starring Elizabeth Taylor, Richard Burton, and Rex Harrison, garnered four Awards in color categories for cinematography, art direction, costume design, and special effects.

AWARDS

Best Picture: "Tom Jones," Woodfall, United Artists, Lopert.

Actor: Sidney Poitier in "Lilies Of The Field," Rainbow, United Artists.

Actress: Patricia Neal in "Hud," Salem-Dover, Paramount.

Supporting Actor: Melvyn Douglas in "Hud."

Supporting Actress: Margaret Rutherford in "The V.I.P.s" Metro-Goldwyn-Mayer.

Direction: Tony Richardson, "Tom Jones."

Foreign Language Film Award: Federico Fellini's "8½," Cineriz, Embassy.

Writing (screenplay based on material from another medium): John Osborne, "Tom Jones."

Writing (best story and screenplay written directly for the screen): James R. Webb, "How The West Was Won," Metro-Goldwyn-Mayer, Cinerama.

Cinematography (black-and-white): James Wong Howe, "Hud."

Cinematography (color): Leon Shamroy, "Cleopatra," 20th Century-Fox, MCL, WALWA.

Art Direction (black-and-white): Gene Callahan, "America America," Athena, Warner Brothers.

Art Direction (color): John DeCuir, Jack Martin Smith, Hilyard Brown, Herman Blumenthal, Elven Webb, Maurice Pelling, Boris Juraga (art direction), Walter M. Scott, Paul S. Fox, Ray Moyer (set decoration), "Cleopatra."

Costume Design (black-and-white): Piero Gherardi, Federico Fellini's "8½."

Costume Design (color): Irene Sharaff, Vittorio Nino Novarese, Renie, "Cleopatra."

Sound: "How The West Was Won," Metro-Goldwyn-Mayer Studio Sound Department, Franklin E. Milton, Sound Director.

Sound Effects: "It's A Mad, Mad, Mad, Mad World," Walter G. Elliott, Casey, United Artists.

Film Editing: Harold F. Kress, "How The West Was Won."

Special Effects: Emil Kosa, Jr., "Cleopatra."

Music (score—substantially original): John Addison, "Tom Jones."

Music (scoring—adaptation or treatment): Andre Previn, "Irma La Douce," Mirisch-Phalanx, United Artists.

Music (song): Sammy Cahn (lyrics), James Van Heusen (music), "Call Me Irresponsible" from "Papa's Delicate Condition," Amro, Paramount.

Short Subjects (cartoon): "The Critic," Pintoff-Crossbow, Columbia.

Short Subjects (live action): "An Occurrence At Owl Creek Bridge," Films Du Centaure, Filmartic, Cappagariff, Janus.

Documentary (short subject): "Chagall," Auerbach, Flag.

Documentary (feature length): "Robert Frost: A Lover's Quarrel With The World," WGBH Educational Foundation.

Irving G. Thalberg Memorial Award: Sam Spiegel.

SCIENTIFIC AND TECHNICAL AWARD

Douglas A. Shearer and A. Arnold Gillespie, Metro-Goldwyn-Mayer, for the engineering of an improved Background Process Projection System.

290

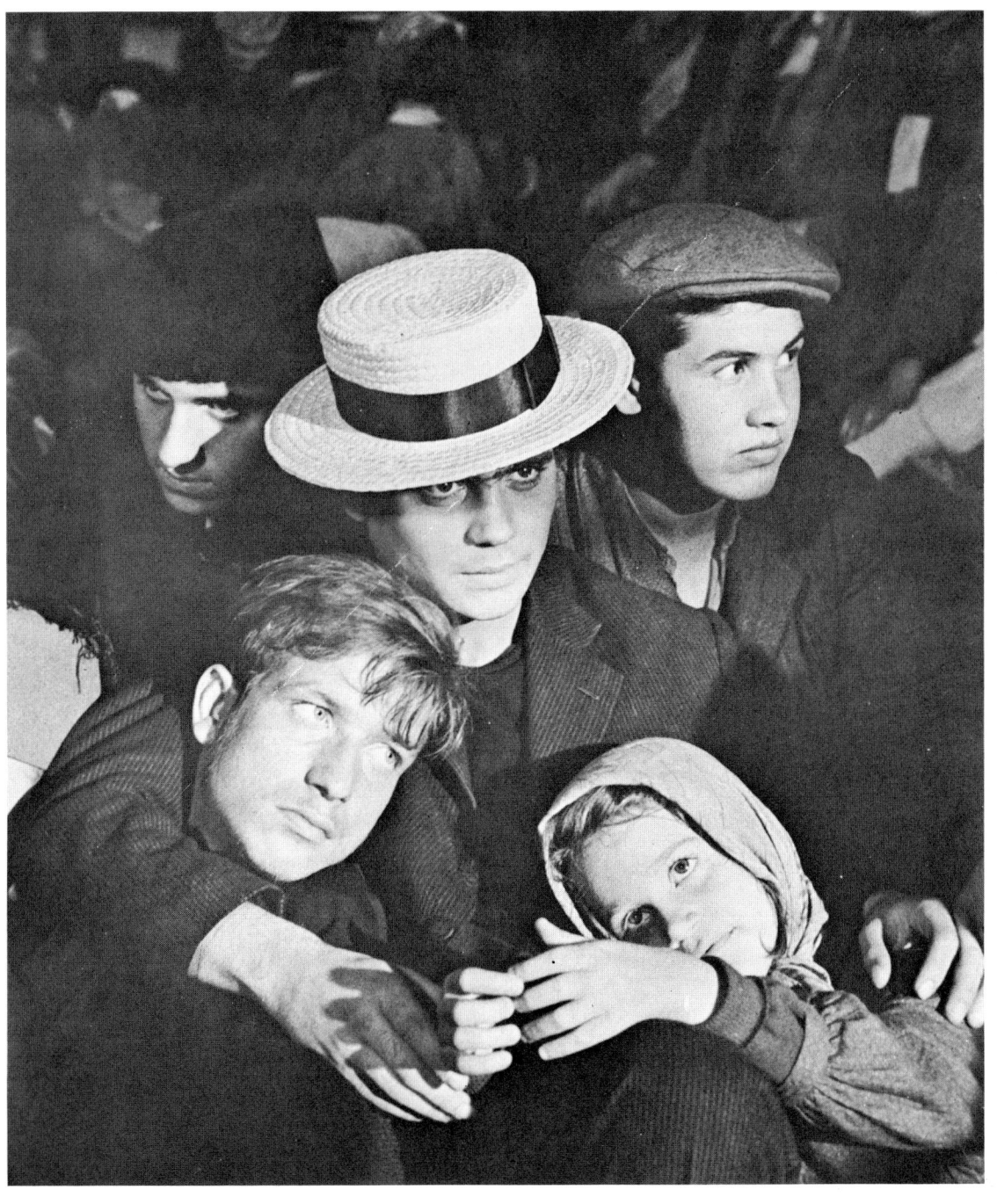

"Tom Jones" (best picture) with Albert Finney and Diane Cilento, below;
Hugh Griffith, Dame Edith Evans, opposite. Woodfall, United Artists, Lopert

Sidney Poitier (best actor) and Lilia Skala in "Lilies Of The Field." Rainbow, United Artists

Melvyn Douglas (best supporting actor),
Brandon De Wilde, and Paul Newman, below;
Patricia Neal (best actress), opposite, in "Hud."
Salem-Dover, Paramount

Federico Fellini's "8½"
(best foreign language film)
with Marcello Mastroianni.
Italy, Cineriz, Embassy

Margaret Rutherford (best supporting actress) in "The V.I.P.s" M-G-M

"Cleopatra"
(best cinematography, color)
with Elizabeth Taylor,
Richard Burton, and Rex Harrison.
MCL, WALWA, 20th Century-Fox

1964

One of the most emotional contests in the history of the Academy Awards began to take shape nearly two years before the 1964 Oscar presentation night. Julie Andrews, the highly acclaimed star of the Broadway and London stage productions of "My Fair Lady," was passed over for the motion picture lead. The most coveted feminine role of the decade was assigned instead to a star of proven stature and super box-office appeal, Audrey Hepburn. Jack Warner, the producer of "My Fair Lady," wanted insurance for his $17,000,000 production. After all, he reasoned, Julie Andrews was unknown outside of New York and London, untried in films, and he just could not take a chance, even though many believed that "My Fair Lady," after 2,717 performances on Broadway, could not possibly fail.

But there was a producer, Walt Disney, who was willing to take a chance with Miss Andrews. He cast her in the title role of "Mary Poppins."

When the nominations for best actress were announced, both Hollywood and the world gasped. Audrey Hepburn was not even nominated. The nominees were Anne Bancroft for "The Pumpkin Eater," Sophia Loren for "Marriage—Italian Style," Julie Andrews for "Mary Poppins," Debbie Reynolds for "The Unsinkable Molly Brown," and Kim Stanley for "Seance On A Wet Afternoon."

The applause was almost deafening when Miss Andrews stepped up to take her Oscar—it was "Supercalifragilistic-expialidocious."

However, the brilliant production of "My Fair Lady" was not to be denied. It was named best picture of the year, even though the caliber of the other four nominees was extremely high: "Becket," "Dr. Strangelove," "Mary Poppins," and "Zorba The Greek."

In all, "My Fair Lady" garnered eight Oscars. George Cukor was honored as best director for the first time in his thirty-six-year film career, and Rex Harrison walked away with best acting laurels for his superb characterization of Professor Henry Higgins. Other "My Fair Lady" Oscars were for best color cinematography, art direction, costume design, musical score, and sound.

Peter Ustinov, in perhaps the biggest upset of the night, was named best supporting actor for his fine performance in "Topkapi." With the apparent sweep for "My Fair Lady," it had seemed almost certain that Stanley Holloway would get the nod for his marvelous music-hall-style performance as Mr. Alfred Doolittle. John Gielgud, Edmond O'Brien, and Lee Tracy were the other nominees.

"Zorba The Greek" was triply honored. Lila Kedrova was named best supporting actress for her poignant performance opposite Anthony Quinn, while the film was named for best black-and-white cinematography and art direction.

"Yesterday, Today And Tomorrow," from Italy and starring Sophia Loren and Marcello Mastroianni, was named best foreign-language production.

AWARDS

Best Picture: "My Fair Lady," Warner Brothers.

Actor: Rex Harrison in "My Fair Lady."

Actress: Julie Andrews in "Mary Poppins," Disney, Buena Vista.

Supporting Actor: Peter Ustinov in "Topkapi," Filmways, United Artists.

Supporting Actress: Lila Kedrova in "Zorba The Greek," International.

Direction: George Cukor, "My Fair Lady."

Foreign Language Film Award: "Yesterday, Today And Tomorrow," Champion-Concordia.

Writing (screenplay adapted from another medium): Edward Anhalt, "Becket," Wallis, Paramount.

Writing (original story and screenplay): Story by S. H. Barnett. Screenplay by Peter Stone, Frank Tarloff. "Father Goose," Universal.

Cinematography (black-and-white): Walter Lassally, "Zorba The Greek."

Cinematography (color): Harry Stradling, "My Fair Lady."

Art Direction (black-and-white): Vassilis Fotopoulos, "Zorba The Greek."

Art Direction (color): Gene Allen, Cecil Beaton, Art Directors; George James Hopkins, Set Decorator; "My Fair Lady."

Costume Design (black-and-white): Dorothy Jeakins, "The Night Of The Iguana," Seven Arts, Metro-Goldwyn-Mayer.

Costume Design (color): Cecil Beaton, "My Fair Lady."

Film Editing: Cotton Warburton, "Mary Poppins."

Music (original score): Richard M. Sherman, Robert B. Sherman, "Mary Poppins."

Music (scoring - adaptation or treatment): Andre Previn, "My Fair Lady."

Music (song): Music and lyrics by Richard M. Sherman and Robert B. Sherman, "Chim Chim Cher-ee" from "Mary Poppins."

Short Subjects (cartoon): "The Pink Phink," Mirisch-Geoffrey, United Artists.

Short Subjects (live action): "Casals Conducts," Thalia.

Sound: "My Fair Lady," Warner Brothers Studio Sound Department, George R. Groves, Sound Director.

Sound Effects: "Goldfinger," Eon, United Artists, Norman Wanstall.

Special Visual Effects: Peter Ellenshaw, Hamilton Luske, Eustace Lycett, "Mary Poppins."

Documentary (feature): "World Without Sun," Columbia.

Documentary (short subject): "Nine From Little Rock," USIA, Guggenheim.

SPECIAL AWARD

William Tuttle, for his outstanding make-up achievement for "7 Faces Of Dr. Lao."

SCIENTIFIC AND TECHNICAL AWARDS

Petro Vlahos, Wadsworth E. Pohl and Ub Iwerks, for the conception and perfection of techniques for Color Traveling Matte Composite Cinematography.

Sidney P. Solow, Edward H. Reichard, Carl W. Hauge and Job Sanderson of Consolidated Film Industries for the design and development of a versatile Automatic 35mm Composite Color Printer.

Pierre Angenieux, for the development of a ten-to-one Zoom Lens for cinematography.

Milton Forman, Richard B. Glickman and Daniel J. Pearlman of ColorTran Industries, for advancements in the design and application to motion picture photography of lighting units using quartz iodine lamps.

Stewart Filmscreen Corporation, for a seamless translucent Blue Screen for Traveling Matte Color Cinematography.

Anthony Paglia and the 20th Century-Fox Studio Mechanical Effects Department, for an improved method of producing Explosion Effects for motion pictures.

Edward H. Reichard, Leonard L. Sokolow and Carl W. Hauge of Consolidated Film Industries, for the design and application to motion picture laboratory practice of a Stroboscopic Scene Tester for color and black-and-white film.

Nelson Tyler, for the design and construction of an improved Helicopter Camera System.

Julie Andrews (best actress) with Dick Van Dyke, Karen Dotrice and Matthew Garber in "Mary Poppins." Disney, Buena Vista

"My Fair Lady" (best picture)
with Rex Harrison (best actor)
and Audrey Hepburn
opposite
Warner Brothers

"The Night Of The Iguana"
(best black-and-white
costume and design) with
Ava Gardner and
Richard Burton.
M-G-M

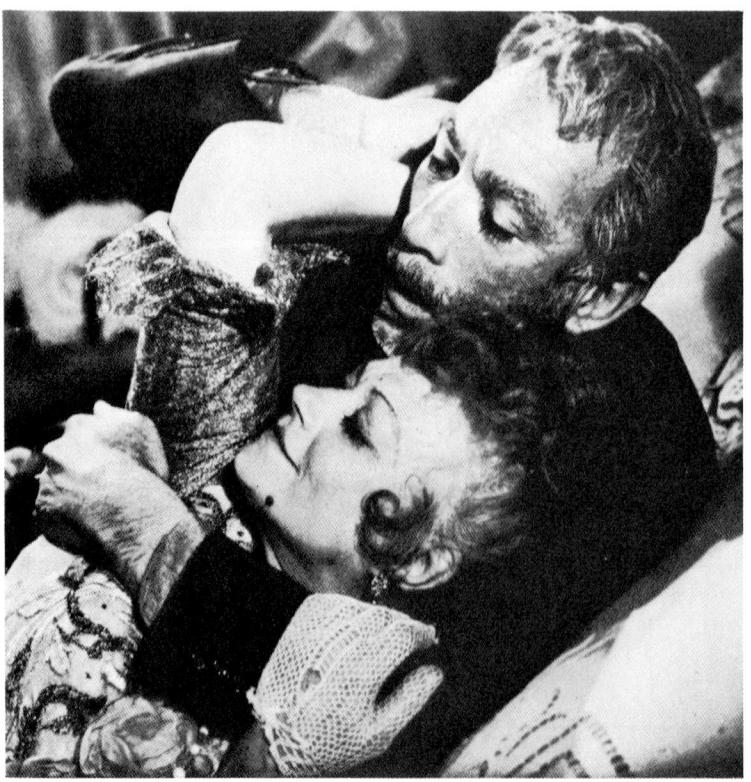

Lila Kedrova (best supporting actress) and Anthony
Quinn in "Zorba The Greek"
(best black-and-white
cinematography and art
direction).
International

Peter Ustinov (best supporting actor), Maximilian Schell and Melina Mercouri in "Topkapi." Filmways, United Artists, above; "Yesterday, Today and Tomorrow" (best foreign language film) with Marcello Mastroianni and Sophia Loren. Embassy, below

"Father Goose" (best original story and screenplay) with Cary Grant and Leslie Caron, Universal, above; "Becket" (best screenplay adapted from another medium) with Richard Burton and Peter O'Toole, Paramount, below

AWARDS

Best Picture: "The Sound Of Music,"
Argyle Enterprises, 20th Century-Fox.

Actor: Lee Marvin in "Cat Ballou,"
Hecht, Columbia.

Actress: Julie Christie in "Darling,"
Anglo-Amalgamated, Embassy.

Supporting Actor: Martin Balsam in "A Thousand
Clowns," Harrell, United Artists.

Supporting Actress: Shelley Winters in
"A Patch Of Blue," Berman-Green,
Metro-Goldwyn-Mayer.

Direction: Robert Wise, "The Sound Of Music."

Foreign Language Film Award: "The Shop On
Main Street," Ceskoslovensky.

**Writing (screenplay based on material
from another medium):** Robert Bolt, "Doctor
Zhivago," Sostar, Metro-Goldwyn-Mayer.

Writing (original story and screenplay):
Frederic Raphael, "Darling."

Cinematography (black-and-white): Ernest Laszlo,
"Ship Of Fools," Columbia.

Cinematography (color): Freddie Young,
"Doctor Zhivago."

Art Direction (black-and-white): Robert
Clatworthy, Art Director; Joseph Kish,
Set Decorator; "Ship Of Fools."

Art Direction (color): John Box, Terry Marsh,
"Doctor Zhivago."

Costume Design (black-and-white): Julie Harris,
"Darling."

Costume Design (color): Phyllis Dalton,
"Doctor Zhivago."

Film Editing: William Reynolds,
"The Sound Of Music."

Music (original score): Maurice Jarre,
"Doctor Zhivago."

Music (score—adaptation or treatment):
Irwin Kostal, "The Sound Of Music."

Music (song): Paul Francis Webster (lyrics),
Johnny Mandel (music), "The Shadow Of Your
Smile" from "The Sandpiper,"
Filmways-Venice, Metro-Goldwyn-Mayer.

Short Subjects (cartoon): "The Dot And The
Line," Metro-Goldwyn-Mayer.

Short Subjects (live action): "The Chicken,"
Renn, Pathe Contemporary.

Sound: "The Sound Of Music," 20th Century-Fox
Studio Sound Department, James P. Corcoran,
Sound Director; Todd-AO Sound Department,
Fred Hynes, Sound Director.

Sound Effects: "The Great Race,"
Patricia-Jalem-Reynard, Warner Brothers,
Tregoweth Brown.

Special Visual Effects: John Stears,
"Thunderball," Broccoli-Saltzman-McClory,
United Artists.

Documentary (feature): "The Eleanor Roosevelt
Story," Glazier, American International.

Documentary (short subject): "To Be Alive!"
Johnson Wax.

Irving G. Thalberg Memorial Award:
William Wyler.

Jean Hersholt Humanitarian Award:
Edmond L. DePatie.

SPECIAL AWARD

Bob Hope, for unique and distinguished service
to the motion picture industry
and the Academy.

SCIENTIFIC AND TECHNICAL AWARDS

Arthur J. Hatch of The Strong Electric
Corporation, subsidiary of General Precision
Equipment Corporation, for the design and
development of the Air Blown Carbon Arc
Projection Lamp.

Stefan Kudelski, for the design and development
of the Nagra portable ¼" tape recording
system for motion picture sound recording.

1965

thirty-eighth annual awards

When "The Sound Of Music" was named best picture of the year, it was no real surprise, even though at the premiere it was greeted with a mixture of sugar-coated adjectives by some of the reviewers and outright disdain by others. But "The Sound Of Music" was a motion picture phenomenon. There could be no doubt that it was a pleasant film with a pretty musical score and a nice performance by Julie Andrews. It was only after the film started to rack up box-office records across the nation and around the world that the Academy members took another, and more serious, look at it. Just what was it that accounted for more than $60,000,000 in paid admissions in the first year? That question has never been answered. The only thing certain was that it was honored over such films as "Darling," a British-made film; "Doctor Zhivago," M-G-M's $13-million film based on the Boris Pasternak novel; "Ship Of Fools," from the novel by Katherine Anne Porter; and "A Thousand Clowns," a low-budget United Artists release.

Perhaps the most widely acclaimed film from the artistic viewpoint was not even nominated as best picture of the year—but it was nominated and honored as the best foreign-language production. "The Shop On Main Street" was a distinguished film in every sense of the word—brilliantly directed by Jan Kadar and Elmar Klos, and starring the magnificent Ida Kaminska.

Julie Christie was the only foreign winner in a performing category, although there had been more than twenty foreign nominees. She was named best actress of the year for her outstanding performance in "Darling" as the footloose, amoral model who relentlessly moves through different levels of contemporary society in her search for self-identity.

Lee Marvin was the surprise winner in the best actor category. All the other nominees were given a better chance of taking the honors: Rod Steiger for his brilliant portrayal in "The Pawnbroker," Laurence Olivier for "Othello," Richard Burton for "The Spy Who Came In From The Cold," and Oskar Werner for "Ship Of Fools." But Marvin, in the dual role of brothers, one good and one evil, in "Cat Ballou," was the comedy-gem winner.

The Award for best supporting actress went to Shelley Winters for her performance in "A Patch Of Blue," a film dealing with the romance between a blind white girl and a Negro man. Miss Winters played the girl's slatternly mother with great power.

Martin Balsam took the supporting actor Oscar for his portrayal of an earthy businessman in "A Thousand Clowns."

The moving film, "The Eleanor Roosevelt Story," took the honor as the best feature-length documentary.

"The Sound Of Music" (best picture) with Julie Andrews,
Christopher Plummer and Peggy Wood, 20th Century-Fox, above;
Julie Andrews, below.

Lee Marvin (best actor) in
"Cat Ballou."
Columbia

Julie Christie (best actress)
with Laurence Harvey
in "Darling."
Embassy

Shelley Winters (best
supporting actress) with
Elizabeth Hartman in
"A Patch Of Blue."
M-G-M

"The Shop On Main Street"
(best foreign language film)
with Ida Kaminska and
Josef Kroner.
Ceskoslovensky

"Thunderball" (best special visual effect) with Sean Connery.
United Artists

1966

The brilliantly conceived and magnificently presented story of the embattled Sir Thomas More, "A Man For All Seasons," was selected by the members of the Academy as the best picture of the year—and the selection received unanimous praise from every sector of the motion picture industry and from the critics. This was true even though the competition in the category was particularly strong. Such fine films as "Alfie," "The Russians Are Coming, The Russians Are Coming," "The Sand Pebbles," and "Who's Afraid Of Virginia Woolf?" had also received nominations. But, under the Oscar-winning directorial hand of Fred Zinnemann, "A Man For All Seasons" walked off with the majority of the Awards —a total of six in all.

Paul Scofield was honored as best actor for his almost perfect performance as Sir Thomas More, the man of principle locked in a life-and-death struggle with the monarch, Henry VIII. Scofield, who had played the role in the Robert Bolt drama on Broadway, etched an unforgettable character on the screen, and in the end, true to this character, he chose to die rather than to submit when placed on trial for his life. Robert Bolt was honored for his screenplay, and the film garnered Awards for best color cinematography and best costuming.

"Who's Afraid Of Virginia Woolf" ran a close second in the Oscar derby. Elizabeth Taylor topped the "Virginia Woolf" winners. She was cited as best actress for her powerful delineation of the explosively antagonistic wife of the college professor in the film adaptation of Edward Albee's drama. Here was Elizabeth Taylor in a screen portrayal unlike anything she had ever done—hideous, dissolute, egocentric, devoid of a redeeming trait—a performance that will live in the memory of everyone who sees it.

Sandy Dennis was named best supporting actress for her "Virginia Woolf" performance as the young wife, drunk and prone to hysterical pregnancy. "Virginia Woolf" was also cited for best black-and-white cinematography, costume design, and art direction.

One of the most popular Awards went to Walter Matthau as best supporting actor for his performance as the ambulance-chasing legal eagle in Billy Wilder's "The Fortune Cookie." Matthau, who had long been familiar as a screen villain, was cited for his first big film comedy role.

Underscoring the international flavor of the Awards were the prizes won by the French "A Man And A Woman"— honored not only as best foreign-language film, but also for its original story and screenplay by Pierre Uytterhoeven and Claude Lelouch. It was the first time that a foreign-language production had been so honored.

AWARDS

Best Picture: "A Man For All Seasons,"
Highland, Columbia.

Actor: Paul Scofield in "A Man For All Seasons."

Actress: Elizabeth Taylor in "Who's Afraid Of
Virginia Woolf?" Chenault, Warner Brothers.

Supporting Actor: Walter Matthau in
"The Fortune Cookie," Phalanx-Jalem-Mirisch,
United Artists.

Supporting Actress: Sandy Dennis in
"Who's Afraid Of Virginia Woolf?"

Direction: Fred Zinnemann,
"A Man For All Seasons."

Foreign Language Film Award:
"A Man And A Woman," Les Films 13.

**Writing (screenplay—based on material from
another medium):** Robert Bolt, "A Man For
All Seasons."

Writing (original story and screenplay):
"A Man And A Woman." Story by Claude
Lelouch. Screenplay by Pierre Uytterhoeven
and Claude Lelouch.

Cinematography (black-and-white):
Haskell Wexler, "Who's Afraid Of Virginia
Woolf?"

Cinematography (color): Ted Moore,
"A Man For All Seasons."

Art Direction (black-and-white): Richard Sylbert,
Art Director; George James Hopkins, Set
Decorator; "Who's Afraid Of Virginia Woolf?"

Art Direction (color): Jack Martin Smith, Dale
Hennesy, Art Directors; Walter M. Scott,
Stuart A. Reiss, Set Decorators;
"Fantastic Voyage," 20th Century-Fox.

Costume Design (black-and-white): Irene Sharaff,
"Who's Afraid Of Virginia Woolf?"

Costume Design (color): Elizabeth Haffenden,
Joan Bridge, "A Man For All Seasons."

Film Editing: Fredric Steinkamp, Henry Berman,
Stewart Linder, Frank Santillo, "Grand Prix,"
Douglas-Lewis-Frankenheimer-Cherokee,
Metro-Goldwyn-Mayer.

Music (original score): John Barry, "Born Free,"
Open Road, Atlas, Columbia.

Music (adaptation or treatment): Ken Thorne,
"A Funny Thing Happened On The Way To The
Forum," Frank, United Artists.

Music (song): Don Black (lyrics), John Barry
(music), "Born Free" from "Born Free."

Short Subjects (cartoon): "Herb Alpert And The
Tijuana Brass Double Feature," Hubley.

Short Subjects (live action): "Wild Wings,"
British Transport, Manson.

Sound: "Grand Prix," Metro-Goldwyn-Mayer
Studio Sound Department, Franklin E. Milton,
Sound Director.

Sound Effects: Gordon Daniel, "Grand Prix."

Special Visual Effects: Art Cruickshank,
"Fantastic Voyage."

Documentary (short subject): "A Year Toward
Tomorrow," Sun Dial for the Office of
Economic Opportunity.

Documentary (feature): "The War Game,"
British Film Institute, Pathe Contemporary.

Irving G. Thalberg Memorial Award:
Robert Wise.

Jean Hersholt Humanitarian Award:
George Bagnall.

SPECIAL AWARDS

Y. Frank Freeman, for unusual and outstanding
service to the Academy during his
thirty years in Hollywood.

Yakima Canutt, for achievements as a stunt man
and for developing safety devices
to protect stunt men everywhere.

SCIENTIFIC AND TECHNICAL AWARDS

Mitchell Camera Corporation, for the design and
development of the Mitchell Mark II 35mm
Portable Motion Picture Reflex Camera.

Arnold & Richter KG, for the design and
development of the Arriflex 35mm Portable
Motion Picture Reflex Camera.

Panvision Incorporated, for the design of the
Panatron Power Inverter and its application
to motion picture camera operation.

Carroll Knudson, for the production of a
Composers Manual for Motion Picture
Music Synchronization.

Ruby Raksin, for the production of a
Composers Manual for Motion Picture
Music Synchronization.

Elizabeth Taylor (best actress) with Richard Burton and George Segal in "Who's Afraid Of Virginia Woolf?" (best black-and-white cinematography, costume design). Warner Brothers

Sandy Dennis (best supporting actress) in "Who's Afraid Of Virginia Woolf?"

Walter Matthau (best supporting actor), right, with Maryesther Denver and Jack Lemmon in "The Fortune Cookie." United Artists

Paul Scofield (best actor)
in "A Man For All Seasons"
(best direction, color cinematography, art direction,
costume design). Paul
Scofield and Susannah
York.
Columbia

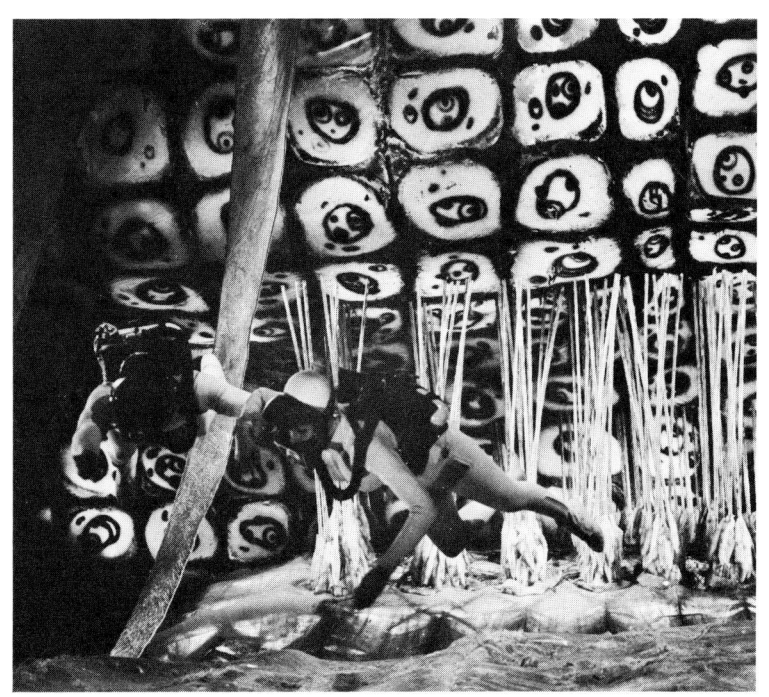

"Fantastic Voyage" (best
color art direction, special
visual effects).
20th Century-Fox

"Grand Prix" (best film
editing) with Brian Bedford,
center.
M-G-M

AWARDS

Best Picture: "In The Heat Of The Night,"
Mirisch, United Artists.

Actor: Rod Steiger in
"In The Heat Of The Night."

Actress: Katharine Hepburn in
"Guess Who's Coming To Dinner,"
Kramer, Columbia.

Supporting Actor: George Kennedy in
"Cool Hand Luke," Jalem,
Warner Brothers-Seven Arts.

Supporting Actress: Estelle Parsons in
"Bonnie And Clyde," Tatira-Hiller,
Warner Brothers-Seven Arts.

Directing: Mike Nichols, "The Graduate,"
Nichols-Turman, Embassy.

Foreign Language Film Award:
"Closely Watched Trains," Barrandov,
Sigma III.

**Writing (screenplay—based on material from
another medium):** Stirling Silliphant,
"In The Heat Of The Night."

Writing (original story and screenplay):
William Rose, "Guess Who's Coming
To Dinner."

Cinematography: Burnett Guffey,
"Bonnie And Clyde."

Art Direction: John Truscott, Edward Carrere,
Art Directors; John W. Brown, Set Decorator;
"Camelot," Warner Brothers-Seven Arts.

Costume Design: John Truscott, "Camelot."

Film Editing: Hal Ashby,
"In The Heat Of The Night."

Music (original score): Elmer Bernstein,
"Thoroughly Modern Millie," Hunter, Universal.

Music (adaptation or treatment): Alfred Newman,
Ken Darby, "Camelot."

Music (song): Music and lyrics by
Leslie Bricusse, "Talk To The Animals" from
"Doctor Dolittle," Apjac, 20th Century-Fox.

Short Subjects (cartoon): "The Box,"
Murakami, Wolf, Brandon.

Short Subjects (live action): "A Place To Stand,"
T.D.F., Columbia.

Sound: "In The Heat Of The Night,"
Samuel Goldwyn Studio Sound Department.

Sound Effects: John Poyner, "The Dirty Dozen,"
MKH, Metro-Goldwyn-Mayer.

Special Visual Effects: L. B. Abbott,
"Doctor Dolittle."

Documentary (short subject): "The Redwoods,"
King.

Documentary (feature): "The Anderson Platoon,"
French Broadcasting System.

Irving G. Thalberg Memorial Award:
Alfred Hitchcock.

Jean Hersholt Humanitarian Award:
Gregory Peck.

SCIENTIFIC AND TECHNICAL AWARDS

Electro-Optical Division of the Kollmorgen
Corporation, for the design and development
of a series of motion picture projection lenses.

Panvision Inc., for a variable-speed motor for
motion picture cameras.

Fred R. Wilson, Samuel Goldwyn Studio
Sound Department, for an audio level clamper.

Waldon O. Watson and the Universal City Studio
Sound Department, for new concepts in the
design of a music scoring stage.

1967

For the first time in the forty-year history of the Academy Awards, presentation night was postponed. The tragic murder of Dr. Martin Luther King, Jr., not only put the ceremony off for two days but also took a great deal of the excitement and joy from the evening. Academy president Gregory Peck started the proceedings with a moving tribute to Dr. King, and although the voting on the Awards had taken place weeks before the assassination, it seemed as if the Academy members had taken the social upheaval of the times into consideration when they cast their ballots. Several films and performances with racial and integration themes were honored.

"In The Heat Of The Night" was the surprise winner of the Oscar for best picture of the year. This taut, dramatic film, basically a hard-boiled detective story, took on added meaning and significance with its setting in the South and its conflict between a white-racist police chief and a Negro detective from the North. With superb performances by Rod Steiger and Sidney Poitier, this film swept past its competition: "Bonnie And Clyde," "Doctor Dolittle," "The Graduate," and "Guess Who's Coming To Dinner."

And after twenty-five films, many great performances, and several Academy nominations, Rod Steiger was named best actor for his brilliant portrayal of the southern police chief.

The Oscar to Mike Nichols for his direction of "The Graduate" while the best picture prize went to "In The Heat Of The Night" marked the first time in eleven years that the two Awards had not gone hand in hand. The last time the best picture and the best director Awards did not go together was in 1956, when "Around The World In 80 Days" was named best picture and George Stevens was named best director for his work on "Giant."

Katharine Hepburn waited a long time for her second Academy Award. She was named best actress in 1933 for her performance in "Morning Glory," and although she was nominated eight times in the interim (for her performances in "Alice Adams," "The Philadelphia Story," "Woman Of The Year," "The African Queen," "Summertime," "The Rainmaker," "Suddenly, Last Summer," and "Long Day's Journey Into Night"), it was not until the 1967 awards that nomination culminated again in an Oscar for best actress—for her role in "Guess Who's Coming To Dinner."

Estelle Parsons was named best supporting actress for her performance as Clyde Barrow's sister-in-law in "Bonnie And Clyde." One of the big disappointments of the evening, at least for Warner Brothers, was the fact that the often-nominated "Bonnie And Clyde" won only two Oscars.

The Award for best supporting actor went to George Kennedy for his superb performance in "Cool Hand Luke," even though such fine supporting performances had been given by John Cassavetes in "The Dirty Dozen," Gene Hackman and Michael J. Pollard in "Bonnie And Clyde," and Cecil Kellaway in "Guess Who's Coming To Dinner."

"In The Heat Of The Night" (best picture)
with Sidney Poitier and Lee Grant. United Artists

Rod Steiger (best actor) in
"In The Heat Of The Night."
United Artists

Katharine Hepburn (best actress) with Spencer Tracy in "Guess Who's Coming To Dinner." Columbia

George Kennedy (best supporting actor) with Paul Newman in "Cool Hand Luke." Warner Brothers

Estelle Parsons (best supporting actress), second from left, with Gene Hackman, Warren Beatty, Faye Dunaway, Michael J. Pollard in "Bonnie And Clyde." Warner Brothers

"The Graduate" (best direction) with Katharine Ross and Dustin Hoffman. Embassy

"Doctor Dolittle" (best special visual effects) with Rex Harrison. 20th Century-Fox

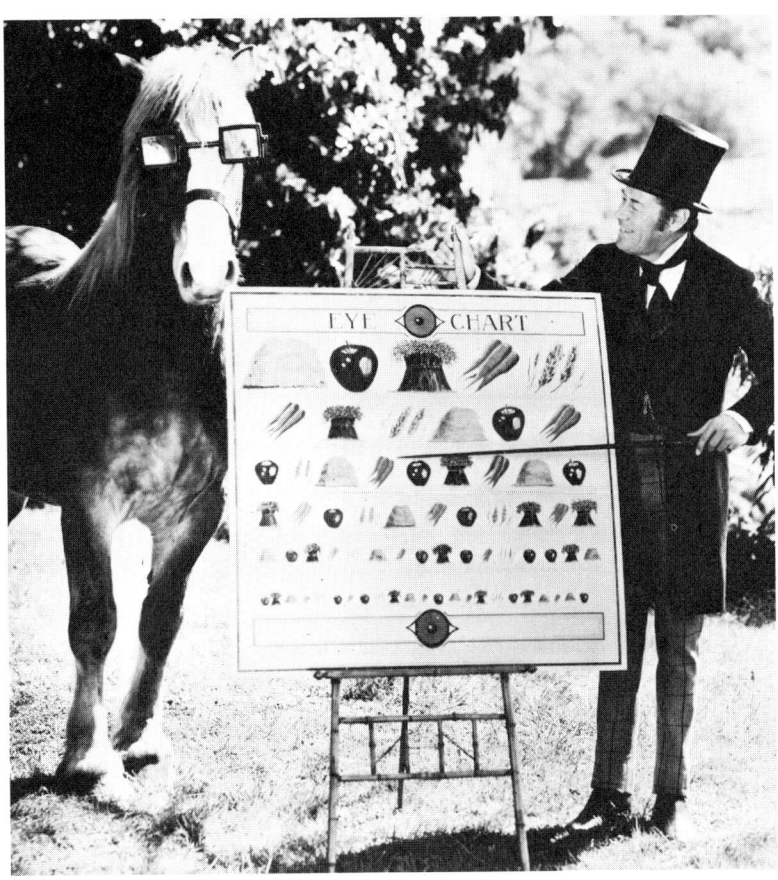

AWARDS

Best Picture: "Oliver!" Romulus Films, Ltd., Columbia.

Actor: Cliff Robertson in "Charly," An American Broadcasting Company–Selmur Pictures Production, Cinerama.

Actress: Katharine Hepburn in "The Lion In Winter," Haworth Productions, Ltd., Avco Embassy. Barbra Streisand in "Funny Girl," Rastar Productions, Columbia.

Supporting Actor: Jack Albertson in "The Subject Was Roses," Metro-Goldwyn-Mayer.

Supporting Actress: Ruth Gordon in "Rosemary's Baby," William Castle Enterprises Production, Paramount.

Directing: Carol Reed, "Oliver!"

Foreign Language Film Award: "War and Peace," A Mosfilm Production (Russia).

Writing (story and screenplay written directly for the screen): Mel Brooks, "The Producers," A Sidney Glazier Production, Avco Embassy.

Writing (screenplay—based on material from another medium): James Goldman, "The Lion In Winter."

Cinematography: Pasqualino De Santis, "Romeo & Juliet," A Franco Zeffirelli Production, B.H.E. Film-Verona Produzione S.r.l.– Dino De Laurentiis Cinematographica S.p.A. Production, Paramount.

Art Direction: John Box, Terence Marsh, Art Directors; Vernon Dixon, Ken Muggleston, Set Decorators; "Oliver!"

Costume Design: Danilo Donati, "Romeo & Juliet."

Film Editing: Frank P. Keller, "Bullitt," A Solar Production, Warner Brothers–Seven Arts.

Music (original score): John Barry, "A Lion In Winter."

Music (score of musical picture—original or adaptation): John Green, "Oliver!"

Music (song): Alan and Marilyn Bergman (lyrics), Michel Legrand (music), "The Windmills Of Your Mind" from "The Thomas Crown Affair," A Mirisch-Solar-Simkoe Production, United Artists.

Short Subjects (cartoon): "Winnie The Pooh And The Blustery Day," Walt Disney Productions, Buena Vista Distribution Company.

Short Subjects (live action): "Robert Kennedy Remembered," Guggenheim Productions, National General.

Sound: Shepperton Studio Sound Department, "Oliver!"

Special Visual Effects: "2001: A Space Odyssey," A Polaris Production, Metro-Goldwyn-Mayer.

Documentary (feature): "Journey Into Self," Western Behavioral Sciences Institute.

Documentary (short subjects): "Why Man Creates," Saul Bass & Associates.

Jean Hersholt Humanitarian Award: Martha Raye.

SPECIAL AWARDS

John Chambers, for his outstanding make-up achievement for "Planet Of The Apes."

Onna White, for her outstanding choreography achievement for "Oliver!"

SCIENTIFIC AND TECHNICAL AWARDS

Philip V. Palmquist of Minnesota Mining and Manufacturing Co., Dr. Herbert Meyer of the Motion Picture and Television Research Center, and Charles D. Staffell of the Rank Organisation, for the development of a successful embodiment of the reflex background projection system for composite cinematography.

Eastman Kodak Company, for the development and introduction of a color reversal intermediate film for motion pictures.

Donald W. Norwood, for the design and development of the Norwood Photographic Exposure Meters.

Eastman Kodak Company and Producers Service Company, for the development of a new high-speed step-optical reduction printer.

Edmund M. DiGiulio, Niels G. Peterson, and Norman S. Hughes of the Cinema Product Development Company, for the design and application of a conversion which makes available the reflex viewing system for motion picture cameras.

Optical Coating Laboratory, Inc., for the development of an improved anti-reflection coating for photographic and projection lens systems.

Eastman Kodak Company, for the introduction of a new high-speed motion picture color negative film.

Panavision Incorporated, for the conception, design and introduction of a 65mm hand-held motion picture camera.

Todd-AO Company and the Mitchell Camera Company, for the design and engineering of the Todd-AO hand-held motion picture camera.

Carl W. Hauge and Edward H. Reichard of Consolidated Film Industries and E. Michael Meahl and Roy J. Ridenour of Ramtronics, for engineering an automatic exposure control for printing-machine lamps.

Eastman Kodak Company, for a new direct positive film and to Consolidated Film Industries for the application of this film to the making of post-production work prints.

1968

The annual Academy Award fete began its fifth decade with several innovations, most geared to facilitate the event's entertainment value for the huge at-home television audience. The ceremony took place not in the Santa Monica Civic Auditorium, but in the new Dorothy Chandler Pavilion of Los Angeles County's Music Center. A special runway was built in the theatre's orchestra area to allow for greater versatility in the show's staging, handled by Gower Champion. Academy president Gregory Peck announced the institution of "ten friends of the Oscar" (Ingrid Bergman, Sidney Poitier, Jane Fonda, Frank Sinatra, Rosalind Russell, Walter Matthau, Natalie Wood, Burt Lancaster, Diahann Carroll, and Tony Curtis) who alternated in announcing and bestowing the winning presentations. Bob Hope, who had so successfully emceed many of the past Oscarcasts, was on hand only briefly to make a special award.

The multimillion dollar musical "Oliver!," which went on to gross over $16.8 million at the box office, was this year's winning picture, beating out such other period-set offerings as "Funny Girl," "The Lion In Winter," and "Romeo & Juliet." "Oliver!" was a retelling on the wide screen of Charles Dickens' touching tale of the waif (Mark Lester) in nineteenth-century London who is rescued in the nick of time from roguish master crook Fagin (Ron Moody). The picturization of the successful London and Broadway stage musical earned five other Oscars. Sir Carol Reed, the distinguished British technician noted for his sensitive handling of such dramatic fare as "Odd Man Out" and "The Third Man," was named best for "Oliver!," his first screen song-and-dance outing. Other "Oliver!" awards were for sound, art-set direction, scoring, and a special Oscar for Onna White's choreography.

Proving that the Academy Award show can have its genuine lighter moments, a chimpanzee was assigned to present John Chambers with a special award for the innovative makeup he used in "The Planet Of The Apes."

The surprise of the evening occurred when presenter Ingrid Bergman announced there had been a tie vote in the best actress category between Katharine Hepburn and Barbra Streisand. It was the first such tie in this category and the second tie in the Academy's history. For her regal performance as Eleanor of Aquitaine in "The Lion In Winter," Hepburn won her third Oscar. It made her the most nominated (eleven times) actress in Oscar's history, and it was the first time an actress had won two Oscars in a row since 1936 and 1937, when Luise Rainer won hers. Unlike Hepburn who remained at home in New York, cowinner Streisand was a vivid participant at the ceremony. When the twenty-six-year-old songstress, who had scored in the Broadway and London versions of "Funny Girl" (the Fannie Brice story), accepted her Oscar, she exclaimed: "Hello, gorgeous."

There was little dispute over the best actor award, going to Cliff Robertson for "Charly." Although he had previously received much publicity for his portrayal of John F. Kennedy in "PT-109," he was best known for his many well-modulated television performances. Because two of his finest video assignments had gone to other actors when the picturizations were made (Paul Newman in "The Hustler," Jack Lemmon in "Days Of Wine And Roses"), Robertson took no chances when he performed in the sensitive TV drama "The Two Worlds Of Charlie Gordon" (1961). He purchased the screen rights and maneuvered for seven years to obtain production financing with himself again portraying the physically mature man who is mentally retarded.

Jack Albertson who began his lengthy show business career as a straight man in burlesque was voted best supporting actor for playing the baffled, frustrated husband and father in "The Subject Was Roses," the film that brought Patricia Neal back to movies. Albertson had previously won a Tony Award for originating the role on Broadway.

In 1915 Ruth Gordon starred in a movie version of "Camille." Fifty-three years later, the septuagenarian performer was named best supporting actress for her capering as the devilish next-door neighbor in the thriller "Rosemary's Baby." "I don't know why it took so long," quipped lively Gordon who had long been a Broadway star and had won a supporting actress nomination for "Inside Daisy Clover" (1965) and had three script writing nominations for collaborating with her playwright-director husband Garson Kanin on "A Double Life" (1947), "Adam's Rib" (1950), and "Pat And Mike" (1952).

Perhaps the evening's most touching moment was when Bob Hope presented big-mouthed, rubber-legged comedienne Martha Raye with the Jean Hersholt Humanitarian Award for her "devoted and often dangerous work in entertaining troops in combat areas almost continuously since World War II." The usually raucous Raye in a very moving acceptance said she would devote the remainder of her life "to deserving this."

"Romeo & Juliet" (best cinematography, costume design) with Milo O'Shea, Olivia Hussey. Franco Zeffirelli, De Laurentiis, Paramount

Cliff Robertson (best actor) in "Charly." American Broadcasting Company–
Selmur Pictures, Cinerama

Katharine Hepburn (best actress) in "A Lion In Winter." Haworth, Avco Embassy and below, Barbra Streisand (best actress) in "Funny Girl." Rastar, Columbia

Ruth Gordon (best supporting actress) with Sidney Blackmer and Mia Farrow in "Rosemary's Baby." William Castle Enterprises, Paramount

Jack Albertson (best supporting actor) with Martin Sheen in "The Subject Was Roses." Metro-Goldwyn-Mayer

"Bullitt" (best film editing) with Steve McQueen, Jacqueline Bisset. Warner Brothers, Seven Arts

"The Producers" (best original screenplay) with Zero Mostel, Kenneth Mars, Gene Wilder

"Winnie The Pooh And The Blustery Day" (best cartoon short subject). Disney, Buena Vista © Walt Disney Productions

"2001: A Space Odyssey" (best special visual effects) with Keir Dullea. Polaris, Metro-Goldwyn-Mayer

"Planet Of The Apes" (special award, make-up achievement). © Apjac Productions, Inc. and Twentieth Century-Fox Film Corporation, 1967

AWARDS

Best Picture: "Midnight Cowboy," A Jerome Hellman–John Schlesinger Production, United Artists.

Actor: John Wayne in "True Grit," A Hal Wallis Production, Paramount.

Actress: Maggie Smith in "The Prime of Miss Jean Brodie," 20th Century-Fox Productions, Ltd.

Supporting Actor: Gig Young in "They Shoot Horses, Don't They?" A Chartoff-Winkler-Pollack Production, ABC Pictures Presentation, Cinerama.

Supporting Actress: Goldie Hawn in "Cactus Flower," Frankovich Productions, Columbia.

Directing: John Schlesinger, "Midnight Cowboy."

Foreign Language Film Award: "Z," A Reggane–O.N.C.I.C. Production (Algeria).

Writing (screenplay—based on material from another medium): Waldo Salt, "Midnight Cowboy."

Writing (original story and screenplay): William Goldman, "Butch Cassidy And The Sundance Kid," a George Roy Hill–Paul Monash Production, 20th Century-Fox.

Cinematography: Conrad Hall, "Butch Cassidy And The Sundance Kid."

Art Direction: John DeCuir, Jack Martin Smith, Herman Blumenthal, Art Directors; Walter M. Scott, George Hopkins, Raphael Bretton, Set Decorators; "Hello, Dolly!" Chenault Productions, 20th Century-Fox.

Costume Design: Margaret Furse, "Anne Of A Thousand Days," A Hal Wallis–Universal Pictures, Ltd. Production, Universal.

Film Editing: Françoise Bonnot, "Z."

Music (original score): Burt Bacharach, "Butch Cassidy And The Sundance Kid."

Music (score): Lennie Hayton, Lionel Newman, "Hello, Dolly!"

Music (song): Hal David (lyrics), Burt Bacharach (music), "Raindrops Keep Fallin' On My Head" from "Butch Cassidy And The Sundance Kid."

Short Subjects (cartoon): "It's Tough To Be A Bird," Walt Disney Productions, Buena Vista Distribution Company.

Short Subjects (live action): "The Magic Machines," Fly-By-Night Productions, Manson Distributing.

Sound: Jack Solomon, Murray Spivack, "Hello, Dolly!"

Special Visual Effects: Robbie Robertson, "Marooned," A Frankovich–Sturges Production, Columbia.

Documentary (feature): "Artur Rubinstein—The Love Of Life," A Midem Production.

Documentary (short subject): "Czechoslovakia 1968," Sanders-Fresco Film Makers, United States Information Agency.

Jean Hersholt Humanitarian Award: George Jessel.

SPECIAL AWARD

Cary Grant, for his unique mastery of the art of screen acting with the respect and affection of his colleagues.

SCIENTIFIC AND TECHNICAL AWARDS

Hazeltine Corporation, for the design and development of the Hazeltine Color Film Analyzer.

Fouad Said, for the design and introduction of the Cinemobile series of equipment trucks for location motion picture production.

Juan De La Cierva and Dynasciences Corporation, for the design and development of the Dynalens optical image motion compensator.

Otto Popelka of Magna-Tech Electronics Co., Inc., for the development of an Electronically Controlled Looping System.

Fenton Hamilton of Metro-Goldwyn-Mayer Studios, for the concept and engineering of a mobile battery power unit for location lighting.

Panavision Incorporated, for the design and development of the Panaspeed Motion Picture Camera Motor.

Robert M. Flynn and Russell Hessy of Universal City Studios, Inc., for a machine-gun modification for motion picture photography.

1969

Bob Hope aptly reflected the tenor of this year's Awards when he stated at the conclusion of the forty-second annual Oscar ceremonies that Hollywood pictures would never again reflect "a lollypop world" but from now on would "hold a mirror up to nature," although he cautioned "the characters in our films may not be ones to emulate." Earlier in the show, there were pretaped shots of such film directors as Federico Fellini, Akiro Kurosawa, and Mike Nichols discussing their views of the screen's "new freedom" in today's very permissive society.

"Midnight Cowboy," an X-rated film (no one under seventeen admitted), was named best picture of the year, despite its very mature subject matter. It pulled no punches in graphically dealing with the ultraseamy aspects of New York City life by focusing on the survival efforts of a Texas-bred male hustler (Jon Voight) and his sickly Bronxite panhandling pal (Dustin Hoffman). Ironically, it took a Britisher— John Schlesinger of "Darling" fame—to really capture the gamy side of big-city life, and for his perceptive handling of "Midnight Cowboy" he was voted best director. Another "Midnight Cowboy" Oscar went to Waldo Salt for the best screenplay from another medium. Voight and Hoffman each received best actor nominations, and Sylvia Miles, as the ex-prostitute who beats naïve Voight at his own game, earned a best supporting actress bid.

It was a popular decision that brought John "Duke" Wayne the best actor's Oscar for playing the one-eyed, whiskey-drinking U.S. Marshal Rooster Cogburn in the western "True Grit." Wayne had made his film debut as an unbilled extra in John Ford's "Mother Machree" (1928) and became a major star in the same director's "Stagecoach" (1939). He is still one of the top ten boxoffice attractions. Said Wayne, who had been previously Oscar-nominated for "Sands Of Iwo Jima" (1949): "If I'd known, I'd have put the eye-patch on thirty-five years earlier."

A dark-horse winner was English Maggie Smith as best actress for "The Prime Of Miss Jean Brodie." She excelled as the unorthodox Scottish schoolteacher, a self-deluded woman whose oversized pride in her cultural "prime" is badly deflated by one of her pupils who woos away her beau (played by her real-life husband, actor Robert Stephens). Favorite contenders in the best actress category had been Jane Fonda as the disillusioned young woman in "They Shoot Horses, Don't They?" and Liza Minnelli in her adult screen debut in "The Sterile Cuckoo." Miss Smith, who much prefers acting in the classics on stage, had first gained filmgoers' notice with her scene-stealing performance as Rod Taylor's lovelorn secretary in "The V.I.P.s" (1961).

Until her best supporting actress Oscar for "Cactus Flower," Goldie Hawn was best known as the giggly dumb blonde on TV's **Rowan And Martin's Laugh-In.** Her screen debut in a small role in Walt Disney's "The One And Only Genuine

337

Original Family Band" (1968) had passed virtually unnoticed. In "Cactus Flower" she performed so ably as the effervescent young miss infatuated with an older man that she often stole the limelight from the picture's stars, Ingrid Bergman and Walter Matthau.

Byron Barr, better known to three decades of filmgoers as sauve screenplayer Gig Young, earned a best supporting actor Oscar on his third try ["Come Fill The Cup" (1951), "Teacher's Pet" (1958)]. He made audiences sit up and take notice of his dramatic talents as the cynical, hard-pressing emcee of an exhausting Depression-days dance marathon in "They Shoot Horses, Don't They?" His closest rival for the award was Jack Nicholson, playing the postadolescent hippie in the youth-market feature "Easy Rider."

There was an effective dose of nostalgia as seventy-one-year-old Fred Astaire, one of this year's seventeen "friends of Oscar," entertained with a few dance routines. Later in the program, self-retired star Cary Grant received a special award for "outstanding artistry and many memorable performances." After clips from several of his films were shown, he left the stage close to tears, saying he would revere his Oscar "until I die. For no honor is greater than the respect of one's colleagues."

"Midnight Cowboy" (best picture, best directing, best screenplay) with Dustin Hoffman and Jon Voight. Below, Brenda Vaccaro and Jon Voight. Hellman-Schlesinger, United Artists

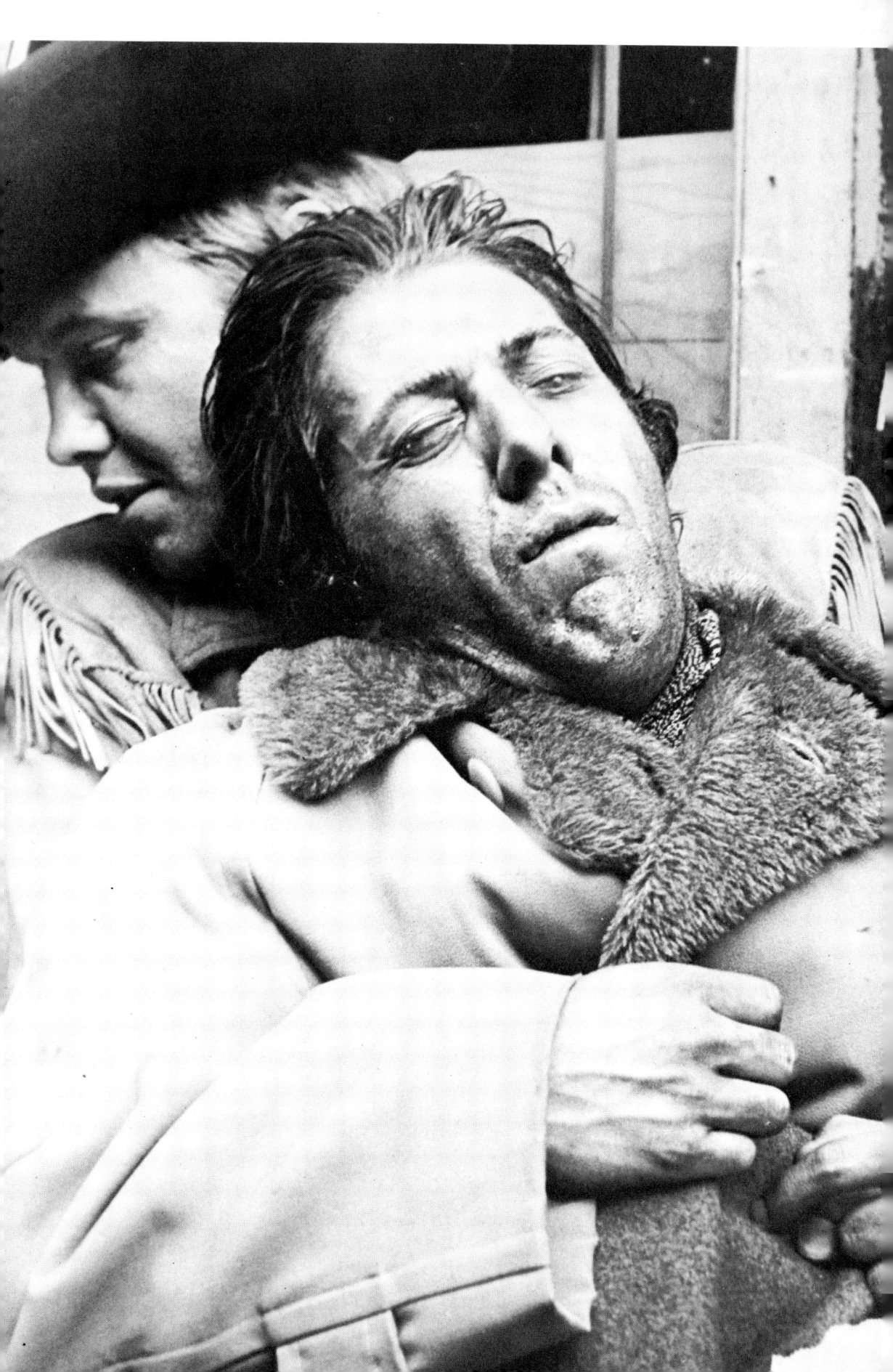

Maggie Smith (best actress) in "The Prime Of Miss Jean Brodie." 20th Century-Fox (© 20th Century-Fox, Ltd., 1968)

Goldie Hawn (best supporting actress) with Walter Matthau in "Cactus Flower." Frankovich, Columbia

John Wayne (best actor) in "True Grit." Hall Wallis, Paramount

Gig Young (best supporting actor) with Albert Lewis in "They Shoot Horses, Don't They?" ABC Pictures, Cinerama

"Butch Cassidy And The Sundance
Kid" (best screenplay) with Paul
Newman, Katharine Ross and Robert
Redford. 20th Century-Fox
(© Campanile Productions, Inc.
and Twentieth Century-Fox
Film Corporation, 1969)

"Z " (best foreign film, best film editing) with Yves Montand and Irene Papas. Algeria

"Hello, Dolly!" (best art direction) with Louis Armstrong and Barbra Streisand. 20th Century-Fox (© Twentieth Century-Fox Film Corporation & Chenault Productions, Inc. 1969)

"Anne Of A Thousand Days" (best costume design) with Genevieve Bujold and Richard Burton. Hal Wallis, Universal

"Artur Rubinstein—The Love Of Life" (best documentary feature). Midem

1970

There was little surprise when "Patton" overran its competitors (including the phenomenally commercial tearjerker "Love Story" and the slick suspense yarn "Airport") to win the best picture of the year award. Producer Frank McCarthy had been engineering this pet project for over twenty years, and the resulting roadshow production fulfilled everyone's artistic and financial expectations. Besides garnering Oscars for sound, editing, screenplay, and art-set direction, director Franklin J. Schaffner was an Academy Award recipient for his controlled handling of this dynamic screen biography set in World War II Europe and Africa. However, nearly everyone was caught off guard when George C. Scott was named best actor of the year for his heady performance as the vituperative, courageous General George S. Patton, Jr., a hero in the decisive Battle of the Bulge. Scott had twice before been nominated for best supporting actor ["Anatomy Of A Murder" (1959), "The Hustler" (1961)], and now for the second time he had asked to have his nomination withdrawn. The Academy, however, stoutly refused his request, insisting upon honoring a dynamic performance rather than paying much heed to tactless behavior.

For the second year in a row, a British performer received the best actress award. Thirty-six-year-old Glenda Jackson was little known to American filmgoing audiences before she portrayed the freethinking sculptress in the sensual picturization of D. H. Lawrence's "Women In Love." A graduate of London's Royal Academy of Dramatic Arts, she had spent several years as a struggling performer in English repertory companies before she made a major breakthrough in 1965, when she appeared in Ophelia in the Royal Shakespeare's production of "Hamlet." Her first film assignment was recreating her stage role in "The Persecution and Assassination of Jean Paul Marat...," followed by meaty cinema parts in "Negatives," "The Music Lovers," "Sunday, Bloody Sunday," and "Mary Queen Of Scots" (again playing the Virgin Queen as she had done on British TV in the series **Queen Elizabeth I**).

Despite the appeal of Chief Dan George as the aged, wise Indian warrior in "Little Big Man," the best supporting actor citation went to British stage and screen veteran John Mills who had so effectively pantomimed the role of the Irish town mute-fool in "Ryan's Daughter." Younger generations of celebrity-followers know him as the dad of Hayley Mills, but he has been turning in quality performances for decades in all the media, including roles in movies such as "In Which We Serve," "Great Expectations," and "The Chalk Garden."

Back in 1931/32, Helen Hayes merited an Oscar for The "Sin Of Madelon Claudet." Forty years later, Miss Hayes was named best supporting actress for essaying the role of the cute old-lady stowaway in "Airport." She made her screen debut in "The Weavers Of Life" (1917), but had appeared in few films over the years, preferring to distinguish herself on the stage.

When Frank Sinatra accepted the Jean Hersholt Humanitarian Award he joked that perhaps his recently announced retirement from show business had earned him this distinction, but presenter Gregory Peck assured all that Sinatra's innumerable charitable contributions made the singer-actor "undeniably the titleholder in the soft-touch department."

Honorary Oscars were bestowed on both Orson Welles and Lillian Gish. Welles, in a pretaped acceptance speech filmed in Europe, concluded his segment with these words: "I accept this Oscar not for what I've done but for what I hope to do. Thank you, with all my heart." Seventy-four-year-old Miss Gish was on hand to receive the respectful appreciation of an industry in which she had performed since 1912. She acknowledged her debt to her recently deceased actress sister Dorothy and to "all the charming ghosts of our movie past."

This was the first year that the Irving G. Thalberg Award (for consistently excellent filmmaking) was given to a director of films in a foreign language. Swedish Ingmar Bergman, in a prefilmed talk in English, stated: "A film goes to your subconscious. That is the secret of the power of cinema's very strange language."

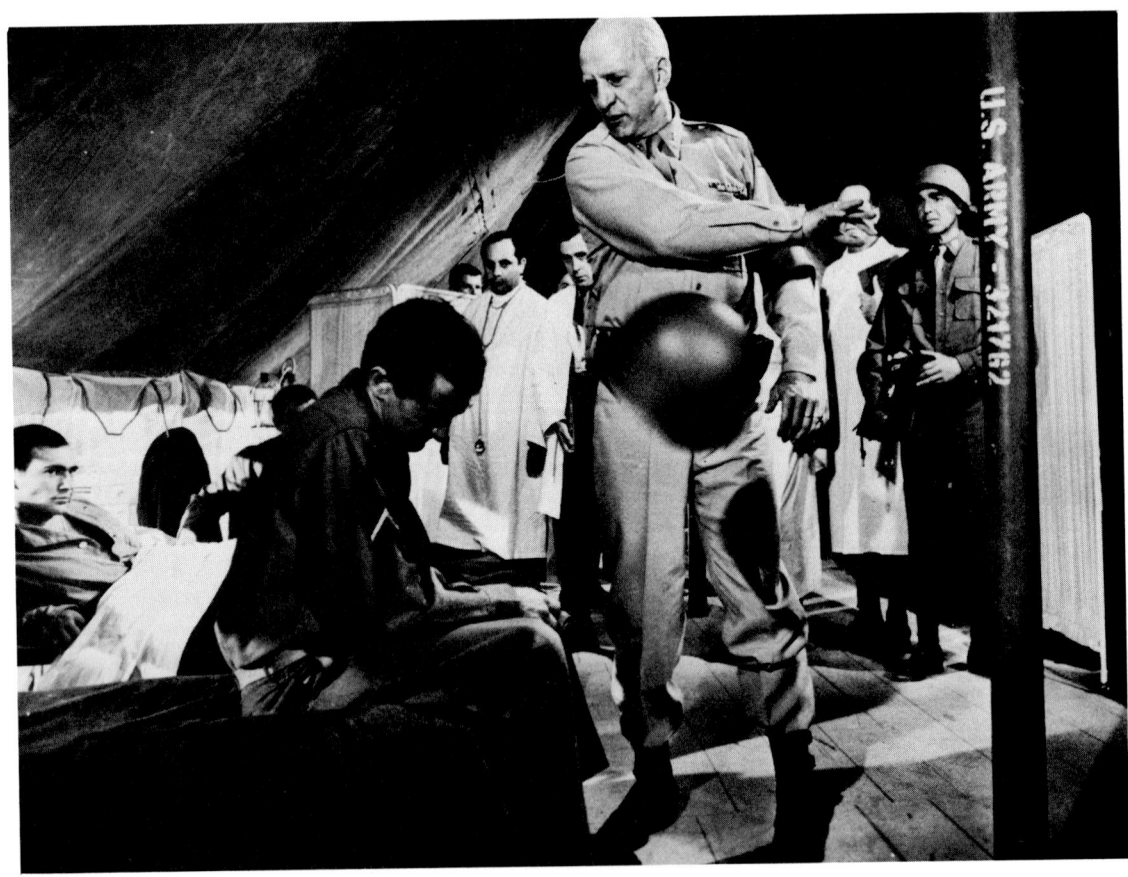

"Patton" (best picture, best direction, best original screenplay, best art direction, best film editing) starring George C. Scott (best actor). (© Twentieth Century-Fox Film Corporation, 1970)

AWARDS

Best Picture: "Patton," 20th Century-Fox.

Actor: George C. Scott in "Patton."

Actress: Glenda Jackson in "Women In Love," A Larry Kramer–Martin Rosen Production, United Artists.

Supporting Actor: John Mills in "Ryan's Daughter," Faraway Productions, A.G., Metro-Goldwyn-Mayer.

Supporting Actress: Helen Hayes in "Airport," A Ross Hunter–Universal Production, Universal.

Directing: Franklin J. Schaffner, "Patton."

Foreign Language Film Award: "Investigation Of A Citizen Above Suspicion," A Vera Films S.p.A. Production (Italy).

Writing (screenplay—based on material from another medium): Ring Lardner, Jr., "M*A*S*H," Aspen Productions, 20th Century-Fox.

Writing (original story and screenplay): Francis Ford Coppola, Edmund H. North, "Patton."

Cinematography: Freddie Young, "Ryan's Daughter."

Art Direction: Urie McCleary, Gil Parrondo, Art Directors; Antonio Mateos, Pierre-Louis Thevenet, Set Decorators; "Patton."

Costume Design: Nino Novarese, "Cromwell," An Irving Allen, Ltd., Production, Columbia.

Film Editing: Hugh S. Fowler, "Patton."

Music (original score): Francis Lai, "Love Story," Love Story Producing Company Production, Paramount.

Music (original song score): The Beatles, "Let It Be," A Beatles–Apple Production, United Artists.

Music (song): Robb Royer, James Griffin (lyrics), Fred Karlin (music), "For All We Know" from "Lovers And Other Strangers," An ABC Pictures Production, Cinerama.

Short Subjects (cartoon): "Is It Always Right To Be Right?" Stephen Bosustow Productions, Lester A. Schoenfeld Films.

Short Subjects (live action): "The Resurrection Of Broncho Billy," University of Southern California Department of Cinema, Universal.

Sound: Douglas Williams, Don Bassman, "Patton."

Special Visual Effects: A. D. Flowers, L. B. Abbott, "Tora! Tora! Tora!" 20th Century-Fox.

Documentary (feature): "Woodstock," A Wadleigh–Maurice, Ltd. Production.

Documentary (short subject): "Interviews With My Lai Veterans," Laser Film Corporation.

Irving G. Thalberg Memorial Award: Ingmar Bergman.

Jean Hersholt Humanitarian Award: Frank Sinatra.

SPECIAL AWARDS

Lillian Gish, for superlative artistry and for distinguished contribution to the progress of motion pictures.

Orson Welles, for superlative artistry and versatility in the creation of motion pictures.

SCIENTIFIC AND TECHNICAL AWARDS

Leonard Sokolow and Edward H. Reichard of Consolidated Film Industries, for the concept and engineering of the Color Proofing Printer for motion pictures.

Sylvania Electric Products, Inc., for the development and introduction of a series of compact tungsten halogen lamps for motion picture production.

B. J. Losmandy, for the concept, design and application of micro-miniature solid state amplifier modules used in motion picture recording equipment.

Eastman Kodak Company and Photo Electronics Corporation, for the design and engineering of an improved video color analyzer for motion picture laboratories.

Electro Sound Incorporated, for the design and introduction of the Series 8000 Sound System for motion picture theatres.

Helen Hayes (best supporting
actress) in "Airport."
Ross Hunter, Universal

John Mills (best supporting
actor) in "Ryan's Daughter."
Faraway, Metro-Goldwyn-Mayer
(© Metro-Goldwyn-Mayer)

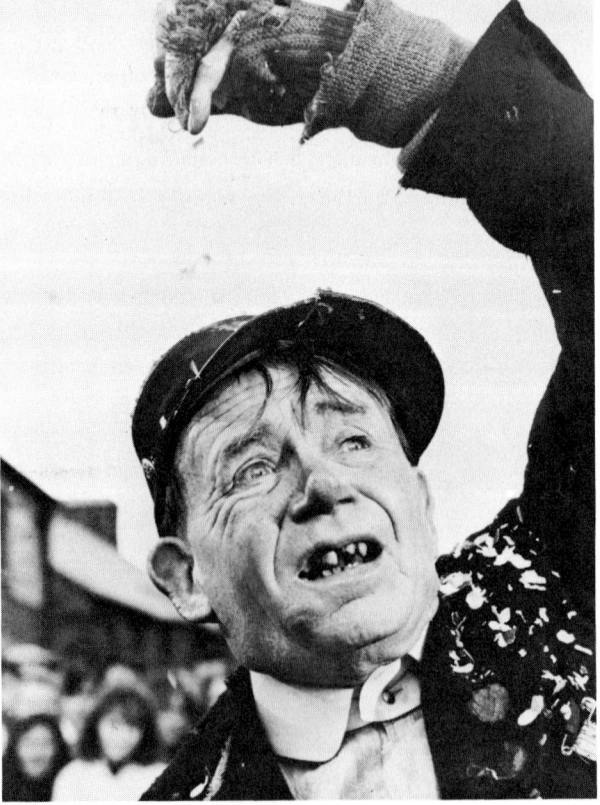

Glenda Jackson (best actress) with Oliver Reed in "Women In Love." Kramer-Rosen, United Artists

"Cromwell" (best costume design) with Richard Harris. Irving Allen, Columbia

"M*A*S*H" (best screenplay) with Elliott Gould, Donald Sutherland, and Sally Kellerman. Aspen, 20th Century-Fox (© Aspen Productions and Twentieth Century-Fox Film Corporation)

"Tora! Tora! Tora!" (best special visual effects). (© Twentieth Century-Fox Film Corporation, 1970)

"Investigation Of A Citizen Above Suspicion" (best foreign film) with Gian Maria Volonte and Florinda Bolkan. Vera, Italy

"Is It Always Right To Be Right?" (best cartoon short subject). Stephen Bosustow, Schoenfeld

"The Resurrection Of Broncho Billy" (best live action short subject). USC Department of Cinema, Universal

1971

An estimated 75 million people viewed the "live from Hollywood" telecast of the forty-fourth annual Academy Award ceremonies. Frequent master of ceremonies Bob Hope was again missing from the show's lineup, a sad loss for the evening's entertainment values. Instead the festivities were presided over by Helen Hayes, Alan King, Sammy Davis, Jr., and Jack Lemmon. Miss Hayes, who had not been present to receive her best supporting actress award for "Airport" (1970), quipped about the still controversial winner of last year's top actor award: "As George C. Scott didn't get around to saying last year, thank you." In general the presenters were ill at ease with their prepared material, and only nightclub/television comedian Alan King managed to ignite some sparks of fun during his on-camera segment, mostly with jokes punning on the ultrapopular new film "The Godfather." In contrast to past years, there were no startling innovations in the show's production format, most of the excitement being generated by the anticipated presence of Charlie Chaplin to receive an honorary Oscar.

This was the first Academy Award competition in which all of the nominees for best supporting actor and best supporting actress were first-time contestants in their categories. The winners, Cloris Leachman and Ben Johnson, won for their performances in "The Last Picture Show," she as the aging, frustrated wife of the small Texas town gym coach and he as the philosophical pool hall owner who dies during the course of the picture. Both are seasoned players, Miss Leachman having been on the Broadway stage, on television soap opera, and in diversified cinema roles ranging from Joanne Woodward's crippled friend in "WUSA" to Gig Young's chic wife in "Lovers And Other Strangers." Johnson, a former stunt rider, has functioned mainly in western movies: "She Wore A Yellow Ribbon," "Wagonmaster," "Major Dundee," "The Rare Breed." In the acceptance speech highlight of the evening, Johnson stated he had put aside his prepared speech because "...the longer I worked on it the phonier it got." He then added: "What I'm about to say will start a controversy around the world: This couldn't have happened to a nicer fella."

Usually the renditions of nominated songs interspersed among the award-giving are hackneyed outings. Not so this year with the dynamic staging of the "Theme From Shaft" performed by Isaac Hayes who composed the music and lyrics for the black detective film. Ron Fields, of "Applause" fame on Broadway, choreographed this segment with imaginative intensity. Hayes won an Oscar for his song. The best original dramatic score was composed by Frenchman Michel Legrand for "Summer of '42."

The Yugoslavian-lensed musical "Fiddler On The Roof," a heavy roadshow contender for best picture of the year, received three Oscars: cinematography, sound, scoring. But it was the New York–filmed detective thriller "The French

Connection" which won the major share (five) of Academy Awards: best picture, director, actor, screenplay, film editing. Thirty-three-year-old William Friedkin who directed the international-narcotics-search film is a former television documentary creator and has handled such diversified features as "The Night They Raided Minsky's" and "The Boys In The Band." Burly Gene Hackman who played rugged detective Popeye Doyle in "The French Connection" was named best actor. He first gained recognition on the Broadway stage in "Any Wednesday." He has been a steady film performer since his cinema debut in "Lilith" (1964), having won best supporting actor nominations for "Bonnie And Clyde" and "I Never Sang For My Father." His closest competitor in this category was Australian Peter Finch for his understated performance as the homosexual Jewish doctor in "Sunday Bloody Sunday."

With Jane Fonda winning the best actress award for "Klute" as the kooky hooker involved in a murder case it was the first occasion in years that all the major Awards were bestowed on Americans. Henry Fonda's daughter has matured quite a bit professionally since her screen bow as the gawky collegian in "Tall Story" (1960). She has been seen as one of the women interviewees in "The Chapman Report," the star of "Barbarella," and as the destruction-bent Depression girl in "They Shoot Horses, Don't They?" (1969) for which she was Oscar-nominated. Because of Miss Fonda's controversial political views, it was expected that should she win, her acceptance speech would contain several topical barbs. However, all she told the audience was: "There's a great deal to say and I'm not going to say it tonight."

"The Garden Of The Finzi-Continis" was selected as best foreign-language film of the year. Its producers, Gianni Hecht Lucari and Arthur Cohn, acknowledged the creative contribution of director Vittorio de Sica, and went on to remark that they had been advised not to produce this film, because the study of the anti-Semitic movement in pre-World War II Italy focused neither on sex nor action.

The long-awaited highlight of the evening was the presentation of a special tribute to Charlie Chaplin, an exile from America for more than twenty years since his political views made him **persona non grata**. The laurel was offered in recognition of "the incalculable effect he has had in making motion pictures the art form it is in this century." After several film clips from his many comedies as the Little Tramp, the soon-to-be-eighty-three-year-old comedian came on stage. He received a four-minute standing ovation from the more than twenty-nine hundred attendees. Throwing kisses and bowing modestly, he haltingly said: "Words are so futile, so feeble. I can only say thank you for the honor of inviting me here. You are wonderful, sweet people."

AWARDS

Best Picture: "The French Connection,"
D'Antoni Productions, 20th Century-Fox

Actor: Gene Hackman in "The French Connection."

Actress: Jane Fonda in "Klute," Gus Production,
Warner Brothers.

Supporting Actor: Ben Johnson in "The Last
Picture Show," BBS Productions, Columbia.

Supporting Actress: Cloris Leachman in
"The Last Picture Show."

Directing: William Friedkin, "The French
Connection."

Foreign Language Film Award: "The Garden Of
The Finzi-Continis," Gianni Hecht Lucari-
Arthur Cohn (Italy).

**Writing (screenplay—based on material from
another medium):** Ernest Tidyman,
"The French Connection."

Writing (original story and screenplay): Paddy
Chayefsky, "The Hospital," Gottfried-
Chayefsky, Arthur Hiller, United Artists

Cinematography: Oswald Morris, "Fiddler On
The Roof," Mirisch-Cartier, United Artists.

Art Direction: John Box, Ernest Archer, Jack
Maxted, Gil Parrondo, Art Directors; Set
Decorator, Vernon Dixon; "Nicholas And
Alexandra," Horizon, Columbia.

Costume Design: Yvonne Blake, Antonio Castillo,
"Nicholas And Alexandra."

Film Editing: Jerry Greenberg, "The French
Connection."

Music (original score): Michel Legrand, "Summer
Of '42," Mulligan-Roth, Warner Brothers.

Music (adaptation or treatment): John Williams,
"Fiddler On The Roof."

Music (song): Isaac Hayes for "Theme From
Shaft," "Shaft," Shaft Productions.
Metro-Goldwyn-Mayer.

Short Subjects (cartoon): "The Crunch Bird,"
Petok, Regency.

Short Subjects (live action): "Sentinels Of
Silence," Paramount.

Sound: Gordon K. McCallum, David Hildyard,
"Fiddler On The Roof."

Special Visual Effects: Danny Lee, Eustace
Lycett, Alan Maley, "Bedknobs And
Broomsticks," Disney, Buena Vista.

Documentary (short subject): "Sentinels Of
Silence."

Documentary (feature): "The Hellstrom Chronicle,"
Wolper, Cinema 5.

SPECIAL AWARD

Charles Spencer (Charlie) Chaplin, for his
unique contribution to motion pictures.

"The French Connection" (best picture) with Gene
Hackman (best actor) and Marcel Bozzuffi, (©D'Antoni
Productions, 20th Century-Fox)

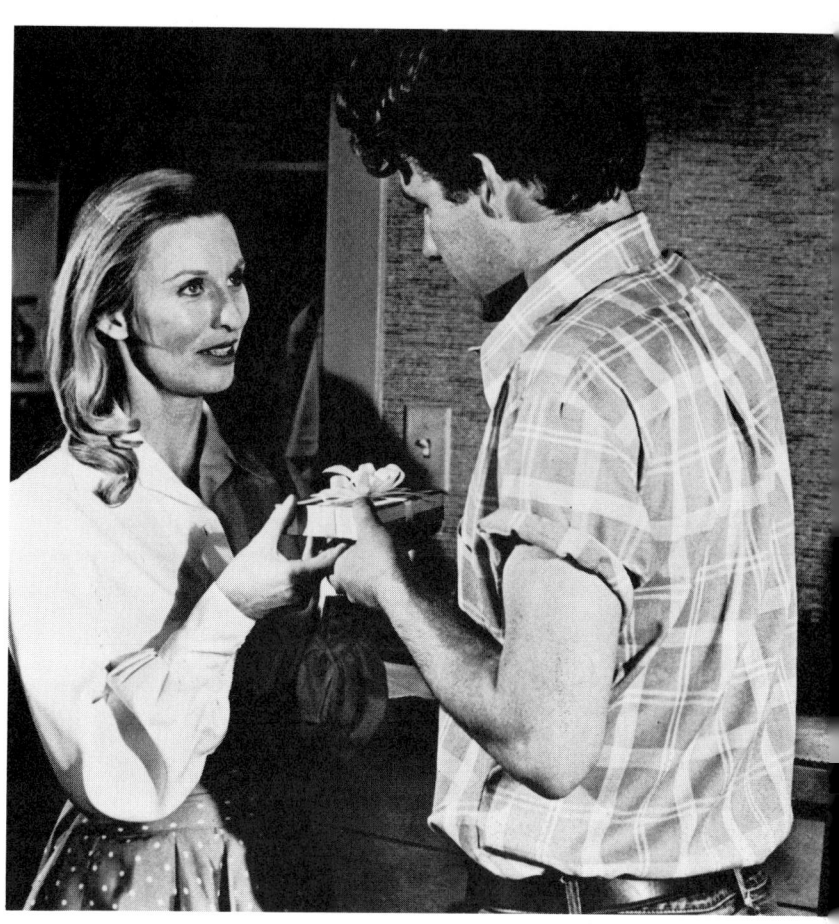

Cloris Leachman (best supporting actress) with Timothy Bottoms. Below, Ben Johnson (best supporting actor) in "The Last Picture Show," BBS, Columbia

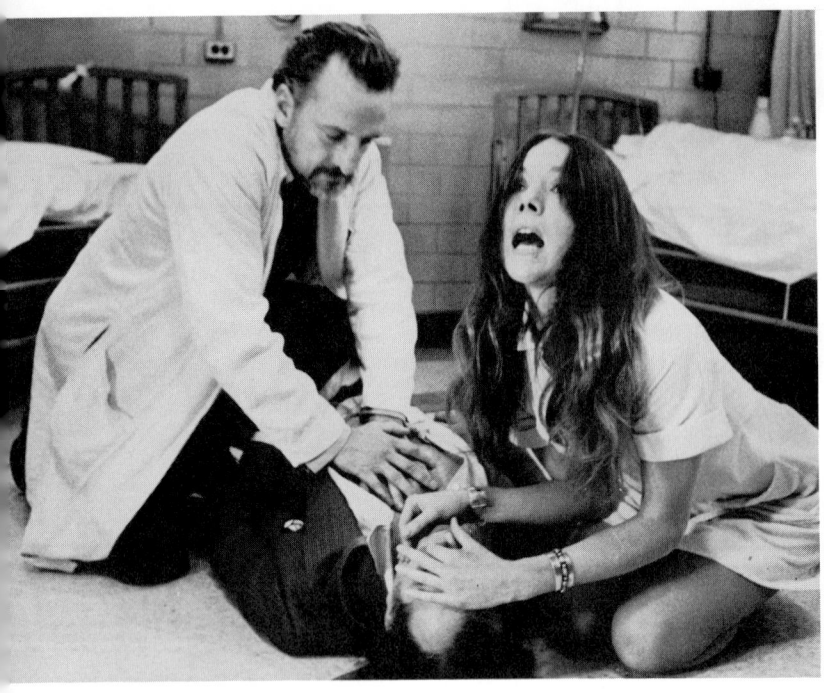

"The Hospital" (best story and screenplay) with George C. Scott and Diana Rigg. Gottfried, Chayefsky, Hiller

"Nicholas And Alexandra" (best art direction, costume design) with Michael Jayston, Janet Suzman. Horizon, Columbia

"The Garden Of The Finzi-Continis" (best foreign language film) with Dominique Sanda, Lino Capolicchio.
Gianni Hecht Lucari-Arthur Cohn (Italy)

Charlie Chaplin (special award) in "The Gold Rush"

1972

There were actually two suspense stories on the TV screens of an estimated 80 million Americans as they watched the forty-fifth annual award ceremonies. First, which one of the two box-office smash hits of the year — "The Godfather" or "Cabaret" — would walk away with the greatest number of Oscars; and second, what would happen if Marlon Brando won the award as best actor.

There were surprises on both scores. In something of an upset, "Cabaret," the musical evocation of pre-Nazi decadence, scooped up a total of eight awards to "The Godfather's" three. And, the worst fears of the Academy were realized when Marlon Brando won the award for Best Actor — and then — by proxy — refused to accept the award. It was pandemonium as a lithe Indian girl, Littlefeather, refused the award in Brando's name.

However, Albert S. Ruddy had no problems when he picked up his best-picture award for "The Godfather," the multi-million dollar, three-hour epic. He was visibly disappointed when his film garnered only one other award, best screenplay based on material from another medium.

"Cabaret" was another story altogether. Bob Fosse was named best director for his efforts, and Liza Minnelli was named best actress for her poignant portrayal of Sally Bowles. It was stiff competition for Liza as she competed with Diana Ross, Maggie Smith, Cicely Tyson, and Liv Ullmann.

Joel Grey won the award for best supporting actor as he repeated his Broadway role of master of ceremonies of the cabaret.

Eileen Heckart, the sentimental favorite, was named best supporting actress for her role as the mother who learns to understand her blind son in "Butterflies Are Free."

"The Discreet Charm Of The Bourgeoisie," a film by Luis Buñuel, was named best foreign film, and a superb film it was; the subject——the protocol of daily bourgeois life, how slavishly the members try to obey it, how easily it is wrecked, and how wretched the values are beneath it.

The most widely acclaimed award of the evening, a special award, went to Edward G. Robinson, who in the words of the Academy citation, "achieved greatness as a player, a patron of the arts, a dedicated citizen...in sum, a Renaissance man." Robinson had appeared in his last film role during the year.

AWARDS

Best Picture: "The Godfather," Albert S. Ruddy Production, Paramount.

Actor: Marlon Brando in "The Godfather."

Actress: Liza Minnelli in "Cabaret," ABC Pictures Production, Allied Artists.

Sporting Actor: Joel Grey in "Cabaret."

Supporting Actress: Eileen Heckart in "Butterflies Are Free," Frankovich Productions, Columbia.

Directing: Bob Fosse, "Cabaret."

Foreign Language Film Award: "The Discreet Charm Of The Bourgeoisie," Serge Silberman Productions (France).

Writing (screenplay—based on material from another medium): Mario Puzo, Francis Ford Coppola, "The Godfather."

Writing (original story and screenplay): Jeremy Larner, "The Candidate," Redford-Ritchie Production, Warner Brothers.

Cinematography: Geoffrey Unsworth, "Cabaret."

Art Direction: Rolf Zehetbauer, Jurgen Kiebach, Art Directors; Set Decorator, Herbert Strabel; "Cabaret."

Costume Design: Anthony Powell, "Travels With My Aunt," Fryer Productions, Metro-Goldwyn-Mayer.

Film Editing: David Bretherton, "Cabaret."

Music (original score): Charles Chaplin, Raymond Rasch, Larry Russell, "Limelight," Columbia.

Music (adaptation): Ralph Burns, "Cabaret."

Music (song): Al Kasha, Joel Hirschhorn, for "The Morning After," "The Poseidon Adventure," Irwin Allen Production, 20th Century-Fox.

Short Subjects (animated): "A Christmas Carol," Richard Williams Production, ABC Film Services.

Short Subject (live action): "Norman Rockwell's World ... An American Dream," Concepts Unlimited, Columbia.

Sound: Robert Knudson, David Hildyard, "Cabaret."

Special Visual Effects: L. B. Abbott, A.D. Flowers, "The Poseidon Adventure."

Documentary (short subject): "This Tiny World," Charles Hugeunot van der Linden Production.

Documentary (feature): "Marjoe," Cinema X, Cinema 5 Production.

Jean Hersholt Humanitarian Award: Rosalind Russell.

SPECIAL AWARDS

Charles S. Boren, leader for 38 years of the industry's enlightened labor relations and architect of its policy of nondiscrimination.

Edward G. Robinson, who achieved greatness as a player, a patron of the arts, a dedicated citizen ... in sum, a Renaissance man.

SCIENTIFIC AND TECHNICAL AWARDS

Joseph E. Bluth, for research and development in the field of electronic photography and transfer of video tape to motion picture film.

Edward H. Reichard and Howard T. La Zare of Consolidated Film Industries, and Edward Efron of IBM, for the engineering of a computerized light valve monitoring system for motion picture printing.

Panavision Incorporated, for the development and engineering of the Panaflex motion picture camera.

Photo Research, a Division of Kollmorgen Corporation, and PSC Technology Inc., Acme Products Division, for the Spectra Film Gate Photometer for motion picture printers.

Carter Equipment Company, Inc., and Ramtronics, for the Ramtronics light-valve photometer for motion picture printers.

David Degenkolb, Harry Larson, Manfred Michelson, and Fred Scobey of DeLuxe General Incorporated, for the development of a computerized motion picture printer and process control system.

Jiro Mukai and Ryusho Hirose of Canon, Inc., and Wilton R. Holm of the AMPTP Motion Picture and Television Research Center, for development of the Canon Macro Zoom Lens for motion picture photography.

Philip V. Palmquist and Leonard L. Olson of the 3M Company, and Frank P. Clark of the AMPTP Motion Picture and Television Research Center, for development of the Nextel simulated blood for motion picture color photography.

E. H. Geissler and G. M. Berggren of Wil-Kin Inc., for engineering of the Ultra-Vision Motion Picture Theater Projection System.

Marlon Brando (best actor) in "The Godfather"

"The Godfather" (best picture, best screenplay adaptation) with James Caan. Albert S. Ruddy Production, Paramount

Liza Minnelli (best actress) in "Cabaret" (best direction, best cinematography, best art direction, best editing). ABC Pictures, Allied Artists

Joel Grey (best supporting actor) in "Cabaret"

Eileen Heckart (best supporting actress) with Goldie Hawn in "Butterflies Are Free." Frankovich Productions, Columbia

"The Discreet Charm Of The Bourgeoisie" (best foreign film) with Fernando Rey (right).
© Serge Silberman Productions, 20th Century-Fox

"The Poseidon Adventure" (best special visual effects) with Gene Hackman and Eric Shae. © Erwin Allen Productions, 20th Century-Fox

"The Candidate" (best original screenplay) with Robert Redford. Redford-Ritchie Productions, Warner Brothers

Edward G. Robinson (special award). His last film role. With Charlton Heston in "Soylent Green"

1973

It was almost "no contest." "The Sting," a slick, rollicking comedy starring Paul Newman and Robert Redford walked away with seven Oscars: best picture, best direction, best original screenplay and four minor awards. The film was a sure-fire box office success from the beginning as Redford and Newman romp as a pair of Depression-era con men who bilk a big-time racketeer out of half a million dollars as vengeance for his having bumped off one of their buddies. What chance did the other nominated films, "American Graffiti," "Cries And Whispers," "The Exorcist," and "A Touch Of Class," have with competition such as this?

Jack Lemmon was named best actor for his portrayal of a middle-aged dress manufacturer, a high liver and high-pressure salesman, a financial juggler in "Save The Tiger." His performance was nothing short of superb, and it had to be to win out over Marlon Brando in "Last Tango In Paris"; Jack Nicholson in "The Last Detail"; Al Pacino in "Serpico"; and Robert Redford in "The Sting."

Glenda Jackson was named best actress for the second time in three years for her fast-and-funny light comedy performance in "A Touch Of Class"—quite a change of pace from her past performances in films.

A tremendously popular choice was director John Houseman as best supporting actor for his controlled performance in "The Paper Chase," his first acting role. Almost equally as popular was the choice of 10-year-old Tatum O'Neal as best supporting actress for her role in "Paper Moon." It made quite a contrast—the 71-year-old Houseman and the 10-year-old O'Neal.

Sometimes the Academy Awards can make an instant success of someone—and that's exactly what happened to Marvin Hamlisch—as he walked away with three Oscars: for the best original score ("The Way We Were"), the best musical adaptation ("The Sting"), and the best song ("The Way We Were").

And, the irrepressible Groucho Marx walked away with a special award, in recognition of his brilliant creativity and achievements in motion picture comedy.

AWARDS

Best Picture: "The Sting," Universal–Bill/Phillips–George Roy Hill Film Production, Zanuck/Brown Presentation, Universal.

Actor: Jack Lemmon in "Save The Tiger," Filmways–Jalem–Cirandinha Productions, Paramount.

Actress: Glenda Jackson in "A Touch Of Class," Brut Productions, Avco Embassy.

Supporting Actor: John Houseman in "The Paper Chase," Thompson-Paul Productions, 20th Century-Fox.

Supporting Actress: Tatum O'Neal in "Paper Moon," Directors Company Production, Paramount.

Directing: George Roy Hill, "The Sting."

Foreign Language Film Award: "Day For Night," Les Films Du Carrosse-P.E.C.F.–P.I.C. Production (France).

Writing (screenplay—based on material from another medium): William Peter Blatty, "The Exorcist," Hoya Productions, Warner Brothers.

Writing (original story and screenplay): David S. Ward, "The Sting."

Cinematography: Sven Nykvist, "Cries And Whispers," Svenska Filminstitutet–Cinematograph AB Production, New World Pictures.

Art Direction: Harry Bumstead, Art Director; Set Decorator, James Payne, "The Sting."

Costume Design: Edith Head, "The Sting."

Film Editing: William Reynolds, "The Sting."

Music (original score): Marvin Hamlisch, "The Way We Were," Rastar Productions, Columbia.

Music (adaptation): Marvin Hamlisch, "The Sting."

Music (song): Marvin Hamlisch, music; Allan and Marilyn Bergman, lyrics; "The Way We Were," from "The Way We Were."

Short Subject (animated): "Frank Film," Frank Mouris Production.

Short Subject (live action): "The Bolero," Allan Miller Production.

Sound: Robert Knudson, Chris Newman, "The Exorcist," Hoya Productions, Warner Brothers.

Documentary (short subject): "Princeton: A Search For Answers," Krainin-Sage Productions.

Documentary (feature): "The Great American Cowboy," Keith Merrill, Rodeo Films Production.

SPECIAL AWARDS

Henri Langlois, for his devotion to the art of film, his massive contributions in preserving its past and his unswerving faith in its future.

Groucho Marx, in recognition of his brilliant creativity and for the unequaled achievements of the Marx Brothers in the art of motion picture comedy.

Jean Hersholt Humanitarian Award: Lew Wasserman.

Irving G. Thalberg Memorial Award: Lawrence Weingarten.

SCIENTIFIC AND TECHNICAL AWARDS

Joachim Gerb and Erich Kastner of the Arnold and Richter Company, for the development and engineering of the Arriflex 35BL motion-picture camera.

Magna-Tech Electronic Co., Inc., for the engineering and development of a high-speed re-recording system for motion-picture production.

William W. Valliant of PSC Technology Inc., Howard F. Ott of Eastman Kodak Company, and Gerry Diebold of The Richmark Camera Service Inc., for the development of a liquid-gate system for motion-picture printers.

Harold A. Scheib, Clifford H. Ellis, and Roger W. Banks of Research Products Incorporated, for the concept and engineering of the Model 2101 optical printer for motion-picture optical effects.

Rosco Laboratories, Inc., for the technical advances and the development of a complete system of light-control materials for motion-picture photography.

Richard H. Vetter of the Todd-AO Corporation, for the design of an improved anamorphic focusing system for motion-picture photography.

"The Sting" (best picture, best
direction) with Paul Newman.
Universal–Bill/Phillips–George
Roy Hill Film, Zanuck/Brown
Presentation, Universal

"The Sting" (best original
screenplay, best art direction,
best costumes, best film
editing, best music) with
Robert Redford, Eileen Brennan

Jack Lemmon (best actor)
in "Save The Tiger." Filmways–
Jalem–Cirandinha Productions,
Paramount

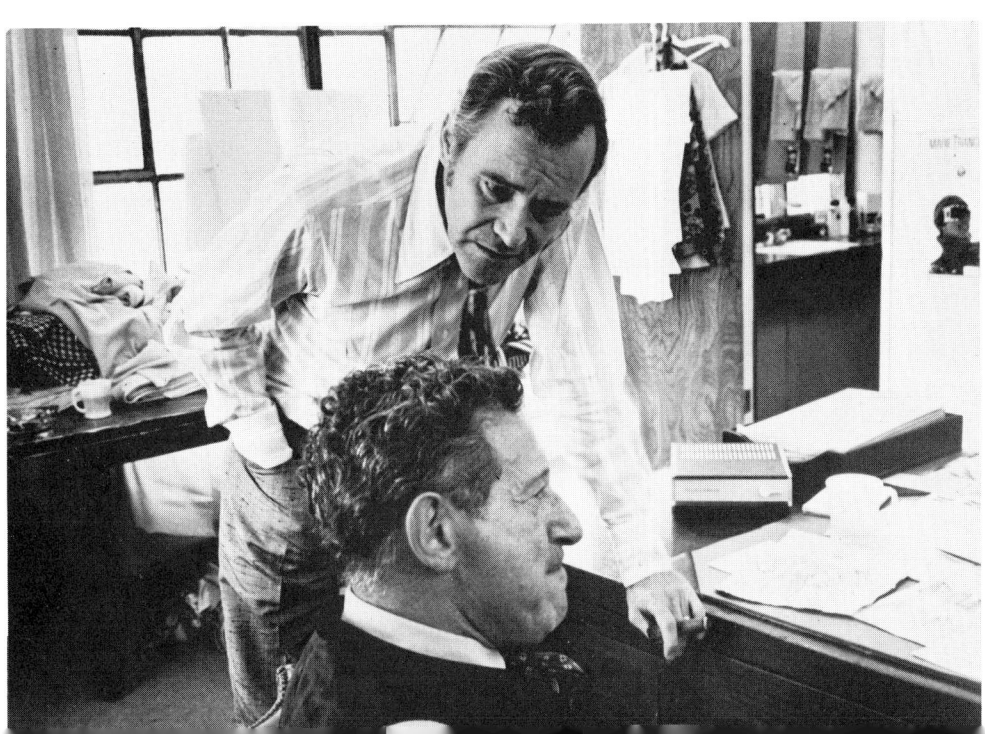

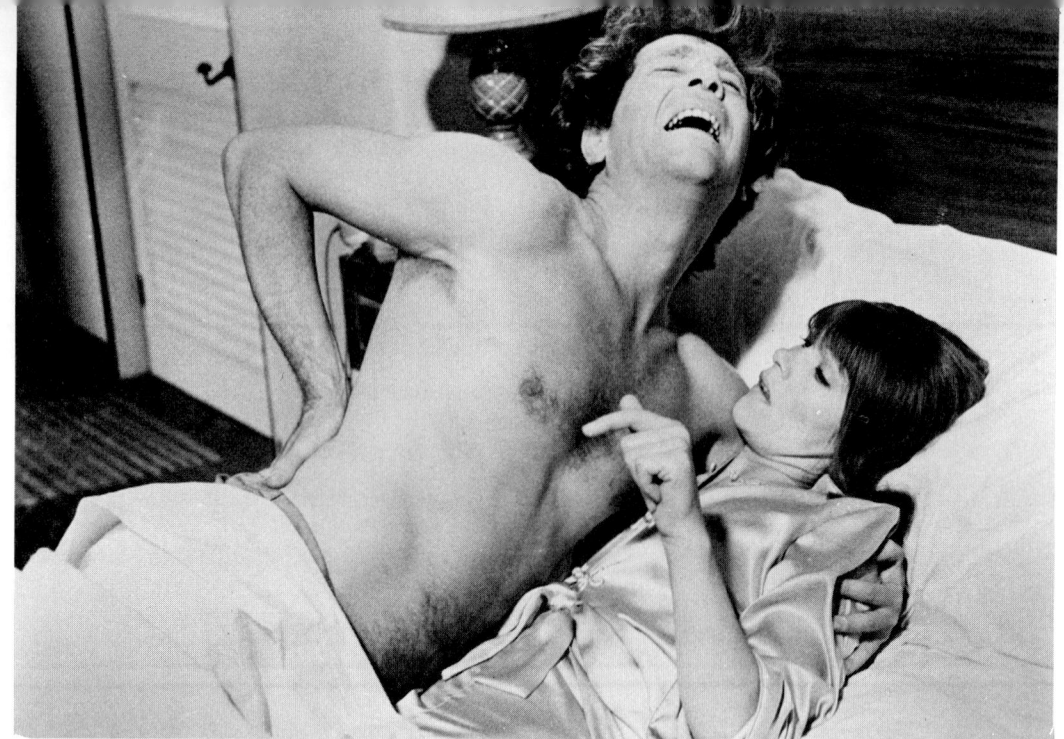

Glenda Jackson (best actress) with George Segal in "A Touch Of Class." Brut Productions, Avco Embassy

John Houseman (best supporting actor) in "The Paper Chase." © Thompson–Paul Productions, 20th Century-Fox

Tatum O'Neal (best supporting actress) with Ryan O'Neal in "Paper Moon." Directors Company Production, Paramount

"Day For Night" (best foreign film) with Jean-Pierre Aumont, Jacqueline Bisset. Les Filmes Du Carrosse–P.E.C.F.–P.I.C. Production (France)

Groucho Marx (special award) in one of his early films, "The Big Store."
© Metro-Goldwyn-Mayer

1974

From the moment that the Oscar nominations were announced, newspaper and magazine writers all agreed: "The Godfather, Part II" will never win—not with the original version already a big winner. The magazine and newspaper writers were wrong as "The Godfather, Part II" swept away all competition and walked off with six Oscars in all. It was named Best Picture and Francis Ford Coppola was selected Best Director. It was a great night for Mr. Coppola. He also captured the award (with Mario Puzo) for Best Screenplay adaptation—and he cheered as his father, Carmine Coppola, won the Oscar (with Nino Rota) for the Best Original Dramatic Score.

The biggest surprise of the night came in the Best Actor category. Jack Nicholson had been nominated for his performance in "Chinatown" and Al Pacino for his portrayal in "The Godfather, Part II." Both had been nominated several times in the past without winning. But it was Art Carney, in his very first nominated performance, who was named Best Actor for his stunning portrait of the self-sufficient widower in "Harry And Tonto." The choice was one of the favorites of the evening.

Ellen Burstyn faced stiff competition—Diahann Carroll, Faye Dunaway, Valerie Perrine, and Gena Rowlands—but she was given the Best Actress Oscar for her performance in "Alice Doesn't Live Here Anymore."

In the supporting roles—a newcomer, Robert De Niro, was honored for his role as the brooding, young Mafia chieftain in "The Godfather, Part II"—while Ingrid Bergman won her third Oscar (her first for a supporting role) for her work in "Murder On The Orient Express." She had already garnered top honors for her performances in "Gaslight" in 1944, and for "Anastasia" in 1956. Miss Bergman joined Helen Hayes as the second actress to have won Oscars for both Best Actress and Best Supporting Actress.

Perhaps the biggest disappointment of the evening was the fact that "Chinatown"—the picture that had received a total of 11 nominations—captured only one award. Robert Towne was cited for his original story and screenplay.

AWARDS

Best Picture: "The Godfather, Part II," A Coppola Company Production, Paramount.

Actor: Art Carney in "Harry And Tonto," 20th Century-Fox.

Actress: Ellen Burstyn in "Alice Doesn't Live Here Anymore," Warner Brothers.

Supporting Actor: Robert De Niro in "The Godfather, Part II."

Supporting Actress: Ingrid Bergman in "Murder On The Orient Express," G. W. Films, Paramount.

Directing: Francis Ford Coppola, "The Godfather, Part II."

Foreign Language Film Award: "Amarcord," F.C.–P.E.C.F. Production (Italy).

Writing (screenplay—based on material from another medium): Francis Ford Coppola, Mario Puzo, "The Godfather, Part II."

Writing (original story and screenplay): Robert Towne, "Chinatown," Robert Evans Production, Paramount.

Cinematography: Fred Koenekamp, "The Towering Inferno," Irwin Allen Productions, 20th Century-Fox/Warner Brothers.

Art Direction: Dean Tavoularis, Angelo Graham; Set Decorator, George R. Nelson, "The Godfather, Part II."

Costume Design: Theoni V. Aldredge, "The Great Gatsby," David Merrick Productions, Paramount.

Film Editing: Harold F. Kress, Carl Kress, "The Towering Inferno."

Music (original score): Nino Rota, Carmine Coppola, "The Godfather, Part II."

Music (adaptation): Nelson Riddle, "The Great Gatsby."

Music (song): Al Kasha, Joel Hirschhorn, "We May Never Love Like This Again," from "The Towering Inferno."

Short Subjects (animated): "Closed Mondays," Lighthouse Productions.

Short Subjects (live action): "One-Eyed Men Are Kings," C.A.P.A.C. Productions.

Sound: Ronald Pierce, Melvin Metcalfe, Sr., "Earthquake," Universal–Mark Robson–Filmmakers Group Production, Universal.

Documentary (short subject): "Don't," R.A. Films.

Documentary (feature): "Hearts And Minds," Touchstone–Audjeff–BBS Production.

Jean Hersholt Humanitarian Award: Arthur Krim.

SPECIAL AWARDS

Jean Renoir, for his outstanding contributions to the world of cinema.

Howard Hawks, for his career-long directorial genius.

"The Godfather, Part II" (best picture, best direction, best screenplay adaption) with Al Pacino. Coppola Company, Paramount

Art Carney (best actor)
in "Harry And Tonto,"
© 20th Century-Fox

Ellen Burstyn (best actress) in
"Alice Doesn't Live Here
Anymore," Warner Brothers

Robert De Niro (best
supporting actor) in "The
Godfather, Part II"

Ingrid Bergman (best
supporting actress) in "Murder
On The Orient Express," G. W.
Films, Paramount

"Amarcord" (best foreign film),
F.C.–P.E.C.F. Production (Italy)

"Chinatown" (best original
screenplay) with Jack
Nicholson, Faye Dunaway.
Robert Evans Production,
Paramount

"The Towering Inferno" (best
film editing) with Steve
McQueen. Irwin Allen, 20th
Century-Fox/Warner Brothers

the losers

1927-28: "The Last Command," "The Racket," "Seventh Heaven," "The Way Of All Flesh."
1928-29: "Alibi," "Hollywood Revue," "In Old Arizona," "The Patriot."
1929-30: "The Big House," "Disraeli," "The Divorcee," "The Love Parade."
1930-31: "East Lynne," "The Front Page," "Skippy," "Trader Horn."
1931-32: "Arrowsmith," "Bad Girl," "The Champ," "Five Star Final," "One Hour With You," "Shanghai Express," "Smiling Lieutenant."
1932-33: "A Farewell To Arms," "Forty-Second Street," "I Am A Fugitive From A Chain Gang," "Lady For A Day," "Little Women," "The Private Life Of Henry VIII," "She Done Him Wrong," "Smilin' Through," "State Fair."
1934: "The Barretts Of Wimpole Street," "Cleopatra," "Flirtation Walk," "The Gay Divorcee," "Here Comes The Navy," "The House Of Rothschild," "Imitation Of Life," "One Night Of Love," "The Thin Man," "Viva Villa," "The White Parade."
1935: "Alice Adams," "Broadway Melody Of 1936," "Captain Blood," "David Copperfield," "The Informer," "Les Miserables," "Lives Of A Bengal Lancer," "A Midsummer Night's Dream," "Naughty Marietta," "Ruggles Of Red Gap."
1936: "Anthony Adverse," "Dodsworth," "Libeled Lady," "Mr. Deeds Goes To Town," "Romeo And Juliet," "San Francisco," "The Story Of Louis Pasteur," "A Tale Of Two Cities."
1937: "The Awful Truth," "Captains Courageous," "Dead End," "The Good Earth," "In Old Chicago," "Lost Horizon," "One Hundred Men And A Girl," "Stage Door," "A Star Is Born."
1938: "The Adventures Of Robin Hood," "Alexander's Ragtime Band," "Boy's Town," "The Citadel," "Four Daughters," "Grand Illusion," "Jezebel," "Pygmalion," "Test Pilot."
1939: "Dark Victory," "Goodbye, Mr. Chips," "Love Affair," "Mr. Smith Goes To Washington," "Ninotchka," "Of Mice And Men," "Stagecoach," "Wizard Of Oz," "Wuthering Heights."
1940: "All This And Heaven Too," "Foreign Correspondent," "The Grapes Of Wrath," "Kitty Foyle," "The Great Dictator," "The Letter," "The Long Voyage Home," "Our Town," "The Philadelphia Story."
1941: "Blossoms In The Dust," "Citizen Kane," "Here Comes Mr. Jordan," "Hold Back The Dawn," "The Little Foxes," "The Maltese Falcon," "One Foot In Heaven," "Sergeant York," "Suspicion."
1942: "The Invaders," "Kings Row," "The Magnificent Ambersons," "The Pied Piper," "The Pride Of The Yankees," "Random Harvest," "The Talk Of The Town," "Wake Island," "Yankee Doodle Dandy."
1943: "For Whom The Bell Tolls," "Heaven Can Wait," "The Human Comedy," "In Which We Serve," "Madame Curie," "The More The Merrier," "The Ox-Bow Incident," "The Song Of Bernadette," "Watch On The Rhine."
1944: "Double Indemnity," "Gaslight," "Since You Went Away," "Wilson."
1945: "Anchors Aweigh," "The Bells Of St. Mary's," "Mildred Pierce," "Spellbound."
1946: "Henry V," "It's A Wonderful Life," "The Razor's Edge," "The Yearling."
1947: "The Bishop's Wife," "Crossfire," "Great Expectations," "Miracle On 34th Street."
1948: "Johnny Belinda," "The Red Shoes," "The Snake Pit," "Treasure Of Sierra Madre."
1949: "Battleground," "The Heiress," "A Letter To Three Wives," "Twelve O'Clock High."
1950: "Born Yesterday," "Father Of The Bride," "King Solomon's Mines," "Sunset Boulevard."
1951: "Decision Before Dawn," "A Place In The Sun," "Quo Vadis," "A Streetcar Named Desire."
1952: "High Noon," "Ivanhoe," "Moulin Rouge," "The Quiet Man."
1953: "Julius Caesar," "The Robe," "Roman Holiday," "Shane."
1954: "The Caine Mutiny," "The Country Girl," "Seven Brides For Seven Brothers," "Three Coins In The Fountain."
1955: "Love Is A Many-Splendoured Thing," "Mister Roberts," "Picnic," "The Rose Tattoo."
1956: "Friendly Persuasion," "Giant," "The King And I," "The Ten Commandments."
1957: "Peyton Place," "Sayonara," "12 Angry Men," "Witness For The Prosecution."
1958: "Auntie Mame," "Cat On A Hot Tin Roof," "The Defiant Ones," "Separate Tables."
1959: "Anatomy Of A Murder," "The Diary Of Anne Frank," "The Nun's Story," "Room At The Top."
1960: "The Alamo," "Elmer Gantry," "Sons And Lovers," "The Sundowners."
1961: "Fanny," "The Guns Of Navarone," "The Hustler," "Judgment At Nuremberg."
1962: "The Longest Day," "The Music Man," "Mutiny On The Bounty," "To Kill A Mockingbird."
1963: "America America," "Cleopatra," "How The West Was Won," "Lilies Of The Field."
1964: "Becket," "Dr. Strangelove Or: How I Learned To Stop Worrying And Love The Bomb," "Mary Poppins," "Zorba The Greek."
1965: "Darling," "Doctor Zhivago," "Ship Of Fools," "A Thousand Clowns."
1966: "Alfie," "The Russians Are Coming, The Russians Are Coming," "The Sand Pebbles," "Who's Afraid Of Virginia Woolf?"
1967: "Bonnie And Clyde," "Doctor Dolittle," "The Graduate," "Guess Who's Coming To Dinner."
1968: "Funny Girl," "The Lion In Winter," "Rachel, Rachel," "Romeo And Juliet."
1969: "Anne Of A Thousand Days," "Butch Cassidy And The Sundance Kid," "Hello Dolly!," "Z."
1970: "Airport," "Five Easy Pieces," "Love Story," "M*A*S*H."
1971: "A Clockwork Orange," "Fiddler On The Roof," "The Last Picture Show," "Nicholas And Alexandra."
1972: "Cabaret," "Deliverance," "The Emigrants," "Sounder."
1973: "American Graffiti," "Cries And Whispers," "The Exorcist," "A Touch Of Class."
1974: "Chinatown," "The Conversation," "Lenny," "The Towering Inferno."

1927-28: Richard Barthelmess in "The Noose" and "The Patent Leather Kid," Charles Chaplin in "The Circus."
1928-29: George Bancroft in "Thunderbolt," Chester Morris in "Alibi," Paul Muni in "The Valiant," Lewis Stone in "The Patriot."
1929-30: Wallace Beery in "The Big House," Maurice Chevalier in "The Love Parade" and "The Big Pond," Ronald Colman in "Bulldog Drummond," and "Condemned," Lawrence Tibbett in "The Rogue Song."
1930-31: Jackie Cooper in "Skippy," Richard Dix in "Cimarron," Fredric March in "The

Royal Family Of Broadway," Adolphe Menjou in "The Front Page."

1931-32: Leslie Howard in "Berkeley Square," Alfred Lunt in "The Guardsman," Paul Muni in "I Am A Fugitive From A Chain Gang."

1934: Frank Morgan in "Affairs Of Cellini," William Powell in "The Thin Man."

1935: Clark Gable in "Mutiny On The Bounty," Charles Laughton in "Mutiny On The Bounty," Franchot Tone in "Mutiny On The Bounty."

1936: Gary Cooper in "Mr. Deeds Goes To Town," Walter Huston in "Dodsworth," William Powell in "My Man Godfrey," Spencer Tracy in "San Francisco."

1937: Charles Boyer in "Conquest," Fredric March in "A Star Is Born," Robert Montgomery in "Night Must Fall," Paul Muni in "The Life Of Emile Zola."

1938: Charles Boyer in "Algiers," James Cagney in "Angels With Dirty Faces," Robert Donat in "The Citadel," Leslie Howard in "Pygmalion."

1939: Clark Gable in "Gone With The Wind," Laurence Olivier in "Wuthering Heights," Mickey Rooney in "Babes In Arms," James Stewart in "Mr. Smith Goes To Washington."

1940: Charles Chaplin in "The Great Dictator," Henry Fonda in "The Grapes Of Wrath," Raymond Massey in "Abe Lincoln In Illinois," Laurence Olivier in "Rebecca."

1941: Cary Grant in "Penny Serenade," Walter Huston in "All That Money Can Buy," Robert Montgomery in "Here Comes Mr. Jordan," Orson Welles in "Citizen Kane."

1942: Ronald Colman in "Random Harvest," Gary Cooper in "The Pride Of The Yankees," Walter Pidgeon in "Mrs. Miniver," Monty Woolley in "The Pied Piper."

1943: Humphrey Bogart in "Casablanca," Gary Cooper in "For Whom The Bell Tolls," Walter Pidgeon in "Madame Curie," Mickey Rooney in "The Human Comedy."

1944: Charles Boyer in "Gaslight," Barry Fitzgerald in "Going My Way," Cary Grant in "None But The Lonely Heart," Alexander Knox in "Wilson."

1945: Bing Crosby in "The Bells Of St. Mary's," Gene Kelly in "Anchors Aweigh," Gregory Peck in "The Keys Of The Kingdom," Cornel Wilde in "A Song To Remember."

1946: Laurence Olivier in "Henry V," Larry Parks in "The Jolson Story," Gregory Peck in "The Yearling," James Stewart in "It's A Wonderful Life."

1947: John Garfield in "Body And Soul," Gregory Peck in "Gentleman's Agreement," William Powell in "Life With Father," Michael Redgrave in "Mourning Becomes Electra."

1948: Lew Ayres in "Johnny Belinda," Montgomery Clift in "The Search," Dan Dailey in "When My Baby Smiles At Me," Clifton Webb in "Sitting Pretty."

1949: Kirk Douglas in "Champion," Gregory Peck "Twelve O'Clock High," Richard Todd in "The Hasty Heart," John Wayne in "Sands Of Iwo Jima."

1950: Louis Calhern in "The Magnificent Yankee," William Holden in "Sunset Boulevard," James Stewart in "Harvey," Spencer Tracy in "Father Of The Bride."

1951: Marlon Brando in "A Streetcar Named Desire," Montgomery Clift in "A Place In The Sun," Arthur Kennedy in "Bright Victory," Fredric March in "Death Of A Salesman."

1952: Marlon Brando in "Viva Zapata!," Kirk Douglas in "The Bad And The Beautiful," Jose Ferrer in "Moulin Rouge," Alec Guinness in "The Lavender Hill Mob."

1953: Marlon Brando in "Julius Caesar," Richard Burton in "The Robe," Montgomery Clift in "From Here To Eternity," Burt Lancaster in "From Here To Eternity."

1954: Humphrey Bogart in "The Caine Mutiny," Bing Crosby in "The Country Girl," James Mason in "A Star Is Born," Dan O'Herlihy in "Adventures Of Robinson Crusoe."

1955: James Cagney in "Love Me Or Leave Me," James Dean in "East Of Eden," Frank Sinatra in "The Man With The Golden Arm," Spencer Tracy in "Bad Day At Black Rock."

1956: James Dean in "Giant," Kirk Douglas in "Lust For Life," Rock Hudson in "Giant," Laurence Olivier in "Richard III."

1957: Marlon Brando in "Sayonara," Anthony Franciosa in "A Hatful Of Rain," Charles Laughton in "Witness For The Prosecution," Anthony Quinn in "Wild Is The Wind."

1958: Tony Curtis in "The Defiant Ones," Paul Newman in "Cat On A Hot Tin Roof," Sidney Poitier in "The Defiant Ones," Spencer Tracy in "The Old Man And The Sea."

1959: Laurence Harvey in "Room At The Top," Jack Lemmon in "Some Like It Hot," Paul Muni in "The Last Angry Man," James Stewart in "Anatomy Of A Murder."

1960: Trevor Howard in "Sons And Lovers," Jack Lemmon in "The Apartment," Laurence Olivier in "The Entertainer," Spencer Tracy in "Inherit The Wind."

1961: Charles Boyer in "Fanny," Paul Newman in The Hustler," Spencer Tracy in "Judgment At Nuremberg," Stuart Whitman in "The Mark."

1962: Burt Lancaster in "Bird Man Of Alcatraz," Jack Lemmon in "Days Of Wine And Roses," Marcello Mastroianni in "Divorce—Italian Style," Peter O'Toole in "Lawrence Of Arabia."

1963: Albert Finney in "Tom Jones," Richard Harris in "This Sporting Life," Rex Harrison in "Cleopatra," Paul Newman in "Hud."

1964: Richard Burton in "Becket," Peter O'Toole in "Becket," Anthony Quinn in "Zorba The Greek," Peter Sellers in "Dr. Strangelove Or: How I Learned To Stop Worrying And Love The Bomb."

1965: Richard Burton in "The Spy Who Came In From The Cold," Laurence Olivier in "Othello," Rod Steiger in "The Pawnbroker," Oskar Werner in "Ship Of Fools."

1966: Alan Arkin in "The Russians Are Coming, The Russians Are Coming," Richard Burton in "Who's Afraid Of Virginia Woolf?," Michael Cain in "Alfie," Steve McQueen in "The Sand Pebbles."

1967: Warren Beatty in "Bonnie And Clyde," Dustin Hoffman in "The Graduate," Paul Newman in "Cool Hand Luke," Spencer Tracy in "Guess Who's Coming To Dinner."

1968: Alan Arkin in "The Heart Is A Lonely Hunter," Alan Bates in "The Fixer," Ron Moody in "Oliver!," Peter O'Toole in "The Lion In Winter."

1969: Richard Burton in "Anne Of A Thousand Days," Dustin Hoffman in "Midnight Cowboy," Peter O'Toole in "Goodbye, Mr. Chips," Jon Voight in "Midnight Cowboy."

1970: Melvyn Douglas in I Never Sang For My Father," James Earl Jones in "The Great White Hope," Jack Nicholson in "Five Easy Pieces," Ryan O'Neal in "Love Story."

1971: Peter Finch in "Sunday Bloody Sunday," Walther Matthau in "Kotch," George C. Scott in "The Hospital," Topol in "Fiddler On The Roof."

1972: Michael Caine in "Sleuth," Laurence Olivier in "Sleuth," Peter O'Toole in "The Ruling Class," Paul Winfield in "Sounder."

1973: Marlon Brando in "Last Tango In Paris," Jack Nicholson in "The Last Detail," Al Pacino in "Serpico," Robert Redford in "The Sting."

1974: Albert Finney in "Murder On The Orient Express," Dustin Hoffman in "Lenny," Jack Nicholson in "Chinatown," Al Pacino in "The Godfather, Part II."

1927-28: Louise Dresser in "A Ship Comes In," Gloria Swanson in "Sadie Thompson."

1928-29: Ruth Chatterton in "Madame X," Betty Compson in "The Barker," Jeanne Eagels in "The Letter," Bessie Love in "The Broadway Melody."

1929-30: Nancy Carroll in "The Devil's Holiday," Ruth Chatterton in "Sarah And Son," Greta Garbo in "Anna Christie" and "Romance," Gloria Swanson in "The Trespasser."

1930-31: Marlene Dietrich in "Morocco," Irene Dunne in "Cimarron," Ann Harding in "Holiday," Norma Shearer in "A Free Soul."

1931-32: Marie Dressler in "Emma," Lynn Fontanne in "The Guardsman."

1932-33: May Robson in "Lady For A Day," Diana Wynyard in "Cavalcade."

1934: Grace Moore in "One Night Of Love," Norma Shearer in "The Barretts Of Wimpole Street."

1935: Elisabeth Bergner in "Escape Me Never," Claudette Colbert in "Private Worlds," Katharine Hepburn in "Alice Adams," Miriam Hopkins in "Becky Sharp," Merle Oberon in "The Dark Angel."

1936: Irene Dunne in "Theodora Goes Wild," Gladys George in "Valiant Is The Word For Carrie," Carole Lombard in "My Man Godfrey," Norma Shearer in "Romeo And Juliet."

1937: Irene Dunne in "The Awful Truth," Greta Garbo in "Camille," Janet Gaynor in "A Star Is Born," Barbara Stanwyck in "Stella Dallas."

1938: Fay Bainter in "White Banners," Wendy Hiller in "Pygmalion," Norma Shearer in "Marie Antoinette," Margaret Sullavan in "Three Comrades."

1939: Bette Davis in "Dark Victory," Irene Dunne in "Love Affair," Greta Garbo in "Ninotchka," Greer Garson in "Goodbye, Mr. Chips."

1940: Bette Davis in "The Letter," Joan Fontaine in "Rebecca," Katherine Hepburn in "The Philadelphia Story," Martha Scott in "Our Town."

1941: Bette Davis in "The Little Foxes," Olivia De Havilland in "Hold Back The Dawn," Greer Garson in "Blossoms In The Dust," Barbara Stanwyck in "Ball Of Fire."

1942: Bette Davis in "Now, Voyager," Katharine Hepburn in "Woman Of The Year," Rosalind Russell in "My Sister Eileen," Teresa Wright in "The Pride Of The Yankees."

1943: Jean Arthur in "The More The Merrier," Ingrid Bergman in "For Whom The Bell Tolls," Joan Fontaine in "The Constant Nymph," Greer Garson in "Madame Curie."

1944: Claudette Colbert in "Since You Went Away," Bette Davis in "Mr. Skeffington," Greer Garson in "Mrs. Parkington," Barbara Stanwyck in "Double Indemnity."

1945: Ingrid Bergman in "The Bells Of St. Mary's," Greer Garson in "The Valley Of Decision," Jennifer Jones in "Love Letters," Gene Tierney in "Leave Her To Heaven."

1946: Celia Johnson in "Brief Encounter," Jennifer Jones in "Duel In The Sun," Rosalind Russell in "Sister Kenny," Jane Wyman in "The Yearling."

1947: Joan Crawford in "Possessed," Susan Hayward in "Smash Up—The Story Of A Woman," Dorothy McGuire in "Gentleman's Agreement," Rosalind Russell in "Mourning Becomes Electra."

1948: Ingrid Bergman in "Joan Of Arc," Olivia De Havilland in "The Snake Pit," Irene Dunne in "I Remember Mama," Barbara Stanwyck in "Sorry, Wrong Number."

1949: Jeanne Crain in "Pinky," Susan Hayward in "My Foolish Heart," Deborah Kerr in "Edward, My Son," Loretta Young in "Come To The Stable."

1950: Anne Baxter in "All About Eve," Bette Davis in "All About Eve," Eleanor Parker in "Caged," Gloria Swanson in "Sunset Boulevard."

1951: Katharine Hepburn in "The African Queen," Eleanor Parker in "Detective Story," Shelly Winters in "A Place In The Sun," Jane Wyman in "The Blue Veil."

1952: Joan Crawford in "Sudden Fear," Bette Davis in "The Star," Julie Harris in "The Member Of The Wedding," Susan Hayward in "With A Song In My Heart."

1953: Leslie Caron in "Lili," Ava Gardner in "Mogambo," Deborah Kerr in "From Here To Eternity," Maggie McNamara in "The Moon Is Blue."

1954: Dorothy Dandridge in "Carmen Jones," Judy Garland in "A Star Is Born," Audrey Hepburn in "Sabrina," Jane Wyman in "The Magnificent Obsession."

1955: Susan Hayward in "I'll Cry Tomorrow," Katharine Hepburn in "Summertime," Jennifer Jones in "Love Is A Many-Splendored Thing," Eleanor Parker in "Interrupted Melody."

1956: Carroll Baker in "Baby Doll," Katharine Hepburn in "The Rainmaker," Nancy Kelly in "The Bad Seed," Deborah Kerr in "The King And I."

1957: Deborah Kerr in "Heaven Knows, Mr. Allison," Anna Magnani in "Wild Is The Wind," Elizabeth Taylor in "Raintree County," Lana Turner in "Peyton Place."

1958: Deborah Kerr in "Separate Tables," Shirley MacLaine in "Some Came Running," Rosalind Russell in "Auntie Mame," Elizabeth Taylor in "Cat On A Hot Tin Roof."

1959: Doris Day in "Pillow Talk," Audrey Hepburn in "The Nun's Story," Katharine Hepburn in "Suddenly, Last Summer," Elizabeth Taylor in "Suddenly, Last Summer."

1960: Greer Garson in "Sunrise At Campobello," Deborah Kerr in "The Sundowners," Shirley MacLaine in "The Apartment," Melina Mercouri in "Never On Sunday."

1961: Audrey Hepburn in "Breakfast At Tiffany's," Piper Laurie in "The Hustler," Geraldine Page in "Summer And Smoke," Natalie Wood in "Splendor In The Grass."

1962: Bette Davis in "What Ever Happened To Baby Jane?," Katharine Hepburn in "Long Day's Journey Into Night," Geraldine Page in "Sweet Bird Of Youth," Lee Remick in "Days Of Wine And Roses."

1963: Leslie Caron in "The L-Shaped Room," Shirley MacLaine in "Irma La Douce," Rachel Roberts in "This Sporting Life," Natalie Wood in "Love With A Proper Stranger."

1964: Anne Bancroft in "The Pumpkin Eater," Sophia Loren in "Marriage—Italian Style," Debbie Reynolds in "The Unsinkable Molly Brown," Kim Stanley in "Seance On A Wet Afternoon."

1965: Julie Andrews in "The Sound Of Music," Samantha Eggar in "The Collector," Elizabeth Hartman in "A Patch Of Blue," Simone Signoret in "Ship Of Fools."

1966: Anouk Aimee in "A Man And A Woman," Ida Kaminska in "The Shop On Main Street," Lynn Redgrave in "Georgy Girl," Vanessa Redgrave in "Morgan!"

1967: Anne Bancroft in "The Graduate," Faye Dunaway in "Bonnie And Clyde," Dame Edith

Evans in "The Whisperers," Audrey Hepburn in "Wait Until Dark."

1968: Patricia Neal in "The Subject Was Roses," Vanessa Redgrave in "Isadora," Joanne Woodward in "Rachel, Rachel."

1969: Genevieve Bujold in "Anne Of A Thousand Days," Jane Fonda in "They Shoot Horses, Don't They?," Liza Minnelli in "The Sterile Cuckoo," Jean Simmons in "The Happy Ending."

1970: Jane Alexander in "The Great White Hope," Ali MacGraw in "Love Story," Sarah Miles in "Ryan's Daughter," Carey Snodgrass in "Diary Of A Mad Housewife."

1971: Julie Christie in "McCabe And Mrs. Miller," Glenda Jackson in "Sunday Bloody Sunday," Vanessa Redgrave in "Mary, Queen Of Scots," Janet Suzman in "Nicholas And Alexandra."

1972: Diana Ross in "Lady Sings The Blues," Maggie Smith in "Travels With My Aunt," Cicely Tyson in "Sounder," Liv Ullmann in "The Emigrants."

1973: Ellen Burstyn in "The Exorcist," Marsha Mason in "Cinderella Liberty," Barbra Streisand in "The Way We Were," Joanne Woodward in "Summer Wishes, Winter Dreams."

1974: Diahann Carroll in "Claudine," Faye Dunaway in "Chinatown," Valerie Perrine in "Lenny," Gena Rowlands in "A Woman Under The Influence."

index

Page numbers in boldface indicate photographs.